Muslim Mothering

Funded by the Government of Canada
Financé par la gouvernement du Canada

Demeter Press
140 Holland Street West
P. O. Box 13022
Bradford, ON L3Z 2Y5
Tel: (905) 775-9089
Email: info@demeterpress.org
Website: www.demeterpress.org

Demeter Press logo based on the sculpture "Demeter" by Maria-Luise Bodirsky <www.keramik-atelier.bodirsky.de>

Front cover photograph: Sylvat Aziz

MIX
Paper from responsible sources
FSC® C004071

Printed and Bound in Canada

Library and Archives Canada Cataloguing in Publication

     Muslim mothering : global histories, theories, and practices / edited by Margaret Aziza Pappano and Dana M. Olwan.

Includes bibliographical references.
ISBN 978-1-77258-021-1 (paperback)

     1. Motherhood—Religious aspects—Islam. 2. Mother and child—Religious aspects—Islam. 3. Parenting—Religious aspects—Islam. 4. Muslim women. 5. Mothers. I. Pappano, Margaret Aziza, 1967–, author, editor II. Olwan, Dana M., 1981–, editor

BP190.5.M67M88 2016   297.5'77   C2016-902837-2

Muslim Mothering
Global Histories, Theories, and Practices

EDITED BY

Margaret Aziza Pappano and Dana M. Olwan

DEMETER

DEMETER PRESS

Dedicated to our mothers,
JoAnne S. Pappano and Hiyam Abu Dhays

Table of Contents

Acknowledgements

The editors would like to thank the contributors for their work, patience, and responsiveness during the long process towards getting this book ready. In addition, we would like to acknowledge the editorial assistance of Noor Ibrahim and thank Jesse O'Reilly-Conlin for carefully copy-editing this manuscript. We would also like to thank Sylvat Aziz for contributing the cover photograph. We thank the English Department at Queen's University, the Women's and Gender Studies Department at Syracuse University, and the Doha Institute for Graduate Studies for their support. We are also grateful to Andrea O'Reilly for her help and generosity. Both editors are thankful to their families for their love and care.

Introduction

Muslim Mothering: Between Sacred Texts and Contemporary Practices

MARGARET AZIZA PAPPANO AND DANA M.OLWAN

OTHERS OCCUPY A REVERED POSITION in Islamic sacred texts and scriptures. The Muslim mother is deserving of respect, generosity, and kindness, which is afforded to her by her children for her role in birthing and/or raising them. In an often-cited *hadith,* echoed throughout this volume, it is stated that "paradise lies at the feet of the mother," indicating the high status that women who mother occupy in Islam. Scholars have paid considerable attention to Islamic views on mothers, asserting the positive ways in which the role of the mother is described and explicated. In Aliah Schleifer's *Motherhood in Islam* (1986), for example, various textual evidence and scripture are presented and analyzed in order to explore the "lofty position" of mothers who birth, feed, and rear children (47). Schleifer sheds light on the role that mothers play in the day-to-day life of the Muslim family and showcases the important relationship between the work of mothering and religious practice for Muslim women. Although readings that focus on the discursive and scriptural exaltation of Muslim mothers proliferate, less attention has been paid to the experiences, practices, and challenges of Muslim mothers across the globe. How do Muslim mothers mother? What role does the Islamic faith—and Islamic scriptures—play in the shaping of Muslim mothering experiences and practices? How have local and global politics, along with current economic orders and social realities, constituted the practices of Muslim mothers while they negotiate what it means to be both a Muslim and a mother in a variety of contexts? And how has the experience of motherhood itself differed for Muslim women across racial, classed, national, and ethnic lines?

With 1.6 billion Muslims in the world—encompassing a vast range of ethnic, racial, national, class, sectarian identities—it is no straightforward task to outline the constituent features of Muslim mothering or its various practices or address such expansive questions in definitive ways. Indeed, it is important to note that there is no singular way in which Muslim mothers mother. Nor is there a unified way in which Muslim women engage in or disengage from the social institution of motherhood. As Terry Arendell states, "mothering is neither a unitary experience for individual women nor experienced similarly by all women" (1196). Muslim mothering, like all forms of mothering, can elicit a range of experiences and emotions that are themselves marked by contradictions, tensions, and even ambivalence (Arendell; Rich). Although many Muslim mothers look for guidance to the traditional sources of Islamic authority, the Qur'an, *hadith*, and *tafsir*, mothering practices necessarily draw heavily from diverse and multiple cultural and familial experiences and national contexts as well. Today, a white Muslim mother in Europe or North American will have a radically different experience of mothering than a refugee mother struggling to escape war-torn Syria, and, indeed, the experience of mothering in war zones, given the present situation of intervention in and occupation of Muslim-majority territories and states, forms one of the sections of this volume. With such diversity in Muslim experience in the world today, this edited volume focuses on different themes and social formations that affect mothering in both Muslim-majority countries and territories and in European and North American diasporic communities.

Muslim mothers are rarely portrayed and even more rarely allotted speaking roles in dominant media representations. They are perhaps more noticeable by their absence than by their presence, in contrast to the prevalence of mother stereotypes of other ethnic and religious groups. For instance, in her recent study, Joyce Antler demonstrates that there is a particularly enduring and potent stereotype of the Jewish mother, one that has been the subject of sustained attention in American popular culture. Patricia Hill Collins speaks of the "superstrong Black mother" (*Black* 76) stereotype that plagues discourse of African American women. What are the stereotypes of Muslim mothers? Popular Western media portrays them as shadowy, veiled figures in the background, repressed by a violent, domineering patriarchal religious culture and, usually, shown as little more than silent appendages of their husbands. In Leila Abu-Lughod's words, there is an

> almost unquestioned consensus that Islam is the ultimate determinant of women's lives in a part of the world closely associated with the Middle East, but extending to South, Southwest, and Southeast Asia. The "Muslim woman" is a trope of great symbolic power, restricted by her veil or burqa, under the thumb of her religion and her man. (xvi)

Although Muslim mothers, like almost all women, do live in patriarchal cultures, as this volume demonstrates, they tend to identify the oppression that they experience more with structural features endemic to their societies rather than with their religious practice or with the men directly in their lives. As immigrants, they witness the Islamophobia that targets all Muslims, including their fathers, brothers, husbands and sons; in Muslim-majority contexts—such as Palestine, Iran, and Kashmir, India—much of the hardship they suffer is a result of repressive regimes and/or military occupations, which includes incarceration, assault, torture, or "disappearance" of family members. The issue of struggle against patriarchal formations emerges most in the chapters devoted to the ethnically diverse and relatively stable Muslim-majority countries of Malaysia and Indonesia; even there, as in Audrey Elegbede's essay on single mothers in Kuala Lumpur, the mothers identify themselves as having successfully navigated the court systems and the social stigmatization attached to divorce to assert their identity as single mothers.

Given the pervasiveness of representations of the silent and oppressed Muslim woman, this volume seeks to show how Muslim mothers experience mothering in their own words. Many of the chapters include extensive interviews with Muslim mothers to record first hand their experiences with issues as diverse as political oppression, immigration, divorce, violence, Islamophobia, work, and postpartum confinement, and to examine how these various contexts affect children and their relations with their children. These interviews insist on highlighting the voices of women who are often ignored, overlooked, or silenced in mainstream representations of mothering. Other chapters rely on social media forums such as blogs and web comics to access representations of and by Muslim mothers. These works help shed light on the ways in which Muslim mothers shape contemporary practices of mothering, as they challenge assumptions of their invisibility, silence, or oppression, and expand traditional notions of motherhood. Indeed, all of the articles in this work attempt to defy such marginalizations by exploring how Muslim mothers negotiate the labour of mothering or what Irene Oh, in this volume, refers to as "both biological and cultural spheres" of motherhood.

ISLAMIC SOURCES ON MOTHERING

Mothers and fathers are not equal in the Qur'an. Asma Barlas points out that "the Qur'an challenges misrepresentations of fathers as surrogates of a divine patriarch by rejecting the mythos of God-the-Father. Likewise, the Qur'an challenges the concept of father-right by refusing to sacralize the prophets as real or symbolic fathers" (109). In the Qur'an, God's absolute difference from humankind places the divine being beyond gender, and, therefore, although it has become conventional to refer to Allah as "he," it is just as acceptable to use "she." Barlas reads the Qur'an as rejecting patriarchy and suggests that "God's rule displaces rule by the father, whether or not the father is a believer." Even the Prophet Muhammad is not deemed a "symbolic father" of his community. Contrarily, scholars recognize that the Qur'an "privileges" or "extols" mothers (Barlas; Kueny). In the Qur'an, Allah recognizes the difficult tasks and sacrifices of mothers, as he refers to her labour in childbirth and her commitment to breastfeeding, and elevates the special procreative capacity of women. Many commentators have cited the etymological relation between womb (*rahm*) and *rahim*, one of the four major attributes of Allah; in Hinna Upal's words, "the divine attribute of Grace is embodied in the wombs of our mothers, who possess some, albeit a tiny fragment, of God's

4

creative energy" (88). In her work on concepts of maternity in Muslim discourse and practice in the Middle Ages, Katherine Kueny points out how early commentators on the Qur'an sought to circumscribe the relation between the creative process of the divine and maternity. The process of creating children is brought within paternal control, she argues, by a number of postpartum Muslim ritual practices that seek to appropriate the mother's special fertile powers and locate them within paternal power structures. Nonetheless, the dynamic relation between divine creation and maternity adumbrated in the Qur'an does find form in some Muslim thinkers, most notably the writing of the thirteenth-century poet Rumi, who saw in this relation the promise of human closeness to and knowledge of God (Keshavarz).

The Qur'an and *hadith* exalt both biological and non-biological mothers. As Kueny points out, the Qur'an shrouds reproduction in mystery and emphasizes that God creates in wombs whatever and however he pleases (Qur'an 3:6), which leaves humans with little to no control over reproduction (20). Only one of the Prophet's wives, Khadija, bore children to him, four daughters surviving beyond infancy. Khadija is honoured for her nurturing role of both her children and the Prophet himself. The other wives were, with the exception of Ayesha, widows or divorcées, many of whom had previously borne children with former husbands; their lack of reproductive identities in the Prophet's household did not lessen their value in the fledgling Muslim community, however. The Prophet's wives were highly praised and considered examples to the community, especially Ayesha, the Prophet's favourite wife, who never had any children but played a very large role in community affairs and was considered a repository of religious knowledge, narrating more *hadith* than anyone else. Indeed, the childlessness of the Prophet's wives was considered a sign of piety, since lack of male lineage was a necessity for Muhammad's status as "the seal of the prophets" (Powers). The wives played nurturing roles to the community at large and are referred to as "The Mothers of the Believers" in the Qur'an (33:6).

In the Qur'an, Mariam (Mary) is a particularly elevated figure, dedicated in her youth to devotional service that was previously an exclusively male domain. Because of her exceptional piety,

Allah granted her the gift of motherhood with no paternal intervention. Unlike in the Bible, Prophet Isa (Jesus) is not considered the "son of God" but is referred to throughout as "the son of Mary," emphasizing his lack of paternity since Arab identity is registered by patronymic, the father's name. Asiya, the surrogate mother of Musa (Moses), is also singled out as a virtuous figure for her nurturance of and devotion to her son, likewise a prophet. The Qur'an emphasizes her defiance of her husband, Pharaoh, to protect Musa's life, in addition to her care for the infant's welfare, which involved returning him to his biological mother to nurse. Mariam and Asiya are considered the two most venerable women in the Qur'an and, notably, in these two figures, motherhood and mothering are both completely independent of fathers and form the basis of their special status.

Yet Muslim cultural traditions and conservative interpretations of the texts frequently circumscribe mothering roles within the patriarchal family unit. It is commonly held that Islam insists on gender distinction—God created two genders and each is seen as having different, albeit equally important, roles in society (Ali 133; Upal 90). Women's biological capacity for bearing children is frequently taken as the basis for her distinctive role: the caretaker of the family rather than the breadwinner, which is frequently seen as the male role (Schleifer 51-52). Although there is evidence in both the Qur'an and *hadith* that women were important political figures and even military heroines in the prophet's day, this evidence is frequently elided in favour of the sources limiting women's duties to the familial sphere. For instance, Nusaybah b. Ka'b al-Ansariyya, one of the earliest Medinan women to swear allegiance to the Prophet and to teach the religion, armed with sword and shield fought alongside her husband and two sons in the battle of Uhud, heroically defending the Prophet and preserving him from harm. Indeed, she went on to fight in several more battles and also played a role in securing a treaty. In these early sources, motherhood and active public service are not seen as contradictory; however, Nusaybah's example is not commonly cited today as a basis for extrapolating contemporary Muslim gender roles. How such texts become read, interpreted and analyzed affect how we understand the practices of Muslim mothering are understood and viewed in a historical and scriptural contexts. As Irene Oh states in this collection, "This may also mean that our willingness to interpret these texts more or less broadly affects normative conclusions" and may help redraw our assumptions about Muslim mothering practices, both historic and contemporary.

GENDER ROLES AND MUSLIM MATERNAL IDENTITIES

Traditional readings of Islamic sources privilege the patriarchal family unit in which men provide for women and children, and as Amina Wadud has pointed out, this conception of family structure has become the basis for Islamic law, rendering all other familial arrangements "deviant" (145). Because the gendered division of labour is often idealized in Muslim communities, many Muslim mothers view motherwork as their proper work and a religious obligation. In her study of Northern Ontario immigrants, Aurélie Lacassagne finds that "practising Muslim women seem particularly conscious that their mothering practices and experience are indeed work in its entirety." Yet the voices of mothers heard in this volume attest to different realities: many of them provide the primary means, if not the sole means, of support for their children. Single mothers in the studies by Elegbede and Ulrike Lingen-Ali consider that they are doing the work of both parents, mothering and fathering, when they work outside the home for wages. The divorced middle-class women of Elegbede's study "recode" their work so that it becomes "defined as obligatory for quality maternal practice and fulfillment of religious obligations." Some Muslim women experience their work outside the home in less positive terms and in conflict with their mothering duties. Nina Nurmila points out that after the New Order period in Indonesia, which encouraged the expansion of women in the workforce, burdens on women increased as they continued to be responsible for childcare and for wage earning. For the Kashmiri women in Nouf Bazaz's study, the need for their livelihood is not a sign of independence or personal achievement but is a reminder of the fractured structure of the family, as husbands, who traditionally served as the breadwinners, have been lost to violence.

Often perceived as the proper work of women and part of religious identity, motherhood provides a social role for many Muslim women. Indeed, as Nurmila explains, until very recently, it was extremely rare to opt out of motherhood for Indonesian women. For the mothers of Elegbede's study, mothering provides a "source of communal validation" that helps to counter the stigma attached to divorce. Although the literature on mothering oriented around white, middle-class Western women frequently cites the isolation experienced by mothers (Wolf) or almost-oppressive individualistic attachment between mothers and children (Warner), this is, generally, not the case in Muslim communities, where mothering is part of the social fabric and mothers provide support to one another. Collins's perspective on mothering in racialized communities is relevant here, as she proposes that "this type of motherwork recognizes that individual survival, empowerment, and identity require group survival, empowerment and identity" (47). In her essay, Margaret Pappano discusses the notion of "identity governed by group membership" that informs many Muslim majority contexts. At Muslim events, there is generally an expectation that children will be brought along and anyone and everyone will be responsible for their care. In North American mosques, people are accustomed to praying while babies cry and younger children run around, playing chase between rows.[1] Maria Curtis's essay focuses on the extension of the support networks for mothers in the *Hizmet* movement in Turkey to the diasporic communities in the United States, in which other women provide organized childcare, religious instruction, advice and emotional support, becoming like family members. Mothering support in Muslim communities extends to helping others cope with the tragic loss of the mothering role in the event of a child's death. The Kashmiri mothers in Bazaz's study who have lost sons by means of state violence depend on other grieving mothers; as one mother says, without that support, "no mother will survive this." In her study of the "mourning mothers" of Iran, Rachel Fox describes how scores of mothers who have lost children organize in Laleh Park in Tehran to create a "politicized space of communal grief"; their rights of motherhood and the loss of those rights underwrites the potency of their collective activism.

REPRODUCTION AND MOTHERWORK IN MUSLIM CONTEXTS

In the recent context of global Islamophobia, reproduction among Muslims has become a highly contested issue. In her study in this volume, Nazila Isgandarova points to readings of Islamic source texts that suggest an expectation that Muslim women will marry and reproduce. Indeed, Nurmila's case studies document social pressures to have children in Indonesia in previous generations, even when financial and personal circumstances made childrearing difficult; yet she finds within religious texts ways to counter the expectations of reproduction for Indonesian women and suggests that feminist readings of these texts are now helping Indonesian women negotiate more choices for themselves. Nurmila also discusses how Indonesian Muslim leaders have collaborated with the government to support birth control practices for women. Despite such evidence from diverse geographical situations and communities, the reproduction of Muslims has come under scrutiny from right-wing establishments, who speak of the birth rate among Muslims as though it imperiled global order (Michaels; Murray; Tomlin).[2] Such a tendency finds particular form in Israel; Prime Minister Netanyahu, among others, has stated that the "demographic threat" represented by the reproduction of the Palestinian citizens within its borders may compromise the Jewish identity of the state (Alon and Benn).[3] Although there may be strong social pressures to reproduce in many Muslim communities, as in most other faith communities, only Muslims are targeted and condemned for their reproductive practices, and even accused of using childbirth as a political strategy to "take over" (Williams). Childbirth for Muslims, then, must be understood in the context of global politicized discourses that seek to raise alarm of a "Muslim tide." Such racist discourses deny Muslim mothers the human complexities of motherhood experiences and suggest that Muslim women are motivated to become mothers for political expediency and that mother-child relations are somehow less vital and valid than those among non-Muslims.

Linked to these Islamophobic conceptions of Muslim childbearing is the belief that Muslim mothers are willing to sacrifice their children for political causes. In her work on the women of the

Lashkar-i-Tayyebia in Pakistan, Farqat Haq notes the ambivalence expressed by the mothers toward the official narrative of sacrifice. "What is written in the jihadi literature about the mothers is largely not written by the mothers themselves" (1043), she observes. In her essay in this volume, Fox discusses the ways that Iranian mothers counter the sacrificial state narrative by insisting on the personal nature of their loss. Likewise for the Kashmiri mothers of Bazaz's study, losses are mourned, not celebrated, and the repercussions of the deaths are palpably experienced in the fractured lives left in the wake of the absence of family members.

In the context of war, violence, and military occupation, Muslim women do experience maternity differently than those who live in relative peace and safety. For the middle-class Malaysian women of Fatimah Al-Attas's study, childbirth is accompanied by a forty-day confinement period, where new mothers receive special foods and bodily treatments. However, for women in precarious situations in the Muslim world, childbirth rituals and even basic health practices are not possible. For Kashmiri women who have lost husbands in Bazaz's study—through death or the limbo status of "disappearance"—times of birth can be traumatic; she describes how women's bodies may even be policed for signs of reproduction, as the police extend surveillance to all family members. Women in Palestine have been humiliated and their lives put at risk by being forced to give birth at checkpoints, as the Israeli soldiers deny them entry to hospitals (Dowson and Sabbah). The United Nations has documented that "one fifth of pregnant women in Gaza and the West Bank could not receive prenatal care because of the difficulty travelling through checkpoints. Delays at these checkpoints have resulted in dozens of unattended roadside births, some of which ended in deaths" (United Nations Population Fund). In her essay on "Gaza Mom," Laila El-Haddad, Nadine Sinno discusses how even seemingly normal maternal tasks such as breastfeeding and changing diapers take on different meaning in the context of occupation, where movement and access is restricted on a daily basis.

These chapters, then, extend theorizations in the field of mothering in war-torn and conflict-ridden contexts. They explore how mothering practices are routinely imbricated in national struggles, and how this imbrication has shaped the experiences, struggles, and sacrifices of Muslim mothers. In her important study on Palestinian mothering practices and strategies of resistance, Julie Peteet explores how women actively "[reconstituted] the meaning of motherhood." Peteet's work reveals that although women must negotiate with iconic and dominant scripts of mothers as bearers of the nation, they also manage to extend the boundaries of both mothering and resistance. In this context, mothers do not prioritize nurturing and survival over resistance but see them intimately bound up in one another: nurturing, survival, and resistance are constant variables that Palestinian mothers, and mothers who labour in besieged contexts, must negotiate in tandem with one another. It is through this negotiation that Palestinian mothers stake out a position for themselves that compels their fellow compatriots to view the work of mothering Palestinian children as highly political labour that is indivisible from the broader national struggle. In this volume, Sinno's discussion of El-Haddad's decision to merge her personal motherhood blog with her work as a journalist documents this indivisibility.

In the articles in this edited collection, Muslim mothers in contexts of occupation and war enact mothering practices that are highly political. That work does not rest on biological assumptions that inhere women's abilities to birth and nurture. Rather, these texts meticulously show the painful negotiations and hard lessons learned by Muslim mothers who raise Muslim children in contexts in which war, occupation, discrimination, and racism are rife.

RAISING MUSLIM CHILDREN

Writing on the experience of raising Muslim children of mixed racial backgrounds in the U.S., Sylvia Chan-Malik explores the connections between spirituality and motherhood. Discussing her own experience of being a mother to two "mixed-race American Muslim girls" who are the children of a Black American father and a Chinese American mother, Chan-Malik's moving post provides insight into a type of "maternal thinking" that often precedes the act of conceiving children, which reveals that the act of mothering does not begin at birth alone. As with other mothers who wish to raise children with a strong ethical and spiritual foundation,

Chan-Malik inquires into what it means to bring into the world children who are cognizant of the important place that religion can play in their lives, while being aware of their own racialized and gendered positionalities. She asks,

> So how to grow these girls—and other girls like them—into strong and confident Muslim American women? How to teach them Islam as a religion, while also explaining anti-Muslim racism, e.g. that to be Muslim in the post-9/11 U.S. means to be subjected to a process of state-sanctioned racialization? ...How to explain sectarian and doctrinal differences within Islam, and the charged domestic, diasporic, and transnational contexts out of which they have grown?

Chan-Malik's questions, though specific to her own context and positionality, index broader anxieties about the day-to-day experiences of mothers. Yet the very specifics that Chan-Malik addresses regarding the convergence of racial, religious, and gendered identities in the shaping of Muslim mothering experiences and practices appear central to discussions of Muslim mothering: when Muslim mothers raise children in places where their racial and religious identities are routinely scrutinized, what are the questions, worries, and fears that animate their day-to-day practices of being mothers? How is mothering a relational and contextual experience that is inseparable from the gendered, raced, and classed struggles of life in diasporic and multicultural contexts?

The chapters in this edited collection offer insights into such questions. Curtis, Lacassagne, Lingen-Ali, Pappano, Shirazi, and Oh discuss the diverse experiences of mothering in places where anti-Muslim and anti-immigrant sentiments may shape childrearing experiences. Although the struggles that are discussed in these texts are not singular to Muslim mothers and cannot be separated from the work of mothering writ large, the specificities of Muslim experiences shed light on the intersections of motherhood as a social practice with other axes of identity, such as race, religion, and nationality. For instance, Muslim mothers tend to be responsible for most, if not all, of the multiple facets of education in the lives of their children, which involves both liaising with school systems and educating children in the extensive knowledge and religious practices that form part of Muslim identity. In the diaspora, mothers are also often charged with the maintenance of and passing along of cultural identities and native languages, as both Curtis and Lacassagne document in their chapters. Without the buffer of a larger community, immigrant mothers are often alone in their worries and fears about their children's development in the context of systems that seem to support and reproduce Islamophobia. One mother in Mehra Shirazi's study expressed "the heavy emotional, mental responsibility and frustration in supporting her children's ability to deconstruct repressive and orientalist narratives about Arabs and Muslims."

In the last year alone, there have been numerous cases of profiling Muslim students in schools. In France, an eight-year-old Muslim boy was investigated by the police when he disagreed with his teacher's interpretation of the Charles Hebdo murders, and a Muslim girl was sent home for wearing a skirt that was deemed too long. In England, a Muslim boy was interrogated for referring to eco-terrorism during a class discussion on ecology, and a Muslim boy in the United States was suspended for bringing a homemade clock to school when the teacher mistook it for a bomb. How do Muslim mothers help their children to not only become educated but also, and simultaneously, to understand and interrogate the mechanisms of educational systems, especially in countries where they may be new immigrants? What does it mean for mothers to perform this difficult work of "double vision"?

Following the work of Black feminist scholar Kimberle Crenshaw, intersectional approaches to mothering help reveal the multiple levels of work and labour involved in the practices of mothering for mothers who occupy racially and religiously minoritized positions in multiethnic, multiracial and multicultural states. Like the experiences narrated by Chan-Malik, racialized and minoritized mothers use the "private" space of the home to raise children and resist their communities' exclusion from dominant society (Collins; Kershaw; Longman, De Graeve, and Brouckaert). Their mothering work, thus, traverses assumed divides between the private and the public, spaces often theorized to be separate and neatly divided from one another. Writing against forms of theorizing that enshrine the split between the privacy of the home and the world in which it is situated, Collins insists that this binary between the private and the public often helps recast the "normative family household" as a paradigmatic analytic unit, ignoring the racial and economic struggles punctuating mothering experiences for racial minorities in dominant societies (*Shifting* 46). Collins thus calls on feminist theorists to recast their analysis in ways that not only seek to include the experiences of mothers from excluded backgrounds but actually foreground them in ways that challenge the very norms on which mothering has been theorized. For Collins, what is at stake in this approach is not only the ability to decentre white, middle-class mothering experiences as norm but the recognition that the voices and experiences of mothers from racial and ethnic minority backgrounds can help configure the "dialectical nature of power and powerlessness ... structuring mothering practices" (*Shifting* 49). Addressing similar themes, chapters in this volume also portray the complex positions that mothers occupy while emphasizing the ways in which Muslim mothers engage the institution of mothering. In these studies, mothering is not portrayed without an attention to the challenges and struggles that accompany its daily practices—thus, the authors move beyond the scriptural elevation of Muslim mothers to engage the material realities of contemporary Muslim mothering.

The chapters in this edited collection explore a number of struggles and challenges that characterize the experiences of Muslim mothers. Throughout this collection, we have aimed to produce a work that can map some of the ideas, issues, and questions shaping contemporary research on Muslim mothering practices. Our aim is to show the wide range of works available and engage how this literature helps recast, reimagine, and reshape dominant theorizations of mothering, which offers ways to address often asked questions about this universal practice and its manifestation in Muslim societies. This is done by paying attention to the particularities of Muslim mothering experiences and to the ways in which these experiences must be read, not by an attention to Islam alone but by a deep study of its concomitant relationship with other axes of identity, such as race, class, nationality, and gender.

Although these chapters emerge from various racial, economic, and geopolitical contexts, they have in common between them a desire to centre the experiences of Muslim mothers in theorizations of motherwork. They do not offer a singular view of Muslim mothering practices, nor do they exhaust the range of Muslim mothering experiences across the globe or wish to produce a unified theory about Muslim mothering practices. They do not seek to romanticize or exceptionalize Muslim mothering. Instead, they expand our understanding of the institution of mothering and broaden the field's theorizations of this practice as it relates to Muslim women. Their approach is not additive. Following on Collins' important contributions to the field, they help stitch a multiplicity of stories, narratives, and stories that provide rich insights into Muslim mothering practices and its various institutions and entanglements in social, political, historical, and cultural contexts.

NOTES

[1] Mosque attendance varies in Muslim communities. In many Muslim-majority countries nowadays it is normal practice for only men to pray in mosques. However, in North America and Europe, mosques are regularly attended by families, although men and women pray in separate spaces. In recent years, there are a number of new initiatives, like the El-Tawhid Juma Circle in Toronto, that are conscious of the need to provide prayer spaces to those with transgender and other gender identities. These places encourage "mecca-style" prayer, with no gender segregation.
[2] According to the Pew Research Center, Muslims have a birthrate of approximately 3.1, and Christians of 2.7 ("The Future of World Religions").
[3] See also the discussion of the "demographic problem" in Ilan Pappe, *The Ethnic Cleaning of Palestine*, 248-56.

WORKS CITED

Abu-Lughod, Lila. *Writing Women's Worlds: Bedouin Stories.* Berkeley: University of California Press, 2008. Print.
Ali, Kecia. *Sexual Ethics and Islam: Feminist Reflections on Qur'an,*

Hadith, and Jurisprudence. Oxford: Oneworld, 2006. Print.

Alon, Gideon, and Aluf Benn. "Netanyahu: Israel's Arabs Are the Real Demographic Threat." *haaretz.com.* Haaretz Daily Newspaper Limited, 3 Dec. 2003. Web. 9 Apr. 2016.

Antler, Joyce. *You Never Call! You Never Write!: A History of the Jewish Mother.* New York: Oxford University Press, 2007. Print.

Arendell, Terry. "Conceiving and Investigating Motherhood: The Decade's Scholarship." *Journal of Marriage and the Family* 62.4 (2000): 1192-1207. Print.

Barlas, Asma. *"Believing Woman" in Islam: Unreading Patriarchal Interpretations of the Qur'an.* Austin: University of Texas Press, 2002. Print.

Chan-Malik, Sylvia. "'Safe Harbors': On Raising Muslim American Girls." *American Studies Media Culture Program (ASMCP).* WordPress, 7 Apr. 2014. Web.

Crenshaw, Kimberle. "Mapping the Margins: Intersectionality, Identity Politics, and Violence against Women of Color." *Stanford Law Review* (1991): 1241-1299. Print.

Collins, Patricia Hill. *Black Feminist Thought: Knowledge, Consciousness, and the Politics of Empowerment.* New York: Routledge, 2000. Print.

Collins, Patricia Hill. "Shifting the Center: Race, Class, and Feminist Theorizing about Motherhood." *Mothering: Ideology, Experience, and Agency.* Eds. Evelyn Nakano Glenn, Grace Chang, and Linda Rennie Forcey. New York: Routledge, 1994. 45-65. Print.

"The Future of World Religions: Population Growth Projections, 2010-2050." *Pew Research Center Religion & Public Life.* Pew Research Center. 2 Apr. 2015. Web. 9 Apr. 2016.

Kershaw, Paul. "Caregiving for Identity is Political: Implications for Citizenship Theory." *Citizenship Studies* 14. 4 (2010): 395-410. Print.

Keshavarz, Fatemeh. "Pregnant with God: The Poetic Art of Mothering the Sacred in Rumi's *Fihi Ma Fih.*" *Comparative Studies of South Asia Africa and the Middle East* 2.1,2 (2002): 90-99. Print.

Kueny, Kathryn M. *Conceiving Identities: Maternity in Medieval Muslim Discourse and Practice.* Albany: State University of New York Press, 2013. Print.

Longman, Chia, Katrien De Graeve, and Tine Brouckaert. "Mothering as a Citizenship Practice: An Intersectional Analysis of 'Carework' and 'Culturework' in Non-normative Mother–child Identities." *Citizenship Studies* 17.3-4 (2013): 385-399. Print.

Michaels, Adrian. "Muslim Europe. The Demographic Time Bomb Transforming Our Continent." *telegraph.co.uk*. Telegraph Media Group Limited, 8 Aug. 2009. Web. 9 Apr. 2016.

Murray, Douglas. "Is the Startling Rise in Muslim Infants as Positive as the Times Suggests." *The Spectator*. The Spectator, 10 Jan. 2014. Web. 9 Apr. 2016.

Pappe, Ilan. *The Ethnic Cleansing of Palestine*. Oxford: OneWorld, 2006. Print.

Peteet, Julie. "Icons and Militants: Mothering in the Danger Zone." *Signs* 23.1 (1997): 103-129. Print.

Rich, Adrienne. *Of Woman Born: Motherhood as Experience and Institution*. New York: Norton, 1976. Print.

Schliefer, Aliah. *Motherhood in Islam*. Cambridge: The Islamic Academy, 1986. Print.

Tomlin, Gregory. "Cardinal: Islam's Goal Is to Conquer Europe by Faith and 'Birth Rate.'" *Christian Examiner*: Christian Examiner, 9 Nov. 2015. Web. 9 Apr. 2016.

United Nations Population Fund (UNFPA). "Checkpoints Compound the Risks of Childbirth for Palestinian Women." UNFPA, 15 May 2007. Web. 9 Apr. 2016.

Upal, Hinna Mirza. "A Celebration of Mothering in the Qur'an." *Journal of the Association for Research on Mothering* 7.1 (2005): 86-97. Print.

Wadud, Amina. *Inside the Gender Jihad*. Oxford: One World, 2006. Print.

Warner, Judith. *Perfect Madness: Motherhood in the Age of Anxiety*. New York: Riverhead, 2005. Print.

Williams, Thomas. "Patriarch of Antioch: Muslims Want to Conquer Europe with 'Faith and the Birthrate.'" *Breitbart*. Breitbart, 6 Nov. 2015. Web. 9 Apr. 2016.

Wolf, Naomi. *Misconceptions: Truth, Lies, and the Unexpected Journey to Motherhood*. New York: Anchor, 2003. Print.

I.
MUSLIM MOTHERING
AMID WAR AND VIOLENCE

1.
Empowered Muslim Mothering

Navigating War, Border Crossing, and Activism in El-Haddad's *Gaza Mom*

NADINE SINNO

Eclipsed by a dominant discourse that often depicts Arab and Muslim women as faceless victims or instruments of radical Islam, stories of Arab and Muslim women have largely been neglected or misrepresented by the mainstream Western media, American pop culture, and (neo)colonial feminism. Mohja Kahf describes the categorical and distorted framework through which Arab and Muslim women are generally viewed in the West, particularly the United States. She writes:

> The United States reading public, despite promising resistances here and there, takes in data about women from the Arab world mainly by using conventions emergent from a long history of Western stereotypes about the Arab peoples and Islamic religion. I find that these conventions take shape today in three stereotypes about the Arab woman: One is that she is a victim of gender oppression; the second portrays her as an escapee of her intrinsically oppressive culture; and the third represents her as the pawn of Arab male power. (149)

In the wake of 9/11 and the "Global War on Terror," this Orientalist discourse has become even louder and has had far-reaching consequences in places such as Afghanistan, Iraq, and Palestine. In the context of the war in Afghanistan, Lila Abu Lughod warns against the dangers of the "rhetoric of salvation"—inherited from Christian missionaries—of which both well-intentioned feminists and invading governments have been guilty. This discourse continues to posit Muslim women as inherent victims of an oppressive religion (Islam), without acknowledging their specific social, economic, and cultural circumstances or the fact that many voluntarily choose not to adhere to Western lifestyles or worldviews in favour of more Muslim or Arab-centred paradigms. It also facilitates the dissemination of a pro-war narrative that helps justify the global War on Terror in the name of women's rights and global security. A more useful approach, Abu Lughod explains, entails investigating the material realities of women in war-torn countries and acknowledging the culpability of the United States in endangering women's lives and livelihoods in the Muslim and Arab world through perpetuating wars and economic hardships (789-790). Similarly, Judith Butler urges her readers to ponder the mediated images that pervade their television screens—in the context of the wars in Afghanistan, Iraq, and Palestine. She shows how these images are used to determine whose lives count as "human" and, thus, "grieveable," and whose lives fall outside the normative human category and are, thus, disposable. She writes:

> Are the Palestinians yet accorded the status of "human" in U.S. policy and press coverage? Will those hundreds of thousands of Muslim lives lost in the last decades of strife ever receive the equivalent to the paragraph-long obituaries in the *New York Times* that seek to humanize—often through nationalist and familial framing devices—those Americans who have violently been killed? Is our capacity to mourn in global dimensions foreclosed precisely by the failure to conceive of Muslim and Arab lives as lives? (12)

This seemingly omnipotent (neo)Orientalist discourse that seeks to efface the humanity of Arab and Muslim peoples—by reducing Arab men to terrorists and oppressors and Arab women to passive victims, escapees, or pawns—has not gone unchallenged, however.

As many scholars have shown, Arab and Muslim women, for example, have been actively involved in the struggles for women's rights and national self-determination for centuries (e.g., Fernea and Bezirgan; Ahmed; cooke; Badran and cooke; Wadud; Keddie). In addition, Arab and Muslim women have been writing poetry, fiction, memoirs, and, more recently, blogs as a means of coping with violence in their respective countries, intervening in the interpretation of global events, and reaching out to worldwide audiences. These women bear no resemblance to the powerless war "victim" or the "oppressed" woman whose images remain engraved in Western imagination. With the advent of new social media technologies, more Arab and Muslim women are making their voices heard, in an attempt to present alternative narratives about various issues, including the Arab-Israeli conflict, Islam, and the War on Terror.

Indeed, the past decade has witnessed a remarkable increase in Internet-based war diaries by Arab women from countries, such as Iraq, Lebanon, and Palestine. These diaries include Riverbend's *Baghdad Burning: Girl Blog from Iraq,* Rasha Salti's "Siege Notes," and Zena El-Khalil's "Beirut Update." Such personal narratives, though still fairly marginal, are powerful and poignant in their promotion of social justice and cross-cultural understanding. Highlighting such emerging war narratives and analyzing them critically are necessary to complicate mainstream perceptions about the Middle East and to demonstrate Arab women's agency in representing themselves as engaged actors in the world rather than mere victims of war or of "evil" Arab men.

Laila El-Haddad—Palestinian mother, journalist, and activist— is one of those Muslim women who have taken control of their own war narratives to shed light on the lives of women and men in war-torn Gaza. Her blog-turned-book *Gaza Mom: Palestine, Politics, Parenting, and Everything in Between* (2010) is comprised of blog entries written during the years 2004 through 2010. During those years, Gaza witnessed intense political upheaval, including frequent border closures, which led to economic and humanitarian crises, recurrent bombardment (especially during the Gaza War[1]), and internecine fighting between rival factions Fatah and Hamas. El-Haddad vividly records her and other Palestinians' predicament living in the war-torn city, her harrowing border-crossing experiences at airports and checkpoints, and her parenting experiences that, surprisingly perhaps, are often joyful, despite the chaos surrounding her life. At times, El-Haddad focuses on her private life, as she fawns over her child Yousuf's linguistic and potty-training skills. At other times, her private life takes the backburner, such as when she reports to duty as a journalist and interviews Palestinian farmers and fishermen to document their personal devastations as a result of Israel's social, economic, and political control, or when she highlights underreported news about the death of innocent civilians in Gaza.

In this essay, I provide a close reading of El-Haddad's *Gaza Mom* and focus on those narratives that illustrate the larger struggle of Muslim mothers during times of crisis. Rather than feeling utterly victimized by ordeals such as racial profiling, Islamophobia, and even heavy bombardment, El-Haddad exercises her agency through writing, participating in anti-war activism, and even laughing in the face of atrocity. Through documenting her experiences in Gaza, she emphasizes the inextricable link between the personal and the political in the lives of civilians under fire, especially mothers and their children. Her steadfastness, creativity, and activism represent what I refer to as "empowered Muslim mothering," a term that is primarily informed by the notions of "empowered mothering," and "feminist mothering" as conceptualized by contemporary feminists such as Sara Ruddick, Tuula Gordon, Adrienne Rich, and Andrea O'Reilly.

In the introduction to her edited volume *Mother Outlaws: Theories and Practices of Empowered Mothering,* O'Reilly highlights the main features of empowered mothering. She writes:

> The theory and practice of empowered mothering recognizes that both mothers and children benefit when the mother lives her life and practices mothering from a position of agency, authority, authenticity, and autonomy…. [T]his new perspective, in emphasizing maternal authority and ascribing agency to mothers and value to motherwork, defines motherhood as a political site wherein the mother can effect social change. (12-13)

Although El-Haddad may not call herself a feminist (or aspire to a Western-centred type of feminism), her mothering approach, which views mother and child as separate entities capable of enriching each other, echoes what these contemporary feminists refer to as "empowered mothering," as opposed to "patriarchal motherhood," which generally views the mother as an authoritarian yet selfless caregiver and the child as an exclusively passive recipient of a mother's care (O'Reilly 11-15). In using the expression "empowered Muslim mothering," I, therefore, situate the concept of empowered childrearing within a Muslim-centred context and show how a Muslim mother such as El-Haddad demonstrates a conscious and symbiotic mode of parenting—one that draws on her own ethnic background, religious values, and socio-political conditions.

STEADFAST MAMA KEEPS THE FAITH

One of the main strengths of El-Haddad's *Gaza Mom* is its painstaking demonstration of the normalization of violence and the tenacity of civilians, particularly the mothers among them, in deflecting the disruptive effects of the Israeli occupation and attacks on Gaza. El-Haddad's diaries provide a valuable eyewitness and journalistic account about survival in a war zone. Specifically, they demonstrate the critical role that the Islamic faith plays in lifting people's morale and in sustaining them through their darkest moments. The reader quickly learns that El-Haddad's steadfastness is inspired and informed by two main facets of her identity, namely her Islamic faith and her motherly status, since she is unabashed in voicing the strong sense of peace they offer her amidst the chaos surrounding her. For example, one of the most heart wrenching entries is titled "On Breastfeeding and Weaning Under Occupation," in which she discusses how breastfeeding—which is recommended by the Qur'an until the child has reached two years of age—had gotten her and Yousuf through border-crossing journeys,[2] such that weaning him became all the more harder to achieve. She writes:

> Further, my ability to breastfeed him—to be a portable milk machine when Israeli closures resulted in shortages of formula—has gotten us through some tough times.... I

think back to those terrible moments and shiver, comforted only by the fact that the nursing sometimes got Yousuf past the hours-long waits in the painful heat of August or bone-numbing cold of winter at checkpoints or at Rafah crossing, waiting for the Israel "über-wardens" to let us through, as they bellowed out orders to the thousands of desperate travelers, including us. (*Gaza Mom* 182)

In this scene, breastfeeding is presented through a Palestinian Muslim woman's eyes: the act is transformed into empowered resistance, both practically and symbolically. Together, El-Haddad and Yousuf brave the harsh circumstances of checkpoints, and their pain is alleviated. The immediate, calming effect of breastfeeding allows her to pass the time as she and Yousuf "waited and waited—and bam, like magic, he would calm down and sleep. And that meant so could [she]" (*Gaza Mom* 182). Although El-Haddad has no control over the border, or the availability of formula milk, breastfeeding at least allows her a sense of agency over her and Yousuf's body and soul.

Clearly, El-Haddad is anything but disempowered by motherhood. Amber Kinser argues against the reductionist perception of mothering as inherently oppressive and proposes that we contemplate the diversity of mothering acts in context because for many women, especially women of colour, mothering can provide a myriad ways of exercising agency. Invoking the contributions of Jessie Bernard and Adrienne Rich, Kinser discusses the important shift in feminist thought with regards to mothering:

[In] the mid 1970s feminist writers Jessie Bernard and Adrienne Rich made important distinctions between the patriarchal institution of motherhood and women's actual experiences of mothering. Rich in particular argued that these experiences are not necessarily oppressive. Many feminists have argued since then that the degree of women's power in mothering, how it is lived out and experienced in by the women themselves, and the social structures that encourage or discourage maternal agency are important points for consideration. This approach takes us beyond simple questions of whether mothers "have" agency or not and, understanding that they do, invites us to examine a more multilayered image of maternal power. (7)

Breastfeeding is not the only motherly task that El-Haddad takes pride in and broadcasts for the entire world to reassess. Potty training, too, takes on a whole new meaning, as she redefines it in all its nuances, once again in the context of occupation. In an entry titled "My Potty-Training Miracle...and Other Things," she announces the good news of her success at potty training Yousuf and preempts any anticipated counter-arguments about the importance (or lack thereof) of her news:

OK, I know this seems so trivial in the realm of things, but you have no idea what this seemingly insignificant advancement has meant for me: no more changing five diapers a day ... or buying those diapers—which you never realize how much you shell out for until you are through with them; no more changing diapers in extremely uncomfortable settings, such as border crossings with tanks pointed at you. (*Gaza Mom* 211)

El-Haddad's elaborate blog post about Yousuf's potty-training milestones achieves at least two major goals: first, she reminds her readers of all the patience and toil involved in a mother's work inside the home, and, at the same time, she points out the unique sense of relief that a woman raising a "war child" feels upon successful potty training. As she notes, such a news headline is not likely to show up anywhere but on her blog. In other words, her mommy blogging takes potty training to another level. Unlike most mainstream media, El-Haddad takes the reader on an intimate journey inside her own home in war-torn Gaza, where even the most basic human needs are depicted in minute detail so the reader can visualize the effects of conflicts and global politics on civilians. In this scene, she shows how militarization spills into the most intimate of human acts, in this case a child's act of defecating, as soldiers put him and his mother under heavy surveillance. As Cynthia Enloe asserts, "Most of the people in the world who are militarized are not themselves in uniform. Most militarized people are civilians" (4).

El-Haddad also imparts her faith to her child when he is feeling anxious and powerless. One of her spontaneous "teaching moments" occurs in the United States, where she travelled occasionally to visit her husband, who was attending medical school at the time. El-Haddad, Yousuf and Noor (her then newborn daughter), and several peace activists brave inclement weather in order to join a national march named "Let Gaza Live" in Washington, DC. In the car, Yousuf interrupts her conversation to ask if his grandfather is going to die in Gaza because of the bombing. He pleads, "Uleelhum may tukhoo, Mama! (Mom, tell them not to shoot him!)" Without dismissing his fears or patronizing him, El-Haddad placates her son by instructing him to trust God with his grandfather's fate. "I ask him to make a dua, to ask God to keep him—to keep all of Gaza—safe.... That is stronger than any bullet," she assures him (*Gaza Mom* 369). This scene demonstrates how empowered Muslim mothering is embedded in El-Haddad's anti-war activism. Yousuf and Noor are socialized from early on to participate in civic society and to lean on their faith when in a crisis. They also receive a lesson about the merging of faith and political activism.

In addition to finding comfort in their Muslim-centred parenting, many Palestinians seek solace through collective prayer, as *Gaza Mom* demonstrates. In an entry titled "The Gates of Hell, the Window to Heaven," El-Haddad recounts the dark cloud of violence that enveloped Gaza city, as phosphorous bombs dropped all over the city on January 12, 2009. She writes:

> The fear is salient; it is suffocating; it is in the air, friends say, and on one knows what's coming next. There is nowhere to turn to except the heavens above. And so many people in Gaza have taken to doing just that: They are waking up for special predawn prayers qiam al layl in the "last third of the night"—a window of time when believers feel especially close to God and when it is said He is especially close to our calls upon Him, and supplications and prayers are most likely to be answered. And

so they tremble, and they wait, and they pray during this
small window to heaven for the gates of hell to be closed.
(*Gaza Mom* 372)

These Palestinian Muslims raise their voices in prayer in response
to the violence around them. For El-Haddad and many of her
compatriots, Islam is a religion of hope and inspiration. Rather
than feeling apologetic or reserved about a religion that has become
so vilified post-9/11, El-Haddad openly shares her faith with her
readers. Her narrative does not heed the secularist call for Muslims
to underplay or reform their Islamic rituals and belief systems.
Saba Mahmoud notes the militancy and presumptuousness of this
secular wave in its attempts to thwart differing worldviews under
the banner of rationality and tolerance. She writes:

> The fear is that orthodox Islamic practices—from the veil
> to public prayers to abidance by rules of sexual segrega-
> tion—are expressions of a fanatical literalist mentality and,
> as such, a threat to the entire edifice of our liberal political
> system.... Since the events of 9/11, it has become customary
> to hear pleas—in the academy as well as in the popular
> press—for the restoration of secular reasoning, principles,
> and orientations, so that some semblance of order may be
> restored from the havoc religious politics has wrought in
> the world today. (345-347)

El-Haddad's text demonstrates a version of Islam that is rarely
accounted for in the mainstream media. She gives her readers a
glimpse of Islam as lived by average Muslims rather than theorized
by (Orientalist) intellectuals and "experts." Through showing, not
telling, she educates her readers about the ways through which
Islam remains an integral part of many people's lives, one that
shapes things, including but not limited to their parenting, activism,
and responses to disaster. In his discussion of the significance of
Muslim narratives in English, Amin Malak writes:

> Since any narrative reflects, mediates, and even reshapes the
> ethos of the culture from which it emanates, Muslim nar-

ratives in English then represent remarkable achievements of self-actualizing, identity-defining processes. Whatever their political, religious, or aesthetic leanings, these Muslims producing narratives in English, affirm, with varying degrees, their affiliation with Islam as a source of spiritual and/or aesthetic inspiration. (7)

Gaza Mom shows the life-affirming value of faith in people's lives. Empowered by their religious faith and the will to make a better life for themselves and their children, many Gazans go about their day-to-day business as they try to live normal lives in a city that is anything but normal.

In an entry titled "Just another Day in Paradise," on March 31, 2006, El-Haddad describes a beautiful day in Gaza, in which she and a cousin enjoy some mint tea and cookies, while their children play, and as war happens in the background. She writes:

> And swirling all around us, the entertainment for the evening was a "symphony" of war, as people like to describe it here. The distinct double-boom of tank artillery shells—"Boom boom" every few seconds, along with the single explosions of what I would later learn were navy gunship attacks—intercepted with rapid machine-gun fire, a swarm of drones whirring instantly overhead, and Apache helicopters attacking areas in northern and eastern Gaza. My cousin told her daughter they were just fireworks and not to be alarmed, so she (4 years old) casually ignored them. (*Gaza Mom* 162)

This entry is one of many entries dedicated to the assertion that life must go on for average civilians, regardless of challenges such as bombs, check points, and border closures.[3] Over the course of the text, numerous life (and death) events are told, including children being born and raised despite their parents' meager resources, students getting around checkpoints to attend classes, and fishermen finding ways to make a living despite Israeli restrictions and naval bombardment. In her article "Getting by the Occupation: How Violence Became Normal during the Second Palestinian Intifada,"

Lori Allen discusses the significance of this collective sense of stoicism. She writes:

> When a variety of forms of violence are being mobilized to encourage, if not force, people to leave, the deflection of these measures through adaptation and just getting by becomes crucial.... In these conditions where the routine and assumptions of daily life are physically disrupted, purposefully and as part of the political program of Israeli colonialism, everyday life in Palestine—in its everyday-ness—is itself partly the result of concerted, collective production. (456)

At the same time that El-Haddad documents her people's resilience, she protests against the normalization of violence and the forced adaptability of civilians to such surreal conditions to which no human being, let alone a child, should have to get accustomed. In "Anything but Ordinary," an entry titled after a speech given by Condoleezza Rice in which she boasts of a border agreement[4] that would allegedly give Palestinians a chance to "live ordinary lives," El-Haddad rages against this veneer of normalcy:

> Now, maybe it's just me, but six months on, I wouldn't say my life is "ordinary" by any stretch of the imagination... Just ask Yousuf. He often mistakes Israeli gunships for birds, dances to the revolutionary songs blasted during political rallies marching by our house, and has learned to distinguish between Israeli-tank shell and machine-gun banter. (*Gaza Mom* 138)

Darry Li, a former information officer for the Palestinian Center for Human Rights, affirms that contrary to what the term "disengagement" might imply, regular military interventions continue to terrify Palestinian populations in Gaza, particularly children. He asserts, "Since disengagement, Israeli fighter jets have begun regularly breaking the sound barrier at low latitude over the entire Gaza Strip, causing sonic shock waves as loud as actual bombardment, shattering windows and reportedly causing psychological damage to children" (48). By documenting her own son's reactions to Israel's military tactics, *Gaza Mom* puts a human face on the Palestinian child whose voice is rarely heard in mainstream news outlets and who, at best, serves as a mere statistic in studies documenting casualties, poverty, and illness in Gaza.

El-Haddad adamantly shows that the strong sense of steadfastness, which Palestinians have become famous for—and which the rest of the world has come to expect of them—demands substantial sacrifices and often takes its toll on people's psyches. She reminds the reader that the celebrated sense of determination, though admirable, does not come easily and naturally but rather at a high cost of emotional and mental exhaustion on the part of civilians, especially mothers. She writes, "Sometimes it can get exhausting being here.... A border closure here. A milk or diaper shortage there. A travel ban. An aerial assault. Anger, and depression, and despondence.... The air is not yours to breathe. It's suffocating and psychologically demanding" (*Gaza Mom* 142). By documenting the emotional rollercoaster experienced by people in the war zone, in their high moments of resilience as well as low moments of dejection, El-Haddad guards against the romanticizing of an unbroken Palestinian spirit. Furthermore, she humanizes civilians to ensure that they are seen as real humans with a threshold for pain and depression. By doing so, she ensures that Palestinians are not relegated to the heroic realm, where issues of social justice and the actual implementation of human rights may be overlooked.

Gaza Mom provides a valuable contribution to the long tradition (and literature) attesting to Arab women's resistance, particularly Palestinian women's resistance. Although El-Haddad's struggles are certainly unique, she should not be perceived as a lone voice. For decades, Palestinian women have been resisting occupation, negotiating gender roles, and ensuring the daily survival of their families, especially their children, in the Occupied Territories and/or in diasporic communities (Hasso; Peteet; Sharoni; Shalhoub-Kevorkian). Being mindful of this long-existing tradition, and situating El-Haddad within it, helps guard against the risky implication that she is exceptional in her accomplishments or that Arab women did not offer intellectual interventions before the advent of blogging and other social media.

FUNNY MAMA CRACKS UP UNDER PRESSURE

Although *Gaza Mom* is undeniably a text about sad and serious issues, including war, loss, and social injustice, it is not void of laughter and sarcasm. On the contrary, humour serves as necessary ingredient for surviving and writing about devastating events. El-Haddad often employs humour as a means of showing the absurdity of things, such as occupation and border crossing, primarily through the lens of a Palestinian Muslim mother. In affirming the still-existing sense of humour among distressed Palestinians, she also asserts her and her compatriots' sense of humanity.

One of the most humorous entries is titled "Flying While Muslim," in which El-Haddad recounts her trials and tribulations at an American airport in 2006 as she tries to check in for a flight from Minneapolis to Chicago. Although she has become accustomed to airport screening, new airport security measures—especially those that she perceives to be primarily aimed at Muslim travellers like herself—never fail to take her by surprise, which make her travels more memorable, for better or for worse, and create new fodder for her writing. She recounts:

> "Ma'am, have you ever been 'SSSS'ed' before?" [The officer asked]

> "SSSSed? What does that even mean?" I wondered, but I didn't bother to ask, because I guessed it was probably something sinister. Something to do with stopping people who seemed to be suspicious and probably plotting a terrorist attack (that or they probably happen to wear a hijab or "look" Muslim) ...

> "We have a female SS here; someone help, please," the agent bellowed out in front of the long line of nervous onlookers.

> "So now only two Ss?" I thought. I waited and was escorted by another official for a check before being asked about what potentially lethal liquids or gels I had. In my possession was a 4-ounce strawberry Dannon Light & Fit

33

yoghurt ... the potentially lethal weapon of strawberries,
corn syrup, and bacteria. (*Gaza Mom* 216)

When asked if she would like to eat her yoghurt, El-Haddad
says she is fasting. After that, she is questioned more thoroughly,
and she undergoes a torso search. In an attempt to make her feel
better, the airline personnel offers a few possible reasons for her
"SSSS" situation, stating that perhaps she was "SSed" because of
possible last-minute changes to her ticket, which she confirms she
has not done. The whole experience leaves her a little depressed,
yet she perseveres in her wry humour as she explains that she
must have been there during a high-terror alert, which caused
authorities to be suspicious of the "strawberry toting Gazan on
her way to a social forum in Norway" (216). Rather than get
upset, El-Haddad jokes, but her joking is anything but innocent.
Through her airport story, the reader is prodded to contemplate
her subtext on racial profiling, Islamophobia, and civil liberties.
In her book on grief and healing in a post-9/11 world, Judith
Butler discusses the practical and psychological repercussions of
this culture of fear. She writes:

> Various terror alerts that go out over the media authorize
> and heighten racial hysteria in which fear is directed any-
> where and nowhere, in which individuals are asked to be on
> guard but not told what to be on guard against; so everyone
> is free to imagine and identify the source of terror.... The
> result is that an amorphous racism abounds, rationalized
> by the claim of "self-defense." A generalized panic works
> in tandem with the shoring-up of the sovereign state and
> the suspension of civil liberties. (39)

Although Butler's statement adequately describes the ubiquitous
and general sense of fear created by "terror alerts," and other
governmental or media tactics, it does not fully capture the specific
repercussions of such tactics on Arabs and Muslims in the United
States. El-Haddad's experience and the experience of many other
Arabs and Muslims who have been subject to hostility, racial profiling, and discrimination illustrate that this "amorphous racism"

often translates into very "targeted" racism—one that is directed at people who are identified as Arabs and/or Muslims.[5]

Like many Arabs and Muslims, El-Haddad's sense of "double-consciousness," to borrow W. E. Dubois's term, follows her every time that she travels, as she sees herself through other people's eyes: a suspect and an unwelcome outsider who is perceived as a threat at any given moment. According to historian Rashid Khalidi, whom El-Haddad invokes in her text, borders are the "quintessential" experience for many Palestinians. They are the space in which their identity—their paperless, stateless existence—becomes most visible and problematic. However, it is this very denial of their nationhood at borders and airports that unites them as a people and affirms their common fate. He writes:

> The quintessential Palestinian experience, which illustrates some of the most basic issues raised by Palestinian identity, takes place at a border, an airport, a checkpoint: in short, at any one of those many modern barriers where identities are checked and verified. What happens to Palestinians at these crossing points brings home to them how much they share in common as a people. For it is at these borders and barriers that six million Palestinians are singled out for "special treatment," and are forcefully reminded of their identity: of who they are, and of why they are different from others. (1)

El-Haddad's humorous stories are not limited to border-crossings, however. They also include anecdotes about awkward cross-cultural encounters that confirm the power of (neo)Orientalist narratives about the "clash of civilizations" within the American and Israeli imaginary. Among these anecdotes is one in which she reaches out to a woman who had been staring at her suspiciously at a playground in Maryland. Upon asking the woman about her kids' ages and where they are from, the woman blurts out "From Israel—Please don't kill me" (*Gaza Mom* 412). When El-Haddad asks the woman, "And ... why exactly would I do that?," the woman asks El-Haddad where she herself is from, as if searching for more tangible evidence to confirm her initial theory about El-Haddad's bloodthirstiness. Upon hearing that she is from Gaza, the woman feels even more validated and responds, "Well, see, that's why" (*Gaza Mom* 412). This brief exchange between El-Haddad and the woman is painfully illuminating. Being Palestinian and Muslim makes El-Haddad's and other Palestinian Muslims' criminality de facto in this woman's mind. The woman—who initially knows nothing about El-Haddad, except that she is a Muslim (as evidenced by her headscarf)—cannot control herself from blurting out Islamophobic comments. Worse still, she does not even feel the need to apologize for her unwarranted comment at any point during the conversation. Sherryl Cashin's comparative study on American perceptions post-9/11 found evidence that "[i]n the wake of the 9/11 attacks, it is more socially acceptable to express explicit bias against Arabs or Muslims than against blacks or other racial/ethnic groups" (132).

Although El-Haddad chooses to respond politely, she fantasizes in retrospect about what she could have told the woman. She uses her blog as a means of showcasing her wit as she muses about all the things she could have said such as, "Not all Palestinians/Arab bite," or "Shouldn't it be me who's afraid of being killed, given the Israeli track record of violence against Palestinians—1,400 in one month?" (*Gaza Mom* 412-13). El-Haddad may not have told the woman these things, but she does share them with her blog and book readers. She turns a disturbing cross-cultural encounter into a teaching moment about the absurdity of casting Palestinians as the ultimate terrorists while completely overlooking the crimes committed against them. She uses her experience as a case study to show how acceptable it has become to voice racist sentiments so loudly and clearly—even to a mother whose only fault is trying to make small talk in a playground. In his essay "Humor and Resistance in the Arab World and Greater Middle East," Khalid Kishtainy discusses the effectiveness of political humour. He writes:

> Political humor is a low-risk, nonviolent channel for discussing injustice, defying foreign occupation, and challenging defunct percepts and misrule ... [T]he encouragement of meaningful humor should be considered as part of the

repertoire of any nonviolent activist, and is one of the best and cheapest nonviolent means for tackling today's problems. (63)

Following Kishtainy, El-Haddad achieves multiple purposes by resorting to humour. She rallies her readers around her, undermines the discourse of the "clash of civilizations," and invokes laughter in the face of pain.

In addition to writing comically about airport sagas and Islamophobic cross-cultural encounters, El-Haddad adopts humour as a therapeutic, defense mechanism that allows her to cope with daily atrocities and to sustain a positive morale in the face of danger. In the following incident, her humour emerges as a desperate attempt to pacify her bewildered child Yousuf who can no longer bear the sound of shelling. She recounts:

> Fierce battles employing mortars, rocket-propelled grenades (RPGs), and heavy machine-gun fire were raging all around our house today, at times only a block away ... Yousuf, of course, became more and more concerned as the day passed, until I finally told him they were not firing, but rather making an enormous pot of popcorn outside that would fill the streets once it was done. At first he wasn't convinced; then, he later remarked, "Mama, I don't really like this kind of popcorn!" When the firing died down, he ran into my room excitedly shouting, "Mama, Mama! I think the popcorn is done!" (*Gaza Mom* 293)

This tragicomic scene reflects El-Haddad's empowered mothering: she creatively finds a solution, as she transforms a bleak experience, such as bombardment, into a more bearable and almost-exciting adventure for her child. Building on Sara Ruddik's conception of "maternal thinking," Kinser emphasizes the necessity of acknowledging the skills and discipline involved in mothering one's children thoughtfully, as opposed to relying exclusively on what is traditionally referred to as "motherly instinct." She writes, "Understanding women's mothering knowledge to be grounded in maternal thinking rather than maternal instinct positions us to consider the concentrated effort that women put into mothering, rather than to assume that it comes to them as quickly and effortlessly, as say, an instinctive 'fight or flight' response to danger" (19). El-Haddad's crafty way of dealing with stressful situations is an enactment of this maternal thinking par excellence since she is indeed in a dangerous situation. Yet she neither flees nor fights; rather, she creatively gets her child through this predicament. The popcorn scene forces the readers to acknowledge the myriad ways through which Palestinian mothers, like other mothers in war zones, often channel their energy into empowering themselves and their children. Even survival takes on a different meaning as a child is slowly conditioned to live with the sound of bullets and grenades.

El-Haddad's humour establishes a uniquely personal and public voice that rivals the media's cold rendering of news events, thus pulling the reader in and almost forcing him or her to have an emotional investment in the text. Populating *Gaza Mom* with real people and writing humorously about them, and most importantly about one's self, may compel some recalcitrant readers to continue reading *Gaza Mom* despite the temptation to abandon an essentially painful narrative. As miriam cooke notes in the foreword to the book,

> Ironic humor, sometimes at her own expense, is a way to make this terrible saga not only not same old, same old but enticing and compelling. You want to read how Laila is going to manage tomorrow; will it be funny in the midst of tragedy so that you will have to read and not want to just skip the bad parts? (*Gaza Mom* 11)

Of course, readers who are genuinely interested in seeking alternative sources of news and information, such as El-Haddad's blog and book, may not want to "skip the bad parts," (i.e., the tragic parts involving things such as loss and devastation), but these avid readers are not the exclusive audience of El-Haddad's text. cooke's statement perhaps signifies something deeper and worthy of investigation with regard to reader reception. Mindful of El-Haddad's international readership, cooke seems to be addressing a potentially apprehensive segment of audience who might be disturbed by all the "bad parts." Her statement reflects a plausible supposition that El-Haddad's text lies outside the comfort zone of some readers in the West, particularly those who have not experienced living under conditions of war and who are used to consuming much more diluted versions of the events in Gaza. After all, El-Haddad's text is written in English and was first disseminated as a blog, accessible to readers worldwide. It was also later published as a book by an American publisher in the United States. El-Haddad herself perceives her blog as an alternative to the mainstream media and refers to it as a "window into Gaza during some of its most turbulent years." In her preface to the book, she writes:

> Journalists who have covered Palestinian-Israeli conflict at great length often note that the headlines written five or even 10 years ago could have been written today.... Such headlines as "more violence in the Middle East" or "Palestinian terror" have become mainstays of the American nightly news—and of the average American's perceptions of the conflict. Such statements are mistakenly attributed to a vague and misleading notion of "cyclical violence" that seems to have no end and no clear beginning, while most mainstream media fail to delve deeper, to ask why the conflict has persisted for so long, what forces are driving the "violence," or what kinds of lives people can live underneath it all. (17)

Similar to cooke, who must mention humour as she frames El-Haddad's narrative, El-Haddad herself must have had her average American readers in mind when she started her blog. Taking into account their reading sensibilities, she may have resorted to humour as a rhetorical strategy. Not only does El-Haddad keep her readers captivated through her funny narrative, but she also ensures that her readers' expectations of the text are constantly being challenged and disrupted by the text's ups and downs, its seriousness, and its jest. Analyzing the role of humour in Latin American fiction, Dianna Niebylski writes:

One of the most distinguishing features of humor is the way in which it forces us to shift our initial expectations, and this is true whether the source of the humor is a joke's punch line or an unexpectedly comic situation. Shifting expectations requires shifting one's presumed center, and moving one's center forces one to reexamine one's epistemological and cultural assumptions. (12)

The same may be said of *Gaza Mom*. After all, El-Haddad is a Muslim mother who seeks to decentre her average readers' assumptions about Palestine, politics, parenting, and everything in between. Finally, by inviting her readers to laugh occasionally, El-Haddad guards against their desensitization to violence or even their feelings of redemption and relief, after the tears have dried.

MIGHTY MAMA MOBILIZES WORDS

One of the main accomplishments of *Gaza Mom*—regardless of whether or not El-Haddad consciously set out to achieve it—is demonstrating that Muslim mothering does not necessarily deter a woman from actively participating in public life. On the contrary, as the text affirms, being an Arab Muslim mother, let alone living in a war zone, might prompt a mother to take an active role in raising awareness about her religion and her experiences and in working towards a more just world for her children—one that rejects violence and prejudice against a people because of their nationality and/or faith. As this essay continues to emphasize, El-Haddad's mothering and activism are inseparable, and the line between the two is almost always blurred. This becomes especially obvious in the way El-Haddad employs her talents and skills with words to wage an education campaign against the mainstream media's rhetoric with regard to the Israeli-Palestinian conflict.

The rhetoric surrounding the invasion of Iraq was predominantly articulated in the form of artificial dualisms—including "good" versus "evil," "terrorist" versus "victim," "oppression" versus "liberation"—that were proclaimed by government officials and disseminated by a complacent mainstream media (Sinno). Not unlike the rhetoric preceding the war in Iraq, the mainstream discourse about the Israeli-Palestinian conflict is fraught with categorical labels that reduce a complex reality of disputed territories, illegal occupation, and daily turmoil into a morass of binary oppositions and misleading terminology. A quick glance at the daily headlines on the Israeli-Palestinian conflict in mainstream news outlets reveals the regular dissemination of familiar buzzwords that contribute to normalizing and justifying violence in places such as Gaza. These buzzwords include "terrorism," "national security," "retaliation," "collateral damage," and "human shields," among others. In *Gaza Mom*, Laila El-Haddad deconstructs such a discourse to reveal how these terms, though seemingly authoritative and clear in their signification, often camouflage and misrepresent much more complex realities.

Among the terms that El-Haddad problematizes is the term "target," often associated with finding and exterminating militants. In one of her March 2006 entries, she recounts:

> I learned that the explosion I heard was an attack by an unmanned Israeli drone ... It killed the intended "targets"—two members of Islamic Jihad. But it also killed three others, including two children—brothers, 8-year old Raed al-Batch and his 15-year-old brother, Ala. They were with their mother at the time. She lived, only to learn that she lost two boys—at once. (142)

Using "targets," in quotations marks, El-Haddad draws attention to this term, often employed by Israeli officials, to show how it includes both militants and innocent children. By narrating such incidents, Al-Haddad deconstructs the myths about military tactics, such as smart bombs and targeted killings: she shows how the boundaries between the battlefield and the domestic sphere are blurred, which causes death and destruction among the most vulnerable groups, in this case children.

Because her activism is influenced by her mothering (and vice versa), El-Haddad remains especially cognizant of the tragic death of innocent children and its effect on the parents, and she always draws attention to the death of a child, lest the child be forgotten or the news of his or her death be buried under more "popular" news headlines. As Antoinette Pole argues, political blogging needs to be recognized for reducing the media's power at monopolizing news reporting. She writes, "In an era of media consolidation, owned by corporate elites who are largely impervious to public sentiment, bloggers have penetrated the hierarchy of the media, thereby diluting the strength of these omniscient organizations" (16). El-Haddad's deconstruction of the dominant rhetoric on Gaza includes telling untold (or underreported) stories, such as that of Aya, a thirteen-year-old girl who got lost on the way back home and was shot four times by the Israeli army (in January 2006), who shot her because she "got close to the fence" (*Gaza Mom* 128). Aya's tragic story, El-Haddad notes, did not make the headlines as the media was busy covering Hamas's victory in the elections, "the political earthquake that shook the region" (*Gaza Mom* 128).

In addition to reporting about the deaths of innocent children, El-Haddad puts a human face to the victims about whom she reports. When she recounts the death of a nine-year old girl named Hadil, after an Israeli shell hit her family's home, she provides personal details about the dead child. The reader learns that Hadil was a vibrant child who enjoyed reading, writing stories, and playing "make-believe" (*Gaza Mom* 173). Unlike stories about dead Americans or Israelis (whether soldiers or civilians), stories of dead Arabs and/or Muslims are rarely given the attention and empathy that every human being deserves. According to Butler, "A hierarchy of grief could no doubt be enumerated ...we seldom, if ever, hear the names of the thousands of Palestinians who have died by the Israeli military with United States support, or any number of Afghan people, children and adults. Do they have names and faces, personal histories, family, favourite hobbies, slogans by which they live?" (32). In El-Haddad's narrative, the reader is forced to ponder all these things and more about the victims whose deaths—and lives—she so vividly describes.

El-Haddad shows that even the term "human shield," which the Israeli authorities and the media have often used in association with the militant group Hamas, can be turned on its head because it signifies a common practice by the Israeli military itself. El-Haddad speaks of her father's interview with Canadian Broadcasting Corporation (CBC) with candour, backing up her father's comments with evidence provided by B'Tselem, an Israeli human watch organization. She writes:

> My father went on to describe accounts of Palestinians being used as human shields—by the Israelis. The Israeli military has been forcing families out of their homes and making them scope out buildings and rooms for the army to enter and for their snipers to nest in.... The practice was also employed in Jenin, and in Nablus in 2007 (where a young girl and boy were abused). B'Tselem has said "Israeli soldiers routinely used Palestinian civilians as human shields by forcing them to carry out life-threatening military tasks." (*Gaza Mom* 363)

In *Women and the War Story*, miriam cooke highlights the nature of postmodern wars and the necessity of gaining access to civilian war reportage, especially women's, precisely because women writers are often invested in exposing the transformation of the domestic sphere, which they know so closely, into a combat zone. She writes:

> Never before has the fictionality of the War Story been so obvious. In nuclear age wars the women and the children—whom the War Story had described as at home and safe because defended by their men at the front—are increasingly acknowledged to be attractive military targets. They are not being protected. Their men cannot protect them. This fact has never been so openly and widely acknowledged as it is now, because war is no longer the province of military historians and national security analysts and advisers, all of them men, but has now become a magnet for humanists, many of them women and feminists. (38)

Unlike other virtual communities that solely exist in cyberspace and are centred on providing a forum for moral support, experiential perspective, or online alliances—all legitimate goals—*Gaza Mom* goes beyond providing a virtual forum. El-Haddad's online activism is almost always complimented by practical, on-the-ground activism, including giving lectures on various university campuses and institutions worldwide, attending protests (sometimes with her children), writing letters and petitions, making media appearances as well as educating people with whom she crosses paths, such as the Israeli mom in the playground in Maryland or the immigration officers at various airports. In other words, the blog, despite its seemingly ephemeral existence by virtue of its "virtual" location, is rooted in the material realities of its author and inhabitants. It is anything but disembodied. The pictures of El-Haddad's children and other Palestinians also fill the pages of the text, which solidify the particularities of place and time and reinforce the fact that anti-war activism is part and parcel of El-Haddad's empowered mothering.

It is worth noting that El-Haddad's blog came about when one of her cousins pressured her to start a blog so she could connect with her expatriate husband and keep him up to date about Yousuf's development. It was a separate entity from another blog, in which El-Haddad wrote occasionally about Gaza. Ultimately, El-Haddad recognized the inseparability of her personal and political lives and merged the two blogs into one that dealt both with Yousuf and the news (*Gaza Mom* 15). Her attitude towards adopting online activism evolved from reluctance to full-on enthusiasm. In one post, she even discusses her new infatuation with Twitter, the more recent technological breakthrough. She writes, "I should say I feel a little guilty—ever since I've begun Twittering, I've found myself devoting less time to blogging. It's like I'm cheating on my blog! I admit it—I'm having an affair with Twitter" (*Gaza Mom* 387).

When El-Haddad is away from Gaza, she recruits her father in reporting live news from the besieged city. She recounts how a phone call from her distressed father in Gaza becomes alternative world news via technologies such as Skype and Twitter. When Israel bombed Gaza in January of 2009, her father reported on the phone, "The suburb is in flames. Residents are calling out to the Red Cross, but they can't reach them. They say they are bombing with firebombs ... there is a thick black smoke descending on them, choking people." In response to hearing her father's report over the phone, she recalls in her book, "I immediately have my brother update my Twitter account for me. I feel better, empowered in whatever incremental way, knowing that I am broadcasting this piece of information that is at once senseless and meaningful to the world. My brother struggles to condense terror, death, and panic to 140 characters" (*Gaza Mom* 370). In this scene, as father, daughter, and son work together to tell Gaza's story, El-Haddad demonstrates the importance of individual responsibility and collective action. Evidently, El-Haddad realizes both the strengths and limitations of social media, and she chooses to use these technologies and do her part and to mobilize others around her in disseminating the news of destruction in Gaza city.

CONCLUSION

In *Motherhood and Feminism,* Kinser writes:

> Because dominant ideas about mothers and children are derived from white, middle-class perspectives and assumptions, it is particularly important in the study and critique of motherhood that feminists widen the lens through which we view mothers' experiences.... Further, the women representing nondominant cultures, ethnicities, and classes have faced limited access to and acceptance in academic publication outlets. As a consequence, much of what has been written and published about feminism and motherhood has failed to adequately examine the multiplicity of women's experiences and points of view. (22)

This is particularly true in the case of Palestinian mothers, whose long-existing history of resistance must be visited and revisited in academic and activist spheres. As Nadera Shalhoub-Kevorkian notes in the introduction to her book on Palestinian women's resistance, "Despite the severe effect of militarization and violence on women's lives, their bodies and survival strategies, the documentation of women's history and frontline activities in war and conflict zones is generally lacking" (14). El-Haddad's *Gaza Mom* attests to the "multiplicity of women's mothering experiences and points of views" by showing how mothering in a war zone can be similar to yet also very different from, other mothering experiences worldwide. In countries in which mothers must constantly worry about securing basic needs, such as food and drink, electric power, and safety for their children—in addition to everything else—empowered mothering takes on a different form and requires a unique set of skills.

Additionally, the text is filled with references to El-Haddad's support system, including her husband, father, mother, and brother—all of whom work side by side in order to disseminate news about Gaza and alleviate the pain of those around them inside Gaza city. Once again, this picture counters the dominant stereotype of the silenced Arab and/or Muslim woman whose relationship with her family, especially her male relatives, is fraught with tension, abuse, and inequality. As Marsha Hamilton notes:

> Middle Eastern women have seldom been presented in U.S. or Western art, literature, song, theatre, or film as loving daughters, sisters, wives, or mothers. They are not portrayed as bravely struggling for a better life for their families or for women's rights. They are never shown fighting beside men for national independence. We see no Arab women writers, artists, doctors, teachers, politicians, or businesswomen. Women have performed all these roles and more. (178)

In *Gaza Mom*, the reader witnesses the intersection of Laila El-Haddad's multiple identities as a mother, journalist, Palestinian, and Muslim woman, and these parts enrich one another and interconnect by virtue of the overlapping of the "private" and "public" spheres in her and other civilians' lives. In El-Haddad's blog, the domestic sphere is exposed as a space in where war and conflict are pervasive, where sonic booms, heavy shelling, food shortage, and power cuts are common occurrences, and where children learn to adapt to violence and chaos at a very early age. The home front—though never idealized or constructed as flawless—is portrayed as a dynamic site of resistance, creativity, communal support, and constant negotiation. As Suad Joseph notes: "The domestic sphere is a lively arena of social, political, and economic action in the Middle East—far more so than in the

West. Locating Middle Eastern women primarily in the domestic domain does not have the same meaning or outcome as it does for Western women" (4).

El-Haddad's *Gaza Mom* documents a nation's present as it unfolds minute by minute, its history as remembered by its own people, and the rest of the world's reactions to global events with regard to this (stateless) nation—all as perceived through a Muslim mother's eyes. The fact that El-Haddad has earned international respect as an on-the-ground journalist reporting for news outlets, including Al-Jazeera and the *Guardian* and making appearances on CNN, makes her work all the more effective in reaching transnational audiences. She cannot be summarily dismissed, and through her journalistic work and mother-centred activism, she gives legitimacy—and hope—to other civilians living in and/or reporting from the war zone, especially the women among them. Through this blog-turned-book, the reader witnesses the devastating effects of occupation on a people's landscape, economy, and psyche as well as the power of "maternal thinking," laughter, and writing.

NOTES

[1]On December 27, 2008, Israeli forces began a unilateral bombing campaign on the Gaza Strip. The stated aim of the bombing campaign was to put an end to rocket attacks into Israel by armed groups connected to Hamas or Fatah. By the time the ceasefire occurred on January 18, 2009, an estimate of fourteen hundred Palestinians had been killed, and large areas of Gaza had been razed, leaving thousands homeless and destroying Gaza's already-ailing economy (For a detailed account, see "Israel/Gaza: Operation Cast Lead, 22 Days of Death and Destruction," Amnesty International Report, July 2009).

[2]El-Haddad was born in Gaza and therefore holds a Palestinian-authority (PA) issued passport as well as an Israeli-issued ID, which theoretically allowed her entry into Gaza through the Rafah border that was manned by the Israeli and Egyptian military. Often that meant that authorized travellers from and to Gaza, including El-Haddad, would be delayed or barred from entry depending on the political situation and Israeli and Egyptian "security" measures. See

El-Haddad's preface (12-17) for more details regarding her status.
³See Sophie Richter-Devroe's article "Palestinian Women's Everyday Resistance: Between Normality and Normalization" for an
intriguing study investigating the significance of women's practices
of leisurely travel, despite Israeli-imposed restrictions.
⁴During February and March 2006, following Hamas's victory in
the elections, Gaza became subject to an international siege (in the
form of sanctions), intense infighting between Hamas and Fatah,
and Israeli punitive actions, including the closure of commercial
crossings and military tactics.
⁵For critical analyses on the nature and manifestation of ethnic
discrimination in the United States, see Elaine Hagopian's edited
volume *Civil Rights in Peril: The Targeting of Arabs and Muslims*
(2004), Steven Saliata's *Anti-Arab Racism in the U.S.A.: Where
it Comes from and What it Means for Politics Today* (2006), and
Amaney Jamal and Nadine Naber's edited volume *Race and Arab
Americans Before and After 9/11: From Invisible Citizens to Visible
Subjects* (2008). I want to acknowledge Dana Olwan's contribution in helping me problematize Butler's quote by noting that this
generalized sense of hysteria often culminates in the targeting of
specific peoples with Arab or Muslim affiliations.

WORKS CITED

Abu-Lughod, Lila. "Do Muslim Women Really Need Saving?:
    Anthropological Reflections on Cultural Relativism and Its Oth-
    ers." *American Anthropologist* 104.3 (2002): 783-790. Print.
Ahmed, Leila. *Women and Gender in Islam: Historical Roots of a
    Modern Debate*. New Haven: Yale University Press, 1992. Print.
Allen, Lori. "Getting by the Occupation: How Violence Became
    Normal during the Second Palestinian Intifada." *Cultural An-
    thropology* 23.3 (2008): 453-87.
Amnesty International. "Israel/Gaza: Operation 'Cast Lead': 22
    Days of Death and Destruction." Amnesty International, 2 July.
    2009. Web. 15 Apr. 2016.
Badran, Margot and miriam cooke, eds. *Opening the Gates: A
    Century of Arab Feminist Writing*. Bloomington: Indiana Uni-
    versity Press, 1990. Print.

Butler, Judith. *Precarious Life: The Powers of Mourning and Violence*. London: Verso, 2004. Print.

Cashin, Sheryll. "To Be Muslim or 'Muslim Looking' in America: A Comparative Exploration of Racial and Religious Prejudice in the 21st Century." *Duke Forum for Law & Social Change* 2.125 (2010): 125-139. Print.

cooke, miriam. "Foreword." *Gaza Mom: Palestine, Politics, Parenting, and Everything in Between*. By Laila El-Haddad. Charlottesville: Just World Books, 2010. 9-11. Print.

cooke, miriam. *Women and the War Story*. Berkeley: University of California Press, 1996. Print.

cooke, miriam. *War's Other Voices: Women Writers in the Lebanese Civil War*. New York: Cambridge University Press, 1987. Print.

El-Haddad, Laila. *Gaza Mom: Palestine, Politics, Parenting, and Everything in Between*. Charlottesville: Just World Books, 2010. Print.

El-Khalil, Zena. *Beirut Update*. N.p., July 2006. Web. 17. Jan. 2011.

Enloe, Cynthia. *Globalization and Militarism: Feminists Make the Link*. Lanham, Maryland: Rowman & Littlefield, 2007. Print.

Fernea, Elizabeth and Basima Qattan Bezirgan, Eds. *Middle Eastern Muslim Women Speak*. Austin: University of Texas Press, 1977. Print.

Gordon, Tuula. *Feminist Mothers*. New York: New York University Press, 1990. Print.

Hagopian, Elaine, ed. *Civil Rights in Peril: The Targeting of Arabs and Muslims*. Ann Arbor: Pluto Press, 2004. Print.

Hamilton, Marsha. "The Arab Woman in U.S. Popular Culture." *Food for Our Grandmothers: Writings by Arab-American and Arab-Canadian Feminists*. Ed. Joanna Kadi. Boston: South End Press, 1994. 173-180. Print.

Hasso, Frances S. *Resistance, Repression, and Gender Politics in Occupied Palestine and Jordan*. Syracuse: Syracuse University Press, 2005. Print.

Jamal Amaney and Nadine Naber, eds. *Race and Arab Americans Before and After 9/11: From Invisible Citizens to Visible Subjects*. Syracuse: Syracuse University Press, 2008. Print.

Joseph, Suad. "Women and Politics in the Middle East." *Middle East Report* 138 (Jan.-Feb. 1986): 3-7

Kahf, Mohja. "Packaging 'Huda': Sha'rawi's Memoirs in the United States Reception Environment." *Going Global: The Transnational Reception of Third World Women Writers.* Eds. Amal Amireh and Lisa Suhair Majaj. New York: Routledge, 2000. 148-172. Print.

Khalidi, Rashid. *Palestinian Identity: The Construction of Modern National Consciousness.* New York: Columbia University Press, 1997. Print.

Keddie, Nikki R. *Women in the Middle East: Past and Present.* Oxford: Princeton University Press, 2007. Print.

Kinser, Amber E. *Motherhood and Feminism.* Berkeley: Seal Press, 2010. Print.

Kishtainy, Khalid. "Humor and Resistance in the Arab World and Greater Middle East." *Civilian Jihad: Nonviolent Struggle, Democratization, and Governance in the Middle East.* Ed. Maria J. Stephan. New York: Macmillan, 2009. 53-64. Print.

Li, Darry. "The Gaza Strip as Laboratory: Notes in the Wake of the Disengagement." *Journal of Palestinian Studies* 35.2 (2006): 38-55. Print.

Mahmoud, Saba. "Secularism, Hermeneutics, and Empire: The Politics of Islamic Reformation." *Public Culture* 18.2 (2006): 323-347. Print.

Malak, Amin. *Muslim Narratives and the Discourse of English.* Albany: State University of New York P, 2005. Print.

Niebylski, Dianna C. *Humoring Resistance: Laughter and the Excessive Body in Contemporary Latin American Women's Fiction.* Albany: State University of New York Press, 2004. Print.

O'Reilly, Andrea, ed. "Introduction." *Mother Outlaws: Theories and Practices of EmpoweredMothering.* Toronto: Women's Press, 2004. Print.

Pappe, Ilan. *The Ethnic Cleansing of Palestine.* Oxford: Oneworld, 2006. Print

Peteet, Julie. *Gender in Crisis: Women and the Palestinian Resistance Movement.* New York: Columbia University Press, 1991. Print.

Pole, Antoinette. *Blogging the Political: Politics and Participation in a Networked Society.* New York: Routledge, 2010. Print.

Rich, Adrienne. *Of Woman Born: Motherhood as Experience and Institution.* 1976. New York: W.W. Norton, 1995. Print.

Richter-Devroe, Sophie. "Palestinian Women's Everyday Resistance: Between Normality and Normalization." *Journal of International Women's Studies* 12.2 (2011): 32-46. Print.

Riverbend. *Baghdad Burning: Girl Blog from Iraq.* New York: The Feminist Press, 2005. Print.

Ruddick, Sara. *Maternal Thinking: Toward a Politics of Peace.* Boston: Beacon Press, 1989. Print.

Salaita, Steven. *Anti-Arab Racism in the United States: Where it Comes from and What it Means for Politics Today.* Ann Arbor: Pluto Press, 2006. Print.

Salti, Rasha. "Lebanon Siege." Rasha Salti Blog Spot. N.p., July 2006. Web. 17. Jan. 2011.

Shalhoub-Kevorkian, Nadera. *Militarization and Violence against Women in Conflict Zones in the Middle East: A Palestinian Case-Study.* New York: Cambridge University Press, 2009. Print.

Sharoni, Simona. *Gender and the Israeli-Palestinian Conflict: The Politics of Women's Resistance.* Syracuse: Syracuse University Press, 1995. Print.

Sinno, Nadine. "Deconstructing the Myth of Liberation @ riverbendblog.com: Baghdad Burning and the Politics of Resistance." *Feminism and War: Confronting U.S. Imperialism.* Eds. Robin L. Riley, Chandra Talpade Mohanty, and Minnie Bruce Pratt London: Zed Press, 2008. 131-142. Print.

Wadud, Amina. *Inside the Gender Jihad: Women's Reform in Islam.* Oxford: Oneworld, 2006. Print.

2.
"God as My Witness"

Mothering and Militarization in Kashmir

NOUF BAZAZ

*During this turmoil situation last year, one of our neigh-
bors' relatives was pregnant and her husband came home
and then he came out again on the road to have a conversation with their friend. When he was just outside of
his door, suddenly there was firing and he was killed by
a bullet. And after some time, the baby was born.*

—Reema

THIS STORY WAS RECOUNTED TO ME in the summer of
2011, and it was the first of many childbirth stories that
I would hear in the most militarized region in the world:
the disputed territory of Kashmir. That summer, I asked women
across Kashmir about their experiences with pregnancy, childbirth, and mothering. These processes cannot be separated from
the physical and psychological trauma the women experienced
as part of the conflict in Kashmir, nor can they be separated
from the extraordinary strength that mothering necessitates in
this context.

The narratives shared in this essay are testimonies in which
women opened up about the torture, abuse, and almost daily
suffering that they endured. They wanted their words and —and
when words failed to capture their pain, they wanted the fact of
their mere survival to be carried beyond the floor of their living
rooms where our tea sat unfinished. One elderly Kashmiri woman
began by turning towards me, gently placing a hand on my arm,
and urging me to "Tell it like this, my dear."

SOCIO-POLITICAL CONTEXT

A background on militarization is critical for contextualizing any study of trauma in Kashmir because, in contrast to other psychogenic disorders, "[i]t is indeed the truth of the traumatic experience that forms the center of its psychopathology; it is not a pathology of falsehood or displacement of meaning, but of history itself" (Caruth, "Trauma" 5). The word "trauma" originates from the Greek word for "wound" and, in this context, is understood as a wound in the mind that cannot be separated from the physical wounds of war or the fracturing of political, economic, and socio-cultural domains of everyday life.

In 1990, the Indian government enacted an emergency provision, the *Armed Forces (Jammu and Kashmir) Special Powers Act* (AF-SPA), which eliminated the requirement for Indian Armed Forces to have a warrant for either arrest of persons or entering homes in the disputed territory. Furthermore, "for the maintenance of public order," an officer may "fire upon or otherwise use force, even to the causing of death, against any person who is acting in contravention of any law or order for the time being in force in the disturbed area" (Duschinski 701). Such a law suspends internationally accepted criminal law conventions of "innocent until proven guilty" and assumes criminal intent indiscriminately. Extrajudicial killings otherwise coded as human rights abuses are sanctioned through authorized usage of the AFSPA (Duschinski 702). As Kashmir is a Muslim-majority state and because of Muslim-led resistance against Indian rule in Kashmir, the Indian Army has largely targeted Muslims, particularly males of military age.

By conservative estimates, there are approximately eight thousand "disappeared persons" in Kashmir, but the Indian Army maintains that disappeared persons are only "suspected militants" (Association of Parents of Disappeared Persons). A 2011 report titled "Half-Widow, Half-Wife?: Responding to Gendered Violence in Kashmir" compiled by the Association of Parents of Disappeared Persons (APDP), strongly refutes that assertion and maintains that countless civilians are among the disappeared. Many of the women with whom I spoke are mothers or wives of the disappeared, and their grief is compounded by the fact that they have received no confirmation of the deaths of their loved ones. Even decades later, they hold on to the hope that when they hear a knock on the door, it is their husband or son returning home.

TRAUMA NARRATIVES

It is important to note the limitations of trauma narratives to adequately encompass the experience of trauma. Trauma is often resistant to language, as memories may be more sensory than narrative in nature (Van der Kolk, Burbridge, and Suzuki) and, thus, exceed linguistic symbolization, particularly in any linear or coherent fashion (Das, Klienman, and Ramphele). Psychiatrist Robert Lifton maintains that no life experience is experienced in and through itself "nakedly"; rather, the experience is recreated in the cortex based on prior imagery and experience. However, when people talk about extreme levels of destruction (in the case of Lifton's research, the devastation after the bombings of Hiroshima), people have little prior imagery to take in the experience (Caruth, "An Interview" 135). Similarly, Primo Levi, a Holocaust survivor, writes of his experience in the Nazi camps, "for the first time we became aware that our language lacks words to express this offense, the demolition of a man" (26).

This "loss of words" can also be seen in these narratives. When reading these stories, it is imperative to be mindful of the ways that the women's words fail to encapsulate the trauma of the experience. Phrases such as "lose control," "became crazy," "became tense," or "was frustrated" may be mistaken for vague signifiers but are, in fact, potent memory traces or fragments that cannot be encapsulated by language. It is also critical to note where sensory or iconic forms of memory predominate, such as through the use of piercing descriptions of physical sensations and vivid imagery. Lastly, in transcribing these stories, efforts were made to note shifts in emotional and physical states (such as when women began crying, trembling, or calling out in prayer) or to recognize the non-linear and, at times repetitive or fragmented telling of these narratives; however, as these testimonies were translated and transposed into a written text, there are undoubtedly and regrettably elements of the testimonies that exceed frames of representation and, thus, cannot be captured within this essay. In light of these limitations, readers are reminded that these trauma testimonials can neither embody nor convey the totality of the trauma experienced, as such a task would be an impossible undertaking.

NARRATIVES

All the women whose stories are contained within this essay gave consent for the recording and publication of their stories.[1] Names, ages, locations and other identifying details have been changed or omitted to protect their confidentiality and safety, as the telling of these particular narratives can potentially endanger the lives of those involved given the current political context of Kashmir.

A number of Kashmiri advocates were instrumental in the telling of these stories, as they introduced me to these women; a few also co-facilitated several of the interviews with me.[2] It was only through the trust of these advocates that I was allowed into these women's worlds. In order to protect the confidentiality and safety of the women interviewed, I regrettably have had to omit the names of these individuals who granted me this access, in case a connection could otherwise be made to determine the identities of the women interviewed.

The interviews were prompted by a few open-ended questions about women's challenges with pregnancy, childbirth, and mothering so that women could tell their own stories in the manner they felt was best. Women were also asked if they had any guidance or advice for other mothers, which positioned these narratives as stories that would be passed on and heard by others.

GULNAZ

Sixteen years ago, Gulnaz's fourteen-year-old son disappeared shortly after the Indian Army killed her brother. She still holds hope that her son will return and told us, "Now I wish for him to only come back even though so many years have passed by since his disappearance." She thought that maybe he would return one day, as she had heard some disappeared boys had returned even after eighteen years. She has never had any closure, which only compounds her grief. She said to us, "One thing is to die when you know it happened because you have the dead body but we never saw him."

Gulnaz spent years fighting through the legal system for justice, but after five years she abandoned her case as her health, and the health of her husband had drastically deteriorated. She had developed severe pains all over her body, whereas her husband suffered from heart problems that eventually took his life. Of his death, Gulnaz related:

He came back from work, and, suddenly, he had a heart attack at nine in the evening. He had walked a lot of distance that day. He was suffering from a heart ailment, and the doctor had already warned him not to walk too much. But he was in the same sorrow, where has my son gone? If anything happened to any kid anywhere, he would be crying about it later. He would be crying two days before Eid[3] every time. Then our other daughter would tell us not to cry on Eid; otherwise, she would run away as kids have this happiness inside of them when they want to wear new clothes and such. Then her father would go into another room and would stay there crying because men don't share their sorrows as women share. Then later he couldn't last long enough because of it.

For Gulnaz, the community has been both a source of support as well as a strain. When we asked her if she has met other women who have faced the same kind of difficulties, she responded that there have been many and that they meet from time to time, otherwise "no mother would survive this." Recently, Gulnaz went to the home of a mother who had lost her son and told her "may God give patience to you and me, both of us." However, this support system has started to dwindle, as Gulnaz sadly reported that "Now the times are different, the people have become busy now, and if there are ten women in a house, all of them go out to work." As more men are lost to the conflict, the burden of supporting the family has fallen on women, often through their handcrafts making or textile weaving. As the conflict has intensified, so has the cost of living, which has risen drastically. Gulnaz shared with us how difficult it was to earn money for her daughter's marriage after the death of her husband. When Gulnaz began working, she suffered from the stigma of being the mother of a "disappeared." If someone related to a woman she worked with fell ill, Gulnaz was often blamed, as she was accused of bringing bad luck or misfortune to others. Gulnaz told us sadly that she stopped working and is even now reluctant to go to her neighbours to talk about her son. "We don't want to make ourselves look small," she told us. From time to time, Gulnaz is invited to someone's home to talk about her son or to console another mother over a similar loss. However, over time these visits have been more difficult for Gulnaz. "I used to get very emotional when I used to get reminded of my tragedies and the people who have lost their loved ones.... I used to lose control for almost two days after that."

We asked Gulnaz what advice she may have for pregnant women and she responded, "women should give birth to baby girls." She continued, "Boys are victims of nazar [evil eye]." She sighed and whispered, "but that's not up to us, but to God's will." She continued:

> I used to ask God for a son, and then he did give me a son and that, too, a beautiful son, but then later I never saw him again. He must have been dear to God. He was a very nice boy and always used to do good things. One day we were going to [redacted] and suddenly he asked to go home, and when I asked why, he said that there is blood there on the street. He said someone has been killed there yesterday, and he was very scared of those policemen and military here. Now I tell women who have lost their children like this to at least look at them for the last time when they die. That kid who had drowned, I asked his mother whether she saw his face the last time or not, and she replied that yes she did see him. I told her at least you saw your son one last time but I have never seen my son for the last time.

SHAZIA

Shazia's husband Afzal left for work one morning in 1998 and was never seen nor heard from again; she was pregnant with her fourth child, which she eventually miscarried. In the years since Afzal's disappearance, the family has received no answers regarding his whereabouts. Instead, they have experienced harassment, physical and psychological abuse, torture, and destruction to their home property by the Indian army. Shazia told us, "[The army] used to tell me to leave this place but I did not leave. I told them I have kids here, I cannot leave them."

We asked her about how difficult this particular pregnancy was for her, and she responded that she had been in and out of many different hospitals for a number of different ailments. Shazia's mother-in-law added that, "Sometimes she can't even hold a cup properly ... she is shaking so much." When Shazia described one encounter with the Indian army, she stressed one particular image: "They would take [Afzal's] clothes, and throw them out." The emotion that is evoked when describing Indian army encounters, and in particular the handling of his possessions, highlighted the vivid imagery and sensations conjured in these recollection; it appeared as though Shazia and her mother-in-law were reliving those moments as they described them to us. When the Indian army questioned the family about Afzal's whereabouts, "We used to say to them if you find him then please show him to us as well, we also want to see him." Only recently has the Indian army stopped coming regularly: "Now they are tired too, as they too don't know where he is and whether he is dead or alive."

After her husband's disappearance, Indian army officers would return to her home to interrogate her, and they often resorted to violence: "Many came, such interrogation, I'm telling you, they would curse at me too, such curses they would say. Such curses they said against me." Shazia mentioned how one relative that lived nearby tried to intervene: "She came to save me, and they beat her too.... No one at all would stay here, everyone would escape. The army came at night and used to drag me and my mother-in-law out of the house and didn't let any of our neighbours to come to help us."

Neither Shazia nor her mother-in-law elaborated on what happened when they were dragged outside from their homes, and we did not dare to ask. While she was pregnant, Shazia had been physically assaulted by Indian Army officers. When Shazia reported this to other Indian army officials, she was cursed more. "They used to grab our neighbours and told them they knew where my husband was ... they would take them to the army camp."

Shazia and her mother-in-law also went into great detail regarding the abuse that her children endured at this time. When one of Shazia's daughters was a young girl, the Indian army would demand to see her. "Give her to us," they would say. For her safety, she was eventually married off at an early age to which Shazia cried to us, "She was a little girl." Shazia's inability to protect her own children from the violence of the Indian army compounded her grief.

One of her sons, similarly, was tortured by the Indian Army, who would question him about his father's whereabouts and ask, "Where is your dad? Does your dad come here at night? Does he have a gun? ... tell, tell." According to Shazia, "They would instill fear in him. Then his heart became weak, his heart became weak.... His heart would stop almost, when they would torture him like that." Fear had taken over their lives. As the child grew, he experienced more torture, which increasingly shifted from solely psychological to increasingly more physical as well:

> What did they leave him with ... he can't even walk straight. That little child, if he could sleep, if only he could do some work, if only he could do some work on the land, he couldn't do anything. They interrogated him, they interrogated him, here, here, here.

When Shazia said "here, here, here" she did not refer or motion to literal places. Rather, her strained voice suggested that he was tortured with such frequency that every place was seemingly a site of torture. Shazia's mother-in-law elaborated further on her son's torture: "They would cut his penis. They would say we won't keep him fit for marriage, we won't keep him fit for marriage [he would not be worth marrying]." Each repetition of the phrase punctuated the loss. The act of "cutting" the penis refers to the common torture technique of sending shocks into the penis through the insertion of copper wiring. Many boys subjected to this torture suffered from kidney problems and impotency, which did, in fact, prevent them from eventually marrying. Following this description, she cried out "*Khudaah deyitha najaath*," which is roughly translated as "God save them." Eventually, her son was sent to live with distant relatives.

When we asked Shazia more about her pregnancy after her husband disappeared, she said that the Indian army used to physically beat her, and the effects of such abuse were palpable. Shazia stated, "So many difficulties all at once was too much for me, sometimes I would be in one hospital and the next moment I would be in another." Her mother-in-law repeated that Shazia would often faint and had to be taken to the hospital. When we asked Shazia how the pregnancy was different from her previous ones, she responded, "When my husband was nowhere to be found, I had to give [my children] the love of a father as well." The burden that was placed on Shazia as a mother at this time exacerbated her deteriorating physical and mental condition.

We asked Shazia what her fears were during pregnancy and she responded, "[The] military scared me a lot, without food or water we had to flee from home for days. Cook, cook, what could we cook?" When Shazia and her family heard the Indian army coming, they would leave their food uneaten and flee to a neighbour's house. Shazia's mother-in-law noted how eventually it became uncomfortable to impose on those around them and ruminated that "At night, we would say we should sleep, [but] where? Where? When blood would not even finish." The phrase, "when blood would not even finish," was a phrase none of us had heard before, but one that, nonetheless, betrayed unspeakable physical and emotional pain.

Shazia's ill health stemming from the seemingly never-ending cycle of Indian army abuse and her fear of their next encounter was apparent. Even the Indian army would interrogate her if she was ill because she was pregnant (indicating that her husband had returned to impregnate her). The family desperately presented the officers with hospital papers that proved Shazia's ill condition was not connected to pregnancy. Her mother-in-law described her condition as follows:

> Her heart would get weak. Even right now, if she does a very little task even, then she just falls down, and then if we tell her to get up, she can't even stand up ... what could she do? What could she do? So many heart problems. What can a person do? What can a person do?" God ... God ... God will do his own plan, God will do his own plan, God will give his own help. What can I do, you have to get up. Always worried, no sleep at night, sleep burns.

The sensory images in her statement blot out much of everything else. The concept of "burning that sleep brings" is intimately connected to the fire of traumatic experience, which rapidly spreads until the entire environment becomes a source of pain.

Shazia's narrative brings out many of the common challenges of mothering in a conflict zone: mothering while enduring physically and emotionally debilitating torture and trauma; mothering children who have experienced profound pain and loss; and mothering within a family crippled by constant fear.

MUMTAZ

Mumtaz is the mother of four children and looks decades older than her stated age. She was married at the age of sixteen and proudly told us that, it was a "love marriage[4] ... the one you people do these days, that same kind." Over twenty years ago, Mumtaz was pregnant with her fourth child. Her husband left one afternoon to visit a relative and was never seen again. Mumtaz explained to us that, "Police used to come saying that he is here and there but never actually saw him anywhere. I think he was killed, and after that, I don't know, did they throw him in the water or bury him somewhere?" Mumtaz has neither seen his body nor received any closure regarding his death.

We asked Mumtaz if she received any help from anyone when she was pregnant, and she responded:

By God, no one opened their doors to help me. What could I do? I don't have such neighbours here. Then what happened was that a poor lady in my neighborhood gave me some rice to eat with onions. With that onion, I ate my first meal in three days.

Mumtaz's poverty was evident. Even when her husband was alive, they struggled to provide for their family, and after his death, it seemed impossible after losing even his modest wages. Following his disappearance, she worked for other families as a domestic helper. "My youngest daughter still had to learn to walk and my youngest son used to do all the cooking. If there was anything to cook … otherwise we would just be without food." Many nights, they subsisted on a diet consisting of only boiled potatoes. As she described the scarcity of food, she frequently stated that at that time, God and the Prophet Muhammad never left her side. She cried out that there were "so many hardships. Only I know and God knows how many hardships have I faced since then" and that "It is on God and the Prophet, only then have I been able to take care of my children." It was through these cries to God and the Prophet Muhammad that Mumtaz could have a witness to her pain. Her religious beliefs provided the only means of coping with the trauma that she endured and the pressures on her as a mother.

Mumtaz described her state when she was in her last month of pregnancy after her husband disappeared:

At that time in one corner of the room sat my children and in the other, I sat. Then I would think, think… "God, what should I do?" When my daughter would start crying, my brain started to get tense…. When he went missing, we lost food, we lost money. I would hit these things, hit these things, hit. Before this I was very happy, then there was nothing left.

Although the reference to "hitting these things" was not entirely clear, it seemed to reference the physical and psychological pain that she felt at this time. "My mind became frustrated. I was so disturbed that I couldn't even give milk to my child." Too mentally disturbed to breastfeed, Mumtaz relied on another woman to breastfeed her newborn. As the azaan[5] from a nearby mosque faded away, we asked her what her fears were at that time, and she responded, "I was scared that they might kill me too."

When we asked Mumtaz what advice she may have for other women who may be in a similar situation, she responded:

> *I would tell them that I was able to bear it and so should you. And look after your children, then, maybe later, we will see what destiny has in store for us and what it doesn't. I was as good as dead at that time then it was in the destiny of this daughter or the other that God brought me back from death and slowly the time changed, since then my children have been shredding their skin, working so hard to support the family.*

Mumtaz's language of coming "back from death" is suggestive of a psychic death or dissociative experience. Trauma psychiatrist Lifton writes that "numbing" among victims of trauma could be described as a "cessation of feeling" in which "the mind is severed from its own psychic forms [and] there's an impairment in the symbolization process itself" (Caruth "An Interview," 136, 134). What is left is an experience that remains largely mute, unsymbolized, and unintegrated.

Mumtaz shared another story with us of an event that occurred about four or five months after her husband disappeared. A neighbour came to Mumtaz's home and told her that she heard on the radio that her husband's dead body was found. Mumtaz then gathered her children and journeyed to the Indian army camp where her husband was supposedly held. She said that she went because "my brain was not working right so I didn't think about it properly.... I thought anything could happen." The dead body had been taken to a military camp. When she arrived at the camp, she told the officer, "this [body] is the father of my children." The officer informed her that there had been a mix-up and that it was a different man that had been found with the same surname. When Mumtaz returned home alone, she said that she had felt again "frustrated" and she kept repeating to us, "I had a love marriage with him. I did it myself. I did it myself." She went on to say, "I went crazy.... I was crazy because I had married him myself because I had loved him."

In Kashmir, the danger associated with mothering creates a sense of uncertainty and fear that pervades all aspects of life. The role of the mother as a provider becomes severely compromised, as the physiological, psychological and material challenges presented by militarization cannot be met. As illustrated by Mumtaz, the inadequacy felt by mothers paralyzes them as their surroundings crumble under a crushing force that they cannot contain.

REFLECTIONS

In penning this essay, I have rewritten my discussion of these narratives over and over again. Nothing I write can adequately summarize or parcel out the overarching themes and lessons contained within. A part of me has wanted the strength of these women and the horror that they have endured to stand on their own through their words. I have cringed each time I have interjected their testimonies on these pages with my editorializing and cataloging of their grief and trauma. I do not pretend that these testimonies would otherwise have provided an unfettered lens into the lives of these women. Lila Abu-Lughod notes that storytelling inherently reveals perspectives that are partial, since a story's telling is positioned for a particular audience and for a particular purpose (15). I know that I have had a hand in mediating the telling of these stories. However, inspired by Abu-Lughod's efforts to limit generalizations, which she notes leads to "producing the effects of homogeneity, coherence, and timelessness" (9), it seems crass to follow these narratives with a discussion of the ways in which they have contributed to the literature of trauma and violence.

Dominick LaCapra, a historian of trauma studies, cautions against "redemptive narratives" that neatly tie up the process of mourning and rush to resolve the complex tensions explored within (153-158). In the margins of LaCapra's book, I found notes that I had written years ago urging me to focus on my own personal reactions as a witness to these narratives. Dori Laub notes the following levels of witnessing: "the level of being a witness to oneself within the experience; the level of being a witness to the testimonies of others; and the level of being a witness to the process of witnessing itself" (75). I invite the reader to reflect on these levels as it pertains to the narratives that have been presented.

I do not want to objectify these narratives any more than I already have by presuming to know what is most salient to the women who shared these stories or to the reader. Instead, I want to stay true to my promise to the women I interviewed that I would share their stories with others so that we may bear witness to their experiences. To the best of my ability, I have tried to reproduce their stories. I cannot, however, make any claims on their behalf of the meaning that they have attributed to their own experiences or how others should understand their story. I can only begin to make meaning of my own experience as a witness to these narratives and my own individual testimony.

NOUF

From the moment that I started this project, I felt in over my head. I was in my mid-twenties when I conducted these interviews. When I started, everyone I met treated me with nothing but kindness. I think it is because I lacked the sophistication or confidence to actually arouse suspicion or to intimidate anyone. As a non-resident Kashmiri that moved to the U.S. at the height of militarization, I also knew my place. I tried my best to not get in anyone's way and said thank you every few minutes before I was begged to stop. I started by meeting a few journalists and advocates and eventually was driving across Kashmir interviewing women with a team of the most incredible individuals that I have ever met.

I will never forget the women I met who shared their stories with me. For all my insecurities and guilt of being a Kashmiri-American (and not a Kashmiri-Kashmiri, as I called them), they never once made me feel like an outsider. They hugged me and shared the most intimate and painful details of their lives. They showed me framed pictures of their husbands and sons who had been killed or disappeared. A few smiled through their tears and told me that I reminded them of their own daughters. I have struggled with how best to honour their stories while protecting their privacy.

If I could go back and tell them one thing, I would say that they have forever changed me and that it breaks me to know that there is little that I can do to alleviate even an ounce of their grief and that I am so sorry that I could not do more.

One part of these stories that has struck me the most is just how central the role of faith, and having faith, is for these women. After the horror Mumtaz endured when her husband disappeared and she and her children had no food to eat for days, her response that only God remained by her side in those moments still shakes me. As my father and I sat in our kitchen in New York listening to the recordings and double-checking any translations, neither of us could even comprehend that level of faith and strength. As we cried over those words, my father could only say, "women like that will not be questioned on the day of judgement," a sobering consolation that, while unable to alleviate any of our pain, seemed the only appropriate response in the moment. Several people have asked me if the women I interviewed were ever angry with God. I do not know. All I know is that throughout their testimonies, there were continuous supplications to God to grant them strength. They frequently called out to God or the Prophet Muhammad when it seemed that the shock or pain of the traumatic experience left them otherwise speechless. Many told me that God and the Prophet Muhammad were the only witnesses to their pain and the only ones who knew the extent to which they suffered.

Another thing I noticed among almost all of the interviewed women is that they had a similar response when I asked them what advice they had for women who may be going through a painful experience. They responded that these women must "bear" the pain as they had done. The majority of the women used the same word, *bardaash,* which is translated as "to bear, tolerate, or carry." I understood this act of "bearing the pain" not as a passive acceptance or victimization but as an active struggle to survive—an intention each day to not crumble under the weight of their grief but to continue living through their suffering each day, over and over again.

As a witness to these testimonies, I have felt horrified by the atrocities committed. I have been in awe of the strength and survival of these women. And I have felt helpless and grieved through words, art, and silence. Although the weight of these experiences pale in comparison to the load carried by these women, I know it is my pain to bear, my small load to carry.

NOTES

[1]Interview methodology, questions, and consent protocol were reviewed and approved by the Institutional Review Board (IRB) at New York University to protect the rights and welfare of interviewees.

[2]Interviews that were co-facilitated were conducted in Kashmiri. I would like to thank Mir Ubaid, a Kashmiri journalist, who assisted me in the enormous task of transcribing and translating recordings of these interviews.

[3]An Islamic holiday.

[4]"A love marriage" indicates that they had chosen to marry one another independent of being arranged by the family as was customary.

[5]The Islamic call to prayer.

WORKS CITED

Abu-Lughod, Lila. *Writing Women's Worlds: Bedouin Stories.* Berkeley: University of California Press, 2008. Print.

Association of Parents of Disappeared Persons (APDP). *Half Widow, Half Wife?: Responding to Gendered Violence in Kashmir.* Kashmir: APDP, 2011. Print.

Caruth, Cathy. "An Interview with Robert Jay Lifton." *Trauma: Explorations in Memory.* Ed. Cathy Caruth. Baltimore: Johns Hopkins University Press, 1995. 128-147. Print

Caruth, Cathy. "Trauma and Experience: Introduction." *Trauma: Explorations in Memory.* Ed. Cathy Caruth. Baltimore: Johns Hopkins University Press, 1995. 3-12. Print

Das, Veena, Arthur Kleinman, Mamphela Ramphele, and Pamela Reynolds, Eds. *Violence and Subjectivity.* Berkeley: University of California Press, 2000. Print.

Duschinski, Haley. "Destiny Effects: Militarization, State Power, and Punitive Containment in Kashmir Valley." *Anthropological*

Quarterly 82.3 (2009): 691-717. Web. 5 Apr. 2016.

LaCapra, Dominick. *Writing History, Writing Trauma*. Baltimore: Johns Hopkins University Press, 2001. Print

Laub, Dori. "An Event Without a Witness." *Testimony: Crisis of Witnessing in Literature, Psychoanalysis, and History.* Eds. Shoshana Felman and Dori Laub. New York: Routledge, 1992. 57-74. Print

Levi, Primo, *Survival in Auchwitz*. New York: Touchstone, 1995. Print.

Van der Kolk, Bessel A., Jennifer A. Burbridge, and Joji Suzuki, "The Psychobiology of Traumatic Memory." *Annals New York Academy of Sciences* 821.1 (1997): 99-113. Print.

3.
Mourning Mothers in Iran

Narratives and Counter-Narratives
of Grievability and Martyrdom

RACHEL FOX

*Burn, My son, Burn with my rage, Burn through this shroud
of lies.*—*Zahra's Paradise*

*[I]f a life is not grievable, it is not quite a life.... It is already
the unburied, if not the unburiable.*—Judith Butler

AN AMATEUR VIDEO RECORDED and uploaded to YouTube
on 13 July 2009 shows Sohrab Aerabi's distraught mother,
Parvin Fahimi, crying and screaming at her son's funeral.
Sohrab Aerabi was a nineteen-year-old student who disappeared
on 15 June 2009, during the protests that followed Mahmoud
Ahamdinejad's landslide victory in the Iranian presidential election
held that year. Many protestors thought the victory was fraudulent
and called for Ahamdinejad to step down. In the recording, Parvin
Fahimi, shouts that "[t]hey told me he was in Evin [prison] ... But
they killed him." His body was returned to his family after weeks
of searching. Her anger is directed towards the religious-political
regime in Iran, whom she calls "cowards," and she declares that
"I need to tell my story. No one can stop me" (hydrademian).
This video served as the inspiration for Amir and Khalil's (writer
and artist respectively) graphic novel *Zahra's Paradise* (2011), a
fictional narrative based on factual events (Bressanin). The graphic
novel depicts elements of Parvin Fahimi's narrative, with the text
culminating in an angry and bitter tirade, by the eponymous mother
Zahra, that attacks the same "they" that Parvin Fahimi accuses in
her rant.[1] Parvin Fahimi is a "mourning mother," as is the avatar

Zahra. In both these real and fictional representations, it is not just the lost, or martyred, son that stands for pro-democracy but also his mother. "The Mourning Mothers of Laleh Park" (and their supporters) assemble at this eponymous site in Tehran and protest the disappearance and/or death of their children following the arrests that took place during the post-election peaceful demonstrations in 2009.[2]

The role of the mourning mother is not an unfamiliar one to contemporary Iran, and it was especially heralded during and after the Iran-Iraq War (1980-1988). Newsha Tavakolian's photographic series *Mothers of Martyrs* (2006) takes from, and shares an affinity with, the murals of martyrs that populated Iran throughout the Iran-Iraq War.[3] These murals propagated a state-endorsed discourse of grievability that typically valued the martyr for the "sacred defence" of his religion and nation, in which "Shiite sacred history played a significant role in motivating the population to defend Iran, as well as the state's attempts to sustain the Islamic Republic" (Flaskerud 26). Roxanne Varzi argues that in light of the Iran-Iraq War, two things were needed to establish the space of death: "a martyr and a photograph. Martyrdom is meaningless without memorialization, and memorialization is not possible without a photograph" (62). Developing from this, I propose that there are four things of importance in the *Mothers of Martyrs* series that constitute the space of death in Iran: the martyr, the photograph, the frame, and the mother. In particular, my exploration of Tavakolian's photography will focus on these latter two, and I will then carry this investigation across to consider further the role of the mourning mother and the frame of (in)visibility in *Zahra's Paradise* as it constructs a counter-narrative to religious-political state discourses on martyrdom and grievability.

In *Zahra's Paradise*, Zahra's son, Mehdi, falls short in the "hierarchy of grief" that Judith Butler proposes and unlike those men who are idolized as martyrs from the battlefields of the Iran-Iraq War, his life does "not find such fast and furious support" and does "not even qualify as 'grievable'" (*Precarious Life* 32). I will argue that the mourning mother in *Zahra's Paradise* (and at Laleh Park) disputes the idea that these missing demonstrators' lives are non-grievable, and introduces an emotive counter-narrative predicated on a written-visual textual platform through which the mother bids her dead son to "burn through the shroud of lies" (Amir and Khalil 218) and posits him as a martyr standing for truth and democracy within his nation.

Tavakolian's relational images of the mourning mother and her son endorse the grievability of the martyr's life and death and his value within Iranian sovereign discourses, whereas the lives of those demonstrators incarcerated and executed without trial following the protests in 2009 become what Giorgio Agamben calls "homo sacer": someone *"who may be killed and yet not sacrificed"* (8). Butler argues that grievability "is a presupposition for the life that matters" (*Frames of War* 14). It is important to note that Butler's works pertaining to grievability and mourning are written pre-dominantly in consideration of the aftermath of the events of 11 September 2001, and the value attached to U.S. lives as compared to those of other nationalities. Nevertheless, Butler's arguments are still relevant to my discussion on the Islamic Republic of Iran. Butler argues that "[i]f certain lives do not qualify as lives or are, from the start, not conceivable as lives within certain epistemo-logical frames, then these lives are never lived nor lost in the full sense" (*Frames of War* 1). Lives— as social entities—are framed by epistemologies, or discourses, that constitute the value, lack of value, or even a lack of recognition of different human lives. Those lives that are ignored come to constitute not even a lived entity, which Agamben regards as "bare life." Butler identifies the indefinite detention of Guantanamo inmates as an example of bare life (and cites Agamben) and qualifies indefinite detainment as a suspension of the law, in which there is "no definitive prospect for a reentry into the political fabric of life, even as one's situation is highly, if not fatally, politicized" (*Precarious Life* 68). Similarly, those protesters detained in Evin prison in Tehran in 2009 are re-moved from the political field, yet this act of negation is politicized in that it secures the regime's position of power.

Imprisoned at Evin, and later executed, Mehdi, the missing son in *Zahra's Paradise*, represents a "homo sacer" within the context of state discourses, in which his life (and death) is "set outside human jurisdiction without it being brought into the realm of divine law" (Agamben 82). In post-revolutionary Iran "the rule of law be[came] subservient to the rule of God and the hegemonic leadership of a juridico-clerical Islam" (Moallem 101). The supreme leader (Ayatollah Khomeini, 1979-1989; Ayatollah Khamenei, 1989-present) ranks highest in the Iranian government, followed by the president, who is elected by the public. The conflation of human jurisdiction with divine law in Iran constitutes a legislative system in which the category "homo sacer" is realizable. The absent son (Mehdi) in *Zahra's Paradise* is devalued in the epistemological frame of state discourse in the Islamic Republic of Iran. The regime's failure to acknowledge Mehdi's presence (and death), as he does not die in willing service to the state, conceives of a position wherein "[a]n ungrievable life is one that cannot be mourned because it has never lived, that is, it has never counted as a life at all" (*Frames of War* 38), an epitome of bare life. However, although Mehdi's life is not grievable to the state, the personal loss experienced by his mother persists as an inconvenient truth, disrupting the state's hegemony. The purpose of the graphic novel is to deconstruct and reconstruct these narrative *frames* of grievability through the representation of his mourning mother: Zahra.

Before I look at the deconstruction and reconstruction of the Islamic Republic's frames of grievability, I first want to expand on the initial construction of these frames by the state during the Iran-Iraq war. Butler suggests that "[o]pen grieving is bound up with outrage, and outrage in the face of injustice," which "has enormous political potential" for the controlling sovereign power (*Frames of War* 39). Butler notes that these "affective responses ... are highly regulated by regimes of power," and, in particular, she makes reference to that which fuelled public grief following the attacks in the U.S. on 11 September 2001: "Public grieving was dedicated to making these images iconic for the nation, which meant of course that there was considerably less public grieving for non-US nationals" (*Frames of War* 38-39). During the Iran-Iraq War, public mourning in Iran was used by political discourse to call for the "sacred defence" of the nation and was primarily constructed by the—literally visual—epistemological frames that propagated martyrdom through murals, museums, and other manifestations of commemorative and cathartic propaganda in the public spaces of cities.

Shahid, from the root *sh-ḥ-d*, stands for "martyr" or "witness." Martyrdom (*shahādat*) is important to both Sunni and Shi'ite narratives, but particularly in the case of the latter, in which "the dominant attitude towards martyrdom is grief" (Cook 59). Muslim martyrs are ideally individuals killed in a violent situation in which their actions indicate "courage and defiance of the enemy, loyalty towards Islam and the pure intention to please God" (Cook 30). In particular, Hoseyn ibn Ali, the grandson of Prophet Mohammed, is "the martyr *par excellence*" and is often labelled as "The Prince of Martyrs" in Shi'ite traditional narratives for his death on the battlefield of Karbala when he defended "True Islam" (Shi'ism) and challenged the rule of the Umayyad Caliph Yazid in CE 680 (61 AH) (Flaskerud 23-24). The annual commemoration of Hoseyn's martyrdom, known as *Ashura*, represents one of the most important spiritual events of the year for Shia Muslims.

Martyrdom is an established discourse in post-revolutionary Iran, and this was especially so during and after the Iran-Iraq War. The conflict was fuelled by disputes over territory and resources, the political and symbolic value of the contested land, and the Iranian ideology of mounting a "sacred defence" to the Iraqi incursion (Khosronejad 3-4). The Iranian experience of the war was marked by a cultural-religious outlook that had been present in the Islamic Republic of Iran since the 1978-1979 revolution and that heralded the (volunteer) soldiers killed on the battlefield as martyrs.

Pedram Khosronejad indicates that "[n]ational bereavement and the commemoration of martyrs were common due to state policy and social demands during and immediately after the Iran-Iraq War," and calls this commemorative trend a "business arrangement" towards maintaining political influence over Iran's citizens (1-3, 9). Martyrs were propagated and rendered politically profitable by the Islamic Republic, and are still publically recognized in a number of ways: streets are named after martyrs; cemeteries designate spaces solely for martyrs; diplomas exalting martyrdom are rewarded by the state to the deceased's family; museums are dedicated to martyrs (Fromanger 50, 54, 65-66); portrait photographs accompany martyrs tombstones; and murals of martyrs (and mourning mothers) populate public spaces. These commemorative tools signify that what is central to martyrdom "is a particular way of living and dying in relation to the community and its continuity, for which collective memory is crucial" (Talebi, "Martyr's Dilemma" 182). The grievability of the martyr is coded by Shi'ite traditional narratives that serve to support the political-religious sovereign discourses of the regime of the Islamic Republic. The political enactment of grievability works to establish continuity and strength within the national community. In particular, the mourning mothers' public grieving serves to maintain the overt presence of the losses felt by the nation and instils this into national collective memory.

The prominence of the commemorative visualization of martyrdom becomes evident through its depiction in texts that are not primarily engaging with this aspect of Iranian culture. Marjane Satrapi's seminal graphic-memoir, *Persepolis: The Story of a Childhood and The Story of a Return*, depicts a series of panels of the avatar Marjane travelling through Tehran in the aftermath of the Iran-Iraq War. She takes note of "all the images: the sixty-five-foot-high murals presenting martyrs" accompanied with "slogans like 'The martyr is the heart of history'" (252). Alireza Korangy notes that "these murals concentrate[d] on the spiritual, religious, and romantic-epic characteristics of martyrdom" (542); the murals propagate an epic narrative ("the heart of history") in support of the religious-political state of Iran. One panel situates Marjane in the bottom corner of the image while a mural towers above her, depicting a woman holding a dead martyr in her lap (542). This figure, who dominates the space in the panel, might be perceived as a mourning mother, although she might also represent a war widow. Her act of making eye contact with Marjane (and her elevated position) is intimidating and unsettling, and also communicates her grief in a directed message in which state narratives of grievability serve to shape the propagation of martyrdom.

The proliferation of these murals throughout Iran's major cities during and after the Iran-Iraq War is one means through which martyrdom has been "institutionalized" (Varzi 54). The religious discourse of martyrdom was appropriated and visualized for the purposes of establishing the strength of the governing regime in the Islamic Republic: "[i]f power is bound by its visibility, then the power of Iran's clergy was made visible by the Islamic surface they so quickly created" (Varzi 108). Varzi ties the production of

Islamic identity in Iran to the construction of social space as an ideological construct, realized, in particular, through the creation of a "visual state" (107-108). In the example taken from *Persepolis*, it is not just the martyr that is visualized but also the mourner. The simultaneous visualization of martyrdom and grief serves as an instrument of the state. In particular, the visualization of the act of mourning facilitates an affective response towards not just the loss of life but also the loss felt by those left behind. These images of martyrs, which visually rendered the very act of the grieving, were both commemorative and cathartic to the state.

This emphasis on the visualization of both the martyr and the mourner is captured in Tavakolian's photographic series *Mothers of Martyrs*. In each image from the series, Tavakolian has photographed a mother, holding the framed image of her martyred son, killed during the Iran-Iraq War. Both Tavakolian's *Mothers of Martyrs* and the mural featured in *Persepolis* are charged with maternal grief and recall the Pietà that is preeminent in Christian traditions. The Pietà is an image (or icon) that depicts the Madonna holding her son's dead body, which the mural in *Persepolis* can be visually mapped onto. Depicted across different cultural and religious contexts, these images of mother and son symbolize that although maternal loss might be politicized, motherhood and maternal love are universal conditions. Furthermore, in all these cases, maternal identity is not lost with the absence of her child but is rendered visible through the act of grief and remembrance. The act of commemoration on the part of the grieving mother can exist both within and outside of state-endorsed rhetoric.

In Tavakolian's *Mothers of Martyrs*, the photographic frame constructs a barrier that divides the two portraits of mother and son (see figure 1). Ranjana Khanna argues that "[w]hile the frame is therefore all about stasis, capturing a moment or holding a particular instance hostage, it also exceeds itself, through what happens 'off-frame,' ... or through the *punctum*, an apparently insignificant signifier piercing or wounding the viewer" (*Algeria Cuts* 39). Khanna is writing predominantly about the cinematic frame; however, the conceptual premise is useful to my analysis of the still image. The physical frame held by the mother in the photograph represents a moment of stasis. Khanna argues that "[p]hotographs in particular capture something irretrievably lost" and that their contents constitute a "spectral presence" (*Algeria Cuts* 39). This is certainly the case for these photographed martyrs who are captured, or held "hostage," eternally young, and eternally dead. The martyr is memorialized in this image, but this imaging is but a spectre of his real existence. As with the martyrs propagated in murals disseminated by the religious-political Iranian state during the Iran-Iraq War, his visualization comes to represent the very fact that he is absent.

Figure 1: Newsha Tavakolian. "[Untitled]." Photograph. *Mothers of Martyrs.*
Photo exhibition. Newsha Tavakolian Photography. LIVEBOOKS. n. d. Web. 29 Nov 2015.
Reproduced with permission from Newsha Tavakolian.

The frame constructed around the martyred son not only renders stasis but also "exceeds itself." In *Mothers of Martyrs*, what occurs "off-frame" interrupts the framed image; the placement of the mothers' hands literally disrupts the physical frame that surrounds her son, and her physical (and visual) presence in Tavakolian's photographs constitutes an additional frame in itself. The martyr is framed by the presence of his grieving mother. In fact, the central subjects of Tavakolian's photographs are not the martyrs—the sons who appear as a "photo within the photo"—but rather the mothers. As the title of the series suggests, these are images of the *mothers of* martyrs. The mourning mothers are the preeminent focus of the series' title and are also the central foci of the image, even if they are not literally at the centre of Tavakolian's frame. The interruption of the martyrs' image, qualified by the mothers' grief, can be seen to represent the "punctum" of the image, and the emotional interruption can be seen to result in the "piercing" or "wounding" of the viewer (Khanna, *Algeria Cuts* 39) insofar that her action of mourning elicits an emotional rather than passive response from the viewer.[4] Using similar terminology to Khanna (associated with the rhetoric of wounding), Sara Ahmed asserts that pain is "bound up with how we inhabit the world, how we live in relationship to the surfaces, bodies and objects that make up our dwelling places" (27). The mourning mothers not only elicit pain through their presence and interruption of the photographed martyr but perform it, as evidenced by their grieving facial expression. The visualized and, thus, "open" grief of the mothers constitutes the "affective" response utilized by state narratives of grievability when relational images of mourning mothers and martyred sons were depicted in murals. The propagation of not just the martyred son but the openly grieving mother not only commemorated but also legitimized his sacrifice within the context of the "sacred defence." Although the dual-framed images of Tavakolian's photographs are illustrative of this state narrative, the epistemological frame that qualifies *these* lives as grievable, her preeminent focus on the mourning mother introduces a narrative that is led first and foremost by the personal grief of the mother, as opposed to the political ramifications of the son's status as a martyr.

Working outside of the epistemological frame of the Islamic Republic, Amir and Khalil in *Zahra's Paradise* use the role of the mourning mother in their counter-narrative to state discourse. The counter-narrative qualifies not only the mourning mother's son's life (and death) as grievable but as a martyr of a different kind. I have suggested that those incarcerated following the protests in 2009 inhabited a state of bare life. The violence (and execution) enacted on them is "classifiable neither as sacrifice nor as homicide" and belongs to "neither the sphere of *sacrum facere* nor that of profane action" (Agamben 82-83). The incarcerated, as bare life, are neglected in Iranian religious-political discourses, correlating with Butler's suggestion that if violence is enacted on (bare) life that is considered non-grievable then "it fails to injure or negate those lives since those lives are already negated" (*Precarious Life* 33).

Tavakolian's series posits an emotional narrative that is pre-cipitated on the visuality— and, therefore, grievability—of the dead son. By contrast, in *Zahra's Paradise*, Mehdi's presence in the narrative is emphasized by his absence, in which his life (and death) is negated within state discourses. Shahla Talebi recounts a contention between "state martyrs" and (political) "dissident martyrs" following the 1978-1979 Iranian Revolution. The latter definition can also be applied to those who lost their lives during the protests in 2009, who were considered by the ruling regime of the time to be political dissidents. Speaking in the context of the years succeeding the Iranian Revolution, Talebi notes "the stark contrast between the hyper-visibility of the 'state martyrs' vis-à-vis the discriminatory invisibility and lack of recognition of the 'dissident martyrs'" ("From the Light" 122). The murals and other commemorative memorabilia of state martyrs, martyrs valuable to the Islamic Republic of Iran, contrast with the invisibility of those who died standing up for a cause considered politically dissident.

In Tavakolian's *Mothers of Martyrs*, the sons are visually rendered and centrally framed. In *Zahra's Paradise*, Mehdi's face is never seen. The graphic novel emphasizes the extent to which his life (and death) has been negated by his literal invisibility within the text. The first chapter of *Zahra's Paradise* stresses that this is the mother's narrative. The narrative begins with Zahra's search for her son in the aftermath of the protests. At the end of the chapter, Hassan (the narrator and Mehdi's brother) dreams of Mehdi's return, but he is seen only at the margins of the frame, his face always obscured (31-32). In the visualization of Hassan's dream, where Mehdi "walks back into our lives," the mother fills almost the whole of the panel, her arms extended outwards towards her lost son. By comparison, Mehdi resides at the very edge of the frame, with almost the entirety of his profile in shadow, as is continually the case throughout the narrative (31). As a profile that is either outlined or filled in shadow but with no other detailing, Mehdi's paradoxical (and spectral) presence is engendered by his continual absence. Furthermore, Amir and Khalil's depiction of and emphasis on the mother and on maternal loss also mark Mehdi's absence. The narrative is driven by Zahra's need to find her absent son.

Zahra's Paradise visually depicts the invisibility of Mehdi whose "life ... enter[s] into an intimate symbiosis with death without, nevertheless, belonging to the world of the deceased" (Agamben 99-100) and, indeed, vice versa, in that his literal death is unacknowledged. In the cemetery, death is lifted from both the organic and the spiritual, and into the digital. Taghi, one of the assistants at the cemetery, assists Hassan in his search for his brother and proclaims "[w]elcome to the garden of the dead," gesturing to what is plainly visible in the panel: a series of computer terminals (161). The "computerized" cemetery represents "the most efficient bureaucracy in all of Iran" (161). The subversive comment on the "efficiency" of death aligns the regime with violence, and Taghi's dialogue also dehumanizes death: in this representation, death (and burial) is not about spirituality or biology. It is now digital; it is scientific (160). The compartmentalization of human life and death into the digital world also provides the capacity to essentially "delete" human life by removing the record of the physical human body. Lot 309—where Mehdi and other protestors who lost their lives are buried—is a preeminent example of this. Taghi states, with an expression of fear, that Lot 309 "does not exist: it has no name and no record" (163). However, the Lot's lack of presence in the digital, bureaucratic landscape is undermined by its physical presence and, in the graphic medium of *Zahra's Paradise*, its visual presence. In a panel where Hassan takes a photograph of the Lot, both the physical and visual are compounded (163). The act of photo taking captures—holds "hostage" (Khanna, *Algeria Cuts* 39)—the physicality of Lot 309: by capturing an image of the Lot, Hassan lends visibility to it, the adverse of negation.

The unnamed grave used by the regime signifies not just the disavowal of Mehdi's death but also a disavowal of the family's right to grieve: "if a life is not grievable, it is not quite a life ... It is already the unburied, if not the unburiable" (Butler, *Precarious Life* 34). The emphasis placed on the (il)legitimacy of the gravesite by Amir and Khalil underscores the grief of those left behind, and also contests their right to grieve. If the dead body cannot be buried, it could be argued that the grief cannot be substantiated. Designated as bare life and unburiable dead within state rhetoric, Mehdi is non-grievable, and his absence throughout the narrative puts a strain on Zahra's ability to grieve. The narrative of *Zahra's Paradise* follows the mother's search for her dead son in order to allow her to bury him and to legitimize her grief. Mehdi's absence and absent presence fuels the mother's narrative.

Talebi argues that in regards to martyrdom, "the state seeks and devours the sacrifices of its citizens" ("Martyr's Dilemma" 184). In state narratives, and also in state silence, Mehdi is first sacrificed as a dissident in order to "protect" the state; and, second, the state attempt to dissolve Mehdi's dissidence by enfolding him into a discourse of state-endorsed sacrifice and martyrdom. The state attempts to devour Mehdi and make his true actions invisible. As a dissident martyr, Mehdi—as with other protestors, such as Neda Agha-Soltan and Sohrab Aerabi—represents a counter-narrative to state discourses of martyrdom. Mehdi's persistent absence throughout the graphic novel is representative of how he and his cause of martyrdom exist outside of the epistemological frame of martyrdom and grievability in the rhetoric of the Islamic Republic of Iran. However, when Hassan locates previously hidden evidence that Mehdi is deceased, the state changes its stance and makes moves to legitimize Mehdi's death, enfolding it into its own rhetoric. After Hassan's discovery, government officials visit Zahra and posit her son as a state martyr, killed by "a *non*-Iranian bullet," and attempt to persuade her to sign documents attesting to his martyrdom, bribing her with "*top of the line* benefits! Better than we ever gave mothers of martyrs of the Iran-Iraq war!" (210). A signature is needed in order for Mehdi to enter from the margins and into the state's epistemological frame; once again death is entwined with bureaucratic discourses, attached to classifications of martyrdom as well as to the burial of the dead at the cemetery. This offer would make Mehdi grievable, but it would do so on the state's terms, terms that Zahra refuses to accept. Her refusal to make her son into a state martyr rejects the state-ratified discourses of sacrifice that would award Mehdi public visibility and would recognize, even value, Zahra's maternal loss. Zahra proclaims that "I did not raise my son to be the sacrificial lamb on the altar of the Islamic Republic" (211). Her loss is driven by her personal and maternal attachment towards the son; she personalizes him ("my son"), disengaging him from the bureaucratic rhetoric of martyrdom used by the government officials. Furthermore, by refusing to sign, Zahra refutes the regime's attempts to dissolve (to devour) Mehdi's political dissidence that would turn him into their sacrifice.

State discourses had posited Mehdi as bare life—unburiable, ungrievable—and his absence is continually reflected by his shadowy presence in the text. However, in the climactic conclusion to *Zahra's Paradise*, Zahra, the mourning mother, expels her rage and grief in an intensely visible and verbal series of panels that compose a powerful counter-narrative, which draws attention to Mehdi as a dissident martyr and calls for the grievability of her son. Here, the similarities between Amir and Khalil's fictional depiction of events and the video of the vocal and grieving mother Parvin Fahimi are evident. Zahra occupies the majority of the panels in this final chapter, sometimes appearing multiple times in a single one. Zahra's overt presence is particularly noticeable in the panels that appear between pages 216 and 218, where she is in every one. The power of the medium of the graphic novel is particularly pronounced, especially given the emphasis that has been placed on visibility and invisibility by state discourses. In these pages, the visual form bombards the reader with the repeated figure of the mourning mother, shrouded in black: her black clothing, her body, her face, and her speech are empowered by their repeated visibility in these panels (see figure 2). Her words, inked on the page, draws the readers' or viewers' eye as much as her image, again by the powerful repetition of her words and also by the strong, enlarged, often bold typeface: "Did you not run in this dirt? / Did you not play in this dirt? / Did you not ... Did you not ..." and so it goes on (217). In a tirade written on the visual depiction of Zahra's tongue, she repeats, "*Burn*, my son, Burn with rage, Burn through this shroud of lies, Burn, Burn ..." (218). This emphatic, dramatic narrative put forward by the mourning mother reads almost poetically, especially given the emphasis of repetition; it is a dirge and a chant, a pledge and a prayer. Her appeal to "burn" away the lies is accompanied by the revisualization of Mehdi; his

Figure 2: From ZAHRA'S PARADISE © 2011 by Amir. Illustrated by Khalil.
Reprinted by permission of First Second, an imprint of Roaring Brook Press, a division of
Holtzbrinck Publishing Holdings Limited Partnership. All Rights Reserved.

Figure 3: From ZAHRA'S PARADISE © 2011 by Amir. Illustrated by Khalil.
Reprinted by permission of First Second, an imprint of Roaring Brook Press, a division of
Holtzbrinck Publishing Holdings Limited Partnership. All Rights Reserved.

whole body and face are clearly visible, where he is depicted as a swaddled baby in the arms of his mother (see figure 3). Mehdi is re-envisioned through the eyes of his mother, who sees him forever as her child. Grief and, more notably, a discourse (a counter-narrative) of grievability are preeminent. They occupy and overpower the space, dominating in both written text and visual art. Where the lost and absent son is unable to establish his presence, the mourning mother reintroduces visibility and value into the life of her son and others like him. Zahra uses her authority as a mother, as the giver of maternal love and nurturement, to not only authorize her grief but also to qualify the terms of that grief as separate from state discourses, and even openly targets these discourses.

During her monologue in *Zahra's Paradise*, Zahra beseeches her son to "[s]peak that the world may know that *all* of Iran's sons have died, and lie dead in you!" (215). The graphic novel format offers both visibility and vocalization. In the case of *Zahra's Paradise*, this is further accentuated as the text is a hybrid of fiction, citizen journalism, and also a tool for human rights advocacy in Iran. The graphic novel represents a fictional rendition of factual events, drawing from the personal dilemmas and grief of citizens in Iran (for example, Parvin Fahimi's grief): those who are missing, incarcerated, and executed are "*all* of Iran's sons" (215) and "They're *all* Mehdi" (188). What is particularly significant at this juncture is not just the emphasis placed on Mehdi as a representation of "*all*" those lost, but also that those lost are identified as "sons." Those who are missing or dead are categorized by their relationship to another, by their status as children to mothers (and fathers) whose experiences of loss are represented, even validated, through Amir and Khalil's visualization of Zahra in *Zahra's Paradise*. Butler conflates "[o]pen grieving" with "outrage in the face of injustice" (*Frames of War* 39), and in *Zahra's Paradise*, a counter-narrative of grievability is vocalized by Zahra's open grief, which responds to the injustices dealt to a multitude of citizens—of sons and daughters—in Iran. The one lost is the *son*; the one left behind is the *mother*; thus, this grief, though opening up a politicized discourse, is emotively charged and introduces a different valuation to this counter-narrative, which is driven by the familial relationship that has been endangered.

This counter-narrative is intended to be far reaching, and the text was originally produced as a web-comic to be disseminated to a global reading public. Continuing to use the forum of the web, Amir and Khalil orchestrated a campaign "Vote4Zahra," which put Zahra forward as a "virtual candidate" in the 2013 Iranian election ("Declaration of Candidacy" 3), campaigning on a platform advocating human rights and democracy and accompanied by some short comic strips. Mehdi represents the sons and daughters lost, but what becomes clear in this online campaign and in the chapter titled "The Grieving Mothers" in *Zahra's Paradise* is that Zahra also represents all those mothers left behind. Responding to the idea of campaigning, Zahra asks "Who will vote for me?," the response: "Every mourning mother"; and "Your grief is Iran's grief" (Amir and Khalil, "Chapter One" 5). In this online campaign, Zahra's grief and loss are not only legitimized but politicized, no longer a personal counter-narrative to state rhetoric but an overtly political one, too.

Zahra reads her "Declaration of Candidacy" at Laleh Park. Mourning mothers have been gathering at Laleh Park since the protests in 2009, and the group also consists of mothers whose children had gone missing, been imprisoned, or been abused going back to the 1980s. By presenting Zahra's speech here, Amir and Khalil utilize the politicized space of communal grief as a stage to deploy human rights activism. The movement in Laleh Park resembles, in part, the "Madres de la Plaza de Mayo," a group of mothers who gathered to protest the "disappearing" of their children during the "Dirty War" (1976-83) in Argentina. Although the identification of the role as "mother" can be criticized for potentially affirming the traditional perception of feminine "emotionality," Sara Eleanor Howe points out that the "Madres" "came together not for the sake of feminism, but to confront the most appalling violations of human rights" (45, 49). Howe's assertion can also be applied tangentially to "The Mourning Mothers of Laleh Park." The expression of maternal identity and grief does not represent "emotionality" as weakness but rather, as Sara Ruddick argues, the particularity of their personal loss that serves as "the emotional root and source of their protest ... extended mothering to include sustaining and protecting any people whose lives are blighted by violence" (232). The state may utilize "grievability" and "non-grievability" as part of its political rhetoric, but by rooting their protest in their personal experiences of grief, mothers find opportunities to subvert such narratives.

Using Zahra as its figurehead, Amir and Khalil's campaign appropriates the "mourning mother" for polemical and political purposes. However, Zahra's "Declaration of Candidacy" serves to deconstruct the state's deployment of the "mourning mother" figure and Zahra's speech—and Laleh Park—comes to embody both a personal and politicized counter-narrative of grievability. The speech banner that flows out from the microphone signifies a clear indication of her speech act, akin to her "Burn" speech cited earlier. This banner is bordered on one side by the crowd of mothers, holding aloft posters of their children and on the other side, by a mass of gravestones, doubling the prominent value of the gravesites of state martyrs. All the faces and the faces of the gravestones are bare. This can be read in such a way that Zahra is giving voice to the faceless, voiceless, and, of course, the dead. Just as in *Zahra's Paradise* the missing are *"all* Mehdi"* (188), Zahra and her narrative stand in for all mourning mothers who have lost their children. The Islamic Republic validates grievability based on its utility to (politicized) state discourses. For example, in *Zahra's Paradise*, government officials were only willing to publically validate Zahra's grief if it could be used to support their cause (209-211). By contrast, Zahra uses polemical rhetoric in order to draw attention to the personal and emotive experiences of maternal and familial loss. Amir and Khalil's works engage with politics in order to validate the personal and emotional, whereas state discourses in Iran appear to utilize emotive and affective narratives to facilitate their political discourses.

In the introduction to her speech for her "Declaration of Candidacy," Zahra cites her connection to the park, reminiscing about taking Mehdi there in his youth. She reflects that now "this park is a monument and a mirror in which time is a measure of grief, a reflection of our children's absence" (Amir and Khalil, "Declaration of Candidacy" 1). This statement aligns the park with the discourses of commemoration and memorialization preeminent in Iranian culture. In particular, it is the image that reigns supreme in this commemorative, and religious, act that represents the "adoration of a hero, of a martyr for Islam" and which, "based on remembrance of the deceased, ensures the unity of Shiite Islam; individual memory contributes to collective memory" (Fomanger 52). Laleh Park represents the "absence" of their children, invisible and faceless. It is the presence and visibility of the collective Mourning Mothers that is commemorative, and which turns the park into a living and breathing "monument." Khanna, speaking of revolutionary actions in Algeria, argues that "[t]he work of mourning materialized in the monument forms a simulation of the past in the service of political myths serving the state," in which "[t]he monument performs the work of mourning" ("Post-Palliative"). However, in the case of the mourning mothers in Laleh Park, the work of mourning is what constructs the "monument." In Laleh Park, mourning is still *performed*, to use Khanna's rhetoric, but it is not (as)simulated through sovereign discourses but rather grounded in the raw emotive collective of the citizens, the relatives, and, above all, the mothers.

In conclusion, the visualization and presence of the mourning mothers serves to constitute and emphasize the grievability of their lost and martyred children. Although religious-political discourses in Iran posit state martyrdom through overt visibility, (politically) dissident martyrs are all but invisible, existing in a delimited space, non-grievable and unburiable. In *Zahra's Paradise*, in Laleh Park, and in video of Parvin Fahimi, the spectacle of the mourning mothers' outrage and grief constitutes a counter-narrative to state discourses and endorses a narrative of grievability and, thus, visibility, for those children and relatives who are incarcerated, missing, and/or killed. In particular, the graphic novel, particularly when incorporated into a web-comic format, allows for the cutting across of these epistemological frames of grievability, of visibility and of invisibility. The "cut" or "splice" between frames, or between panels, "is the edge that belongs to neither one frame nor to the other" and has the potentiality of "pierc[ing] both ... frames, because it demonstrates its own liminality and therefore the representational structure of the frame itself" (Khanna, *Algeria Cuts* 5). In *Zahra's Paradise*, Mehdi exists in the very margins of the panel frames; and in the concluding chapter, his mother, fuelled by her grief, breaks down these barriers. Her grief becomes both spectre and spectacle as her shrouded figure repeats visually—and verbally—across frames, and within them. The mourning mother cuts through and remakes the Islamic Republic of Iran's epistemological frame regarding grievability.

NOTES

[1] The title of Amir and Khalil's text is also indicative of the cemetery *Behesht-e Zahra* in Tehran, alternatively called Zahra's Paradise.
[2] It should be noted that the texts that I am focusing on predom-

inantly cover the loss of these mothers' sons, but daughters have also lost their lives, with perhaps the most globally recognized female "martyr" of the 2009 protests being Neda Agha-Soltan.
[3]The act of memorializing the martyr, represented in murals and rituals, is not unique to Iran. In Palestine, following the second *Intifada*, the memorialization of the martyr was also politicized and integrated into a Palestinian national identity qualified by "shared suffering ... that is shared ceremonially, conceptually, practically, emotionally" (Allen 128).
[4]The "punctum" is a supplement, an "addition" which is "addd[ed] to the photograph and *what is nonetheless already there*" (Barthes 55).

WORKS CITED

Agamben, Giorgio. *Homo Sacer: Sovereign Power and Bare Life.* Trans. Daniel Heller-Roazen. Stanford: Stanford University Press, 1998. Print.

Ahmed, Sara. *The Cultural Politics of Emotion.* 2nd ed. Edinburgh: Edinburgh University Press, 2014. Print.

Allen, Lori. A. "The Polyvalent Politics of Martyr Commemorations in the Palestinian *Intifada.*" *History & Memory* 18.2 (2006): 107-38. Print.

Amir and Khalil. "Chapter One." *Zahra on the Campaign Trail.* Web Comic. *The Real Candidate.* N.p, n.d. Web. 19 Jun 2015.

Amir and Khalil. "Chapter Two: Declaration of Candidacy." *Zahra on the Campaign Trail.* Web Comic. *The Real Candidate.* N.p., n.d. Web. 19 Jun 2015.

Amir and Khalil. *Zahra's Paradise.* New York and London: First Second, 2011. Print.

Barthes, Roland. *Camera Lucida: Reflections on Photography.* Trans. Richard Howard. London: Vintage Books, 2000. Print.

Bressanin, Anna. "Zahra's paradise: the Iranian woman running for president." BBC, 11 Jun. 2013. Web. 24 Jun. 2015.

Butler, Judith. *Frames of War: When if Life Grievable?* London: Verso, 2009. Print.

Butler, Judith. *Precarious Life: The Powers of Mourning and Violence.* London: Verso, 2004. Print.

Cook, David. *Martyrdom in Islam*. Cambridge and New York: Cambridge University Press, 2007. Print.

Flaskerud, Ingrild. "Redemptive Memories: Portraiture in the Cult of Commemoration." *Visual Anthropology* 25.1-2 (2012): 22-46. Print.

Fromanger, Marine. "Variations in the Martyrs' Representations in South Tehran's Private and Public Spaces." *Visual Anthropology* 25.1-2 (2012): 47-67. Print.

Howe, Sara Eleanor. "The *Madres de la Plaza de Mayo*: Asserting Motherhood; Rejecting Feminism?" *Journal of International Women's Studies* 7.3 (2006): 43-50. Print.

hydrademian. "Sohrab Aerabi's mother at his funeral (English subtitles)." *YouTube*. YouTube, 13 July 2009. Web. 21 July 2015.

Khanna, Ranjana. *Algeria Cuts: Women and Representation, 1830 to the Present*. Stanford: Stanford University Press, 2008. Print.

Khanna, Ranjana. "Post-Palliative: Coloniality's Affective Dissonance." *Postcolonial Text*. 2.1 (2006): n. pag. Web. 5 July 2015.

Khosronejad, Pedram. "Introduction: Unburied Memories." *Visual Anthropology* 25.1-2 (2012): 1-21. Print.

Korangy, Alireza. "A Literary and Historical Background of Martyrdom in Iran." *Comparative Studies of South Asia, Africa and the Middle East* 29.3 (2009): 528-543. Print.

Moallem, Minoo. *Between Warrior Brother and Veiled Sister: Islamic Fundamentalism and the Politics of Patriarchy in Iran*. Berkeley: University of California Press, 2005. Print.

Ruddick, Sara. *Maternal Thinking: Towards a Politics of Peace*. London: The Women's Press, 1989. Print.

Satrapi, Marjane. *Persepolis: The Story of a Childhood and the Story of a Return*. London: Vintage, 2008. Print.

Talebi, Shahla. "An Iranian Martyr's Dilemma: The Finite Subject's Infinite Responsibility." *Comparative Studies of South Asia, Africa and the Middle East* 33.2 (2013) 177-196. Print.

Talebi, Shahla. "From the Light of the Eyes to the Eyes of the Power: State and Dissent Martyrs in Post-Revolutionary Iran." *Visual Anthropology* 25.1-2 (2012): 120-47. Print.

Tavakolian, Newsha. *Mothers of Martyrs*. Photo exhibition. *Newsha Tavakolian Photography*. LIVEBOOKS. n. d. Web. 26 May 2015.

Varzi, Roxanne. *Warring Souls: Youth, Media, and Martyrdom in Post-Revolution Iran.* Durham: Duke University Press, 2006. Print.

II.
REMAKING KINSHIP:
MUSLIM SINGLE MOTHERS,
ADOPTIVE MOTHERS, AND CO-MOTHERS

4.
Constructing Counter-Narratives of the "Good" Muslim Mother in Kuala Lumpur, Malaysia

AUDREY MOUSER ELEGBEDE

THIS CHAPTER EXPLORES WAYS that women look to Islam as a model for quality mothering practice and as site for construction of arguments against social marginalization and stigmatization because of divorced status.[1] Based on ethnographic research conducted among self-identified middle-class[2] Malay[3] mothers in the Klang Valley[4] who are divorced or permanently separated, the chapter examines women's rejection of perceived "old-fashioned" interpretations and cultural corruptions of Islam's unbiased permission to divorce, and investigates ways women obtain and retain social capital by reinforcing religiously sanctioned positions. Malaysia uses both common and *syariah* legal systems in family matters, and the *syariah* system is only applied to Muslims. Women in this study acquired divorce through the *syariah* (Islamic) legal system.[5] This analysis includes an evaluation of the ways women apply the elevated standing of mothers in Islam to their own mothering practice and cite "good" mothering as fulfilling social and religious obligations, and an examination of the court context as a venue for construction of personal counter-narratives supported by religiously sanctioned claims to social acceptance.

In a conference presentation in which I addressed identity construction among divorced middle-class Malay women with children, I indicated that a majority of women with whom I worked in the metropolitan area of Kuala Lumpur, Malaysia, believed Islam to be empowering, validating, and liberating, especially in the context of a social and cultural environment that otherwise stigmatized divorced women. A colleague queried my findings.

Many of her informants, who were married middle-class Malay women, instead found Islam to be a restrictive and cumbersome obstacle in contemporary Malaysian modernity.[6] When I returned to Kuala Lumpur, I asked my informants [7]how these two groups could have such disparate perceptions of the role of Islam in modern lives, and what impact marital status might play in this disjuncture. They were eager to discuss these matters, with one participant stating that "[married] women have not experienced the difficulties [with marriage and social stigmatization as a result of divorced status] that we have. Of course they would see Islam's constraints as restrictive rather than supportive" and "It is not until they [i.e. currently married women] are divorced that they will see the positive image of single-mothers in Islam." Essentially, they argued that one needed the experience of being a divorced woman to fully understand how Islam provides a framework to liberate women from social and cultural obstacles that have little to do with the religion. Divorced women also made the case that Malay women in general have engaged in development agendas (NEP), achieved higher education, built professional careers, and gained political aspirations. They have formulated ethnically conscious identities, participated in an Islamic religious revival known as the *dakwah* movement, and assumed public and powerful roles as new members of the middle and upper-middle classes (Hassan).

In this context, others have confirmed that middle-class values and consumer tastes, increased religious consciousness, and refor-mulation of the nuclear family are social, cultural, religious, and political ideals, as depicted by national development and economic strategist rhetoric within the country. In her exploration of do-mestic labourers in middle-class Malaysian households, Christie B. N. Chin explores how the narrow categorization and practice of gender and sexuality within the context of the heteronormative and reproductive marriage includes a bifurcation of enacted gender roles, with men as breadwinners and heads-of-household. Roziah Omar ("Negotiating"; *State; The Malay Woman)* and Maila Stivens ("Sex"; "Theorizing") explain that within Malay-specific house-holds, women are simultaneously constructed as wives, mothers, and primary social and physical (re)producers of the Muslim *ummah* (community), who may or may not work outside the home for wages.[8] Although practice of these ideals vary in individual lives, conceptions of men as purveyors of the public sphere (employment and engagement outside the home) and women as representatives of the domestic sphere (responsible for molding the next generation of morally upright and productive Malaysian citizens) are often internalized and articulated by members of the larger Malaysian population as goals necessary for living in full accordance with modernist, nationalist, middle-class agendas. They are constructions supported by what Aiha Ong and Michael G. Peletz describe as the paternalism of state-initiated development agendas.

Women in this study are agents who "recode" (Mahmood 6) specific actions as fulfilling valued social and individual identities, and operationalize what Anthony Carter identifies as strategic and "reflexive monitoring and rationalization of a continuous flow of conduct" (61) that provides personalized meanings. Malay women recognize that middle-class identity consists not only of access to material wealth but also includes access to religious and class-based knowledge. Combining key cross-listed elements of social elevation and social capital—namely religious piety and maternal practice—they redefine lived experience and personal choices as fulfilling key social and religious expectations. Divorced women in particular emphasize relational analyses with bordering social groups such as married women or divorced men, a methodology supported by Lois Weis and Michelle Fine, and they locate themselves in key social, economic, and political structures. By constructing positive images of their own maternal practice and by comparing themselves to former spouses and fathers that they interpret as inattentive or not dependable, divorced women with children restake claims to valued social capital and positions in the middle classes based on fulfillment of 'traditional' gender roles that are threatened by the stigma of divorce.[9]

DIVORCE AND SOCIAL STIGMATIZATION

Islamic belief systems and Malay ethnic *adat* (localized cultural logics that outline appropriate behaviours and codes of conduct for individual and communal action) combine in Malaysia to define relative and qualitatively egalitarian gender norms between men and women and to emphasize the importance of family as a fundamental building block of the Malay community, the *ummah* (Karim, *Women*). Marriage, procreation, and childrearing are valued in both Malay and Muslim cultural traditions, and every member of the family and community is expected to nurture and contribute economic and emotional support to members of the extended family. Interplay of the Arabic-derived concepts of *akal*[10] (rationality or self-control; henceforth referred to as *akl*) and *nafsu*[11] (desire or passion; henceforth referred to as *nafs*)[12] are considered in discussions of familial relationships and gendered behaviour.[13] Both men and women are believed to hold elements of *akl* and *nafs*. Men are assumed, however, to articulate more *akl*—the more socially valued attribute—whereas women are believed to express more *nafs* (Peletz, "Neither").

Within the context of marriage, inappropriateness of behaviour on the part of one or both parties (lack of restraint and expression of excessive passion or desire) is popularly associated with the causes for divorce. Marital infidelity, excessive spending on material goods, lack of personal modesty in behaviour or dress, abandonment, or the inability or unwillingness to provide economic support to one's family—are all cited often as examples of perceived lack of *akl* and excessive *nafs* (Banks; Peletz, *Reinscribing* and *Islamic*). They are used as evidence in divorce applications to support a perceived lack of restraint associated with those who divorce.

Although divorce has historically been common within the Malay population, the popular stigma associated with divorce has grown in recent decades and continues to vex government officials, academics, and the populace (Djamour, *Malay*: Jones; Peletz, *Reason* and *Islamic*; Banks; Stivens, *Matriliny*; Karim, "Bilateralism" and *Women*). In 2010, *The New Straits Times* reported a doubling of Malaysian divorce proceedings between 2002 and 2009, of which Muslim divorces comprised 82 percent.[14] In 2011, *The Malay Mail* article "Every 15 minutes, a Muslim couple gets divorced in Malaysia" (Kaos) further engendered concern over divorce frequency within the Malay community. Government representatives, university researchers, and medical personnel often cite unrealistic expectations based on Western models of marriage, individual marriage choice, disillusionment with married life, and unwillingness to work on marital problems as causes for increasing divorce rates. As suggested by Zeenath Kausar in *Social Ills in Malaysia: Causes and Remedies,* increasing divorce within the Malay community is a result of "the ignorance of the type of relationship that Islam visages for married couples (20)." [15]

In the Malaysian *syariah* system, the concept of "no-fault" divorce, which permits a court to grant a divorce without evidence that one or both parties have violated a marital contract, is not present. Both men and women may initiate divorce. Although the guidelines for application for divorce are beyond the scope of this chapter, women are generally granted divorce if a husband is found guilty of violating the marriage contract through cruelty, abuse, the inability to maintain and financially support his wife and children for three consecutive months, or a mental or physical defect that is revealed after marriage. Men, in contrast, have greater access to divorce, and may or may not be required to justify such application before divorce is granted (Peletz, *Reinscribing* and *Islamic*; Hassan and Cederroth; Jones).[16]

Informants argue, however, that women bear the brunt of social stigma of divorce. Using marital infidelity as an example, informants argue that although more women than men cite infidelity in application for divorce, women are often still perceived as responsible for marital breakdown on these occasions because it is the *ummah's* expectation that it is a wife's task to keep her husband sexually satisfied and domestically content. If a husband seeks female companionship outside the marriage, it may be perceived as a lack of restraint on his part and an indication of excessive *nafs,* but it can also be perceived as a reflection on the wife's deficiency as a domestic partner and, therefore, excused as justifiable behaviour on his part. Groups such as the Obedient Wives Club, launched in June 2011 by the conservative Islamic order, *Al-Arqam,* support this claim. The group asserts that divorce can be curbed by teaching women how to be submissive and how to keep their husbands sexually satisfied and claim that "disobedient wives are the cause for upheaval in this world" (Ng).

Single-parent households, primarily headed by women, are further labelled by the general population as "social problems" (Stivens, "Hope") and are associated by political and social organizations with crime and drug abuse and with other Western-influenced social deficits that challenge the functionality of the ideal Malay family (Stivens, "Hope"; Kausar). Teen sexual activity, drug usage, or lack of academic achievement on the part of children are often cited as the result of inattentive parenting, the primary purview of the domestic sphere and the female domain (Stivens, "Hope"). Lack of paternal engagement with children, deficient social resources to address drug usage, and poor decision making on the part of children are generally underexplored as explanations for unde-sirable behaviours. As a result, Malay middle-class allotment of prestige and social capital becomes tenuous for divorced women, as the context of divorce casts doubt on a woman's understanding of the role of the "good" Muslim wife and mother and effectively questions her piety, religious observance, and maternal practice.

Divorced women often are described by members of the Malay community, by media sources, and even by some informants as unwilling to serve husbands and/or children, as too materialistic and too career-oriented, and as inattentive to family obligations and religious responsibilities. These deficiencies highlight her inability either to control *nafs* (passions and desires, in this case for material and personal gain) or to use *akl* (intellect or reasoning) in decision making. Final divorce decrees that designate husbands as petitioners in divorce further identify wives as deficient partners because the husband has been granted his request for divorce.[17] Although this is often done to reduce court fees paid by women (Peletz, *Rein-scribing*), it unintentionally negates women's active engagement in dissolution of marriage. Prevailing patriarchal attitudes in the Malay community indicate that most of its members do "not feel comfortable if a woman divorces a man even on genuine grounds" (Kausar). By divorcing, women are perceived as having refused to "live up to the norms of motherhood and femininity" (Tan 283) and, as a consequence, become "the enemy within" (Tan 283). The physical location of this blame—the religious courts—further solidifies the social marginalization of single mothers. The result is stigma experienced at the public, family, and personal levels.

As practised agents of national modernization agendas, these divorced middle-class women, however, generally have cared for the physical, social, and emotional needs of their families while building professional careers. They have skills (higher education, employment, and experience) that substantiate claims to empowered and socially valued roles as independent women and mothers. Islamic knowledge provides them with socially and religiously fortified foundations needed to rebuff models that assume deficiencies in mothering and maternal practice because of divorce. Rather than accept these models, middle-class Malay women recode daily mothering activities by infusing them with personal, social, and religious meanings, by reclaiming their place at the center of social and national development, and by gaining social capital.

DIVORCE AND THE *SYARIAH* COURTS: A VENUE FOR VALIDATION

Because of the religious authority attributed to Malaysia's *syariah* system and to the availability of divorce in Islam, the *syariah* courts become a critical venue for divorced women's identity construction. As noted earlier, middle-class Malay society tends to attribute social-class status and social capital to individuals with financial and material evidence of upward mobility, with performance of social and gender roles in accordance with the idealized nuclear family, and with command of religious knowledge. Because many divorced women experience significant reduction of wealth post-divorce and are no longer able to claim status associated with the idealized nuclear family, religious validation of positive mothering practice becomes a key venue for Malay middle-class divorced women's identity construction. A woman achieves religious validation in divorce proceedings through the granting of a divorce in which she is not cited as having violated the marital contract. She has supporting evidence that she lives in accordance with Islamic principles, and she is not to blame for the failure of her marriage. She can justifiably argue, therefore, the right to recode religious identity based on successful and religiously appropriate mothering and marital behaviour. This is particularly important given the patriarchal bias often attributed to the court system.

Malaysia's Islamic family courts are sites routinely denounced by informants for holding gender bias in favour of men and for using cultural interpretations of the *syariah* legal system that impede Islam's "true" intent behind women's access to divorce. Aida Melley Tan Mutalib, for example, filed for divorce because her husband was frequently abusive and refused to financially provide for household expenses, both of which she argued were grounds for divorce in the *syariah* system. According to Aida, her husband remarried and created a new family, and the court's leniency permitted him to be absent from court and delay court proceedings indefinitely. She claimed that it was the court's bias against women and not *syariah* law that permitted her husband to delay divorce proceedings and restricted her ability to move forward. Nine years after she initially filed for divorce, the sultan of the State of Selangor and head of Islamic Affairs of the State personally intervened in her case, stating publically that "[T]aking so long to grant a divorce is torturous" (Cruez), thus shaming Aida's husband into granting her a divorce.[18]

Although Aida Melley's case was perhaps notable, other women provide similar evidence. Mariam, a fifty-two-year-old advertising executive, explained that her husband of thirteen years had stated his intention to take a second wife. During the course of a subsequent argument, he publically declared his willingness to provide her with a divorce: "He said [in front of witnesses] that he would divorce me. He didn't want to do it, but he had no choice. If there [had not been] witnesses, the court would have denied my case and he would have been allowed two [wives]. I didn't want to live like that." The court, however, offered her a miniscule settlement of RM13,000 [*ringgit*] [approximately USD 3,500 at time of divorce] and RM60 [USD 13] per month per child for child support. Commenting on this decision, Mariam said, "I was insulted by the *kadi* [judge] and the court at that time ... Only 1000 ringgit per year of marriage! It was nothing ... I rejected the offer." She settled for a letter from her husband relinquishing his rights to their children.

In contrast, Khadijah, a thirty-nine-year-old office administrator, claimed that she did not experience explicit bias in the court, but she also indicated that she had conducted independent research in preparation of court defenses in anticipation of such a bias. According to Khadijah, she perceived her thirteen-year marriage to be unsatisfactory because, according to her understanding of marriage in Islam, her husband did not fulfill financial or emotional obligations to the family. According to Khadijah, "[My husband] didn't support me emotionally ... [and] He only had short-term jobs ... I was always the one with the job." She claimed her husband failed to lead the family in religious practice, and that it was she who encouraged religious observance for herself and their two sons. "According to Islam," she said, "I shouldn't have to wake him for the morning prayer. As husband, *he* should be *my* guide" (informant's emphasis). Confident in her knowledge of gendered and marital roles in a proper Muslim marriage, Khadijah researched contexts under which a woman could seek divorce within the *syariah* system. She also sought legal advice from various sources, including internet resources, *syariah*-trained lawyers, and court officials, and she presented her argument to demonstrate that her marriage had not fulfilled expectations of a proper Muslim marriage. Khadijah was granted divorce on the grounds that her husband was not the family's religious guide, had not provided economic support for the household, and had violated the marriage contract.

Despite the seeming bias in the adjudication of family law, the courts are still sites for the development of counter-narratives by women who refocus identity construction from marital status to quality religious and maternal practices. The preceding cases illustrate that women identify success in divorce proceedings as indicators of righteousness and piety; successful divorce cases are perceived as confirmation of fulfillment of religious roles as wives and mothers. Cases also establish former husbands as less religiously aligned because they were not victorious in quests to retain marriages, despite spousal objection, or were found in violation of elements of the marriage contract.

Khadijah's example also illustrates that women can be armed with interpretations of Islam and Islamic law that are effective in court and that are useful in the construction of counter-narratives that place blame for dissolution of marriage on the husband. Popular web resources that provide theological and/or feminist analyses of Islam's perspective on divorce and single parenting (such as *Sisters in Islam* or *Islam's Women,* or academic websites that outline divorce and child-support proceedings around the world such as the *Ahlul Bayt Digital Islamic Library Project,* an international and collaborative effort to create the world's largest digital Islamic library on the internet) provide information for women seeking judicial information and religious interpretation on divorce and child support. Books such as Norma Kassim's *A Walk Through Life: Issues and Challenges Through the Eyes of a Muslim Woman* identify religious passages and interpretations that support women's arguments that they have fulfilled religious duties as wives and mothers while spouses have failed to fulfill religious responsibilities as husbands and fathers. In this context, women's counter-narratives are forged in the court system and are couched in Islamic terms. Counter-narratives also highlight positive maternal and religious images, are poised to validate life choices, and can be generalized to other contexts.

COUNTER-NARRATIVES: MOTHERHOOD AND QUALITY PARENTING AS RELIGIOUS PRACTICE

As noted earlier, reports about "social problems" frequently identify single mothers as contributing to social delinquency because of a perceived inability or unwillingness to fulfill familial responsibilities. Informants' popular profiles of the "bad" mother, in comparison, describe women who lack concern for children's emotional, physical, or educational needs. These "bad" mothers are rumoured to focus on personal lives and material gain and to leave children with family or household help while seeking companionship or professional development outside the home. That profile, with slight variation, mirrors the one used to describe divorced single mothers and is often considered the cause of divorce.

Having used "success" in the court context as a venue to validate religious observance and fulfillment of familial obligation, women's counter-narratives resist social marginalization, however, and routinely reference the "bad" mother profile as comparison to their own maternal practices. Two ways that women operationalize this process are relevant to our discussion: 1) underscoring prized placement of mothers and mothering in Islam, and 2) highlighting positive maternal practice, often built in relation to familial obligation and in opposition to paternal practice of former spouses.

Mothers and mothering practice are notably honoured in Islam. Informants repeatedly presented versions of Prophet Muhammad's advice that one should honour one's mother above all others, after God, or that heaven and paradise are located at one's mother's feet, as evidence that mothers hold esteemed status in Islam. Kassim, in her personal narrative on life as a Malay single mother, quotes the advice of the Prophet Muhammad to support this point. "A man asked the Prophet: 'Whom should I honour most?' the Prophet replied: 'Your mother.' 'And who comes next?' asked the man. The Prophet replied: 'Your mother'. 'And who comes next?' asked the man. The Prophet replied: 'Your mother'. 'And who comes next?' asked the man. The Prophet replied: 'Your father'" (Kassim 82). Women also refer to Islam's allowance of polygyny as evidence that divorced or widowed women with children should be received in their communities with compassion and full inclusion. As one woman explained, "Islam permitted a man four [wives] so that men could take care of single mothers and their children. There was no bias. Islam [recognizes] the value of moms and doesn't judge [single mothers based on divorced status]." This comment acknowledges an empowered understanding of Islamic principles and the religiously elevated or substantively equal placement of women (compared to men), regardless of marital status. The statement also represents one of the more feminist interpretations of Islamic principles being discussed throughout the Islamic world, and it supports the argument that women with access to Islamic knowledge recode lived experience and claim social capital associated with living in accordance with Islamic principles.[19]

To bolster public perceptions of single mothers, divorced women with children have highlighted the intensified parental investment that occurs after divorce. Noraini, for example, encapsulated this sentiment when she stated, "Everything from A to Zed you have to do on your own." This redirection of public concern is partially achieved through use of the term "*ibu tunggal*," or "single mother." According to an article published in *The Star* ("Singled Out for Discrimination"), the term *ibu tunggal* was introduced in 1995 and has since replaced *janda* (divorcee) and *balu* (widow). According to Hew, the term has also been more broadly applied to include women that are separated from or abandoned by their partners, unmarried adoptive parents, never-married biological parents, and women considered heads of household (with ill or absent partners). These designations, however, are ones that primarily focus on marital status rather than motherhood status. Government programs—such as the National Social Policy and the Family First: Bring Your Heart Home family unity campaign— quickly adopted the use of *ibu tunggal* and began to underscore the central role of mothers in family continuity. By stressing motherhood, the term *ibu tunggal* recognizes emotional bonds between parent and child and aligns single mothers with the designated authority and dignity accorded mothers in Islam, regardless of marital status (Elegbede). In this context, divorced mothers argue that the stigma that they receive in divorce is unwarranted, and that they should retain the dignity, respect, and social capital accorded all mothers in Islam.

In addition to status of mothers and mothering in Islam, women look to individualized parenting as support for resisting stigmatized associations. Divorced women in this study are acutely concerned that children are able to access the same class-based attributes of higher education and extracurricular opportunities that they would have received had their parents remained married. This, women argue, becomes representative of quality parenting and is key to fulfilling both religious and class-based parental responsibilities to children.

Mariam explained, for example, that after her divorce, she needed to prove to herself, her family, and her ex-husband that she was capable of caring for her children and her household. She refused familial support, and each evening, she placed her youngest child safely in a washing tub while she slept with the eldest. Unlike other women she knew, she did not spend money frivolously on personal desires—characteristics associated with a "bad" mother—but instead expended only emotional, physical, and financial resources for the betterment of her children. Having forsaken child support in favour of full custody, Mariam believed that her sacrifice represented fulfillment of religious duty as a "good" mother.

Rahimah, similarly, recoded personal sacrifice and ensuing life difficulties as qualities of a "good" mother. Divorced after twenty years of what she described as an emotionally abusive marriage, Rahimah ran a small home-based business and struggled financially to maintain her apartment and transportation. She tried to ensure that her four children's education, transportation, and basic physical and emotional needs, and she argued that their father refused to pay child support and did not engage them emotionally. She provided financial and religious guidance as would a male head of household, and she believed that her actions on behalf of her children were fulfilling her fate. "How would I answer to God if I did not care for them?," she asked. In comparison, she said, her former husband did not interpret his insufficient child support and guidance as a lack of conformity to social-class expectations or religious obligation. Once his failure to comply with a court order was brought to public attention, her former husband claimed Rahimah caused him shame. "As if *not* paying for his kids *didn't* cause him shame? It should," she replied (informant's emphasis).

Each of these examples illustrates positive maternal practice and religious responsibility in family constructs. Women claim financial and emotional investment and sacrifice as evidence of quality maternal care. Recognizing changing gender roles in household dynamics post-divorce, with particular attention to decreased household income and the necessity (not just option) for women to work outside the home as heads of households, women *recode* personal sacrifice and *change* gendered expectations as continuation of maternal practice. Although work outside the home prior to divorce may have been perceived by the Malay community as an individual desire for self-aggrandizement and as an inability to control one's *nafs*, work outside the home after divorce is defined as obligatory for quality maternal practice and fulfillment of religious obligation—a sign of one's *akl*. Women further code emotional attachment to children, as compared to the lack of emotional attachment on the part of delinquent fathers, as indexes of quality parenting, and, therefore, as acts that warrant elevated social recognition for the divorced mothers.

CONCLUSIONS: ELEVATING THE MUSLIM MOTHER

Emotional and financial obligations to family, particularly children, are constructed as essential elements to social placement in Malaysia's modernist, middle-class, and religious ideals. The seeming "failure" of divorced women with children to fulfill religious and familial obligations as wives and mothers marks them as peripheral. The women in this study acknowledge stigmatizing beliefs about divorced women with children and recognize that to reestablish valued social positions they must locate individual identities in ways that are personally significant and socially defensible. Using the social capital middle-class Malay society grants individuals with command of Islamic knowledge, women in this study argue that Islam provides liberty and equality for all people and that patriarchal continuance in the social marginalization of divorced women is a result of Malay culture, not "true" Islam. Women draw on religious resources as roots of personal power and identify specific experiences within Islamic contexts as religious validation to combat social marginalization. Having achieved religious validation in the *syariah* court system, divorced Malay women construct counter-narratives that combat social stigmatization by using the sanctified role of mother and the performance of "good" mothering as supporting evidence. By also comparing their own mothering practice to stories of men or women who do not provide equal levels of emotional and financial support to children, the women in this study provide counter-narratives that substantiate claims to social and religious position.

Women's attempts to resist social placement on the margins of middle-class Malay society appear to have had a gradual impact in larger Malaysian society. Some women have chosen to remain quiet on issues of marital status for fear of social marginalization; others have chosen to tell their stories publically in an effort to assist others struggling under similar circumstances. The Malaysian state has issued public statements on the status of single mothers and provides budget items for those in financial need. Nevertheless, the stigma of divorce and questions of religiosity and piety for women who are divorced continue for many women. As a result, mothering remains a source of communal and religious validation, for self and social placement. Articulating actions using a culturally salient yet flexible rubric, middle-class divorced women with children couch daily activities in accordance with religious ideals and apply them to the social, economic, political, and religious systems in which they operate. They further dovetail mothering and Muslim images into counter-narratives that are individualized and that ensure social and religious validity to support claims to piety and Islamic morality as accomplished Muslim mothers.

NOTES

[1] This research was supported by a Fulbright Dissertation Grant and a Mellon Dissertation Grant, as well as the Department of Anthropology, the Population Studies and Training Center, and the Graduate School at Brown University. I am grateful to the women who shared their lives and stories in the course of research. For invaluable feedback on this essay, I thank Bruce Mouser, Nancy Mouser, and Munsifah Abdul Latif. Portions of this paper were presented at the 110th Annual Conference of the American Anthropological Association in Montreal, Canada in 2011. Pseudonyms have been used to protect the identity of research participants. Any errors are my own.

[2] "Middle class" is defined in various ways by researchers of Malaysia. More generally, it is characterized by economic indicators, and includes various management, administrative and government occupations. Although it often includes an assumption of higher education, educational attainment is not obligatory if professional and economic achievements have been realized. I argue that although middle-class membership is procedurally professional and economic, near-equal emphasis is given to social policies of increased Islamic identity, nuclear family format, and "traditional" gender roles. More specifically, because of the economic downward mobility of single-parent households, "middle class" for this project was established using educational and professional accomplishments, self-identification, and values and lifestyle, including English proficiency, technological knowledge, international experience or knowledge, and familiarity and comfort with understanding and utilizing various religious interpretations in state-based venues, such as the *syariah* court. "Middle class" in this context is both economic and social, where common values and lifestyle are practiced, reconfigured, and either conferred on or denied members by others of the community.

[3] "Malay" refers to the dominant ethnic group within Malaysia, as opposed to Chinese and Indian populations. "Malaysian"

refers to all people with national citizenship. Malays are almost exclusively Muslim.

[4] Research was conducted in the metropolitan area of Kuala Lumpur and the suburban areas of the Klang Valley, including, but not limited to, Petaling Jaya, Subang Jaya, Shah Alam, Damansara Heights, and Ampang. These multicultural communities are within the state of Selangor and the Federal Territory of Kuala Lumpur and are principal locations of middle-class Malay populations.

[5] Within the state of Selangor, the site of this study, all legal issues outside of family and moral matters are addressed using the common law system, regardless of religious affiliation. This was once the case across the nation. In recent years, however, the states of Kelantan and Terengganu have encouraged and implemented elements of *hudud* and *syariah* for non-Muslims and for non-family matters (Hays; "The 8 Things").

[6] "Modernity" in the Malaysian context is not uniformly understood or defined, but it tends to include an application of a series of economic and social development schemas—such as the New Economic Policy (NEP) (1971-1990), the New Development Policy (NDP) (1991-2000), and Vision 2020—that have propelled Malaysia into industrialized status. Included in such economic programs are the eradication of poverty, technological development, health achievements, and the development of an urban Malay middle class. The Malaysian development project is also social, as it places morality, Islamic religious agendas, and the patriarchal, heteronormative familial construct on the forefront of what is considered "modern" (Embong; Chin).

[7] All interviews were conducted in English.

[8] Many middle-class women who are married work outside the home in professional positions, including advertising, office administration, small business, education, technology services, etc. Dual income households are not uncommon, and represent some of the demand for domestic work, as discussed by Chin. Women usually retain professional positions after divorce.

[9] Claims to middle-class status, as presented by the women in this study, are not meant to indicate that all women lose middle-class status upon divorce, or that opportunities for upward mobility are unavailable post-divorce. The interconnectedness of middle-class

constructions and the nuclear family is so strong, however, that divorced women are threatened with, and most often receive, stigma. Women often perceive this stigma as a risk to class-based status and are, thus, compelled to emphasize areas of middle-class identity to which they continue to lay claim.

[10]*Akal* stems from the Arabic word *'aql* (Peletz, "Neither") or *akl*.

[11]*Nafsu* stems from the Arabic word *nafs* (Peletz, "Neither").

[12]*Akal* and *nafsu*, as discussed in the Malaysianist literature, are referenced as *akl* and *nafs* in the Islamic literature. Although a majority of my sources have been from the Malaysianist perspective, and my work was conducted within the Malay population, *akl* and *nafs* will be used throughout this piece to remain consistent with other contributions to the volume. The contextually understood and utilized definitions of the terms, however, will remain consistent with the Malaysian experience and the Malaysianist literature.

[13]According to Peletz ("Neither"), *akl* and *nafs* "are key symbols in many domains of Malay culture—and among Muslims in Aceh, Java, and elsewhere in Southeast Asia and beyond—and they are frequently invoked in discussions of the similarities and differences between males and females" ("Neither" 82).

[14]The Malaysian *syariah* court system does not enumerate divorce rates based on income or class.

[15]It should be noted that Kausar indicates that she "does not claim that this study is empirical nor is it thoroughly a research-based study" (back cover). Instead the work presents an attempt "to explore some of the social problems that are spreading in Malaysia at an unprecedented scale" (back cover). It should also be noted that my research is primarily concerned with women's constructions of envisioned 'true' Islam, perceived appropriate gendered and marital behaviours, and how personal experience conforms or deviates. This idyllic vision may not be supported by dominant religious interpretation in Malaysia but may stem from marginal religious interpretations within Malaysia or elsewhere in the Muslim world, and may be culturally or individually varied. I, therefore, do not outline a single model of gendered and marital behaviour as proscribed by religion, or by Malay culture, but rather focus on women's perceptions of individual lives in relation to idyllic models.

[16]In Islamic law, a husband can notify his wife, either verbally or

in writing, of an impending divorce by uttering the *talak* (meaning "to release," "to divorce," or "I divorce thee"), and subsequent filing of the divorce within the *syariah* court system. In the Malaysian context, a husband is often (but not always) expected to justify his utterance of the *talak* in court before the divorce is officially granted (Jones; Peletz, *Islamic*; Djamour, *Muslim*; Hassan and Cederroth). A wife, in contrast, is only able to access divorce in one of three scenarios. The first scenario is if the husband is found guilty by the *syariah* court of cruelty, abuse, the inability to support his wife for three consecutive months, or abandonment or neglect for six consecutive months. The second scenario is if the wife offers to provide financial compensation in return for marital release, and the husband can be convinced to utter the *talak*. The third scenario is if a man is unable to financially support his wife or if after marriage, the wife discovers that her husband is impotent, insane, has serious health conditions such as leprosy or elephantiasis, or is sent to jail for three or more years (Jones; Djamour, *Muslim*; Sharifah and Cederroth). In the case of the Kuala Lumpur Federal statutes, cruelty can also qualify under this type of divorce (Horowitz).

[17]Within Malaysia, the sultan of each state is the head of Islamic affairs for his state. The *syariah* family court system in Malaysia, therefore, differs from state to state, without federal standardization, and is, as Peletz (*Reinscribing* and *Islamic*) argues, both Muslim (structural) and Malay (subjective) in nature.

[18]It should be noted that various levels of patriarchy are at work in this context. Divorce tends to be the purview of the husband, and custody of older children is assigned to the father, should he make the request. In the Malaysian context, women usually retain domestic custody of children, even when there is joint retention of parental rights. In addition, the state-based *syariah* system retains patriarchal control by denying women access to divorce without explicit evidence to support how husbands have violated marital contracts, by supporting leniency of husbands contesting divorce, and by permitting husbands extended flexibility with financial obligations to children. For greater detail on the various levels of patriarchy at work in the Malaysian court system, see Peletz (*Islamic*), Sharifah and Cederroth, and Jones.

[19]Within Malaysia, the group Sisters in Islam has come to the fore as a feminist-centred organization that works with and for the rights of women in Islam. For more information, see *Sisters in Islam*.

WORKS CITED

Ahlul Bayt Digital Islamic Library Project. N.p. 1995-2016. Web. 9 April, 2016.

Anwar, Zainah. *Islamic Revivalism in Malaysia: Dakwah Among the Students.* Petaling Jaya: Pelanduk, 1987. Print.

Banks, David J. *Malay Kinship.* Philadelphia: Institute for the Study of Human Issues, 1983. Print.

Carter, Anthony. "Agency and Fertility: For An Ethnography of Practice." *Situating Fertility:Anthropology and Demographic Inquiry.* Ed. Susan Greenhalgh. Cambridge: Cambridge University Press, 1999. 55-85. Print.

Chin, Christie B. N. *In Service and Servitude: Foreign Female Domestic Workers and the Malaysian "Modernity" Project.* New York: Columbia University Press, 1998. Print.

Cruez, Annie Freeda. "Ruler Has Won the Hearts of the Rakyat." *New Straits Times,* 11 Dec. 2002. Web. 6 Apr. 2016.

Djamour, Judith. *Malay Kinship and Marriage in Singapore.* London: Athlone, 1959. Print.

Djamour, Judith. *Muslim Matrimonial Court in Singapore.* London: Athlone, 1966. Print.

Elegbede, Audrey. "Becoming a 'Single-Mom': Featuring Motherhood over Marital Status Among Malays in Muslim Malaysia." *Anthropology of Mothering.* Eds. Michelle Walks and Naomi McPherson. Bradford, ON: Demeter Press, 2011. 240-250. Print.

Embong, Abdul Rahman. *State-Led Modernization and the New Middle Class in Malaysia.* London: Palgrave, 2002. Print.

Hassan, Sharifah Zaleha Syed. "Islamization and the Emerging Civil Society in Malaysia." *Islam and Civil Society in Southeast Asia.* Eds. Nakamura Mitsuo, Sharon Siddique, and Omar Farouk Bajunid. Singapore: Institute of Southeast Asian Studies, 2001. 76-88. Print.

Hassan, Sharifah Zaleha Syed, and Sven Cederroth. *Managing Marital Disputes in Malaysia: Islamic Mediators and Conflict*

Resolution in the Syariah Courts. Richmond: Routledge Curzon, 1997. Print.

Hew Cheng Sim. "Like a Chicken Standing on One Leg: Urbanization and Single Mothers." Village Mothers, City Daughters: Women and Urbanization in Sarawak, Hew Cheng Sim, ed. Singapore: The Institute for Southeast Asian Studies, 2007. 104-119. Print.

Horowitz, Donald L. "The Qur'an and the Common Law: Islamic Reform and the Theory of Legal Change." *American Journal of Comparative Law* 62.1 and 2 (1994): 233-293, 543-580. Print.

Hays, Jeffrey. "Islam in Malaysia." *Facts and Details.* N.p.,2013. Web. 7 Apr. 2016.

Islam's Women. N.p., 2006. Web. 9 April, 2016.

Jones, Gavin W. *Marriage and Divorce in Islamic Southeast Asia.* Kuala Lumpur: Oxford University Press, 1994. Print.

Karim, Wazir Jahan. "Bilateralism and Gender in Southeast Asia. "'Male' and 'Female' in Developing Southeast Asia.* Ed. Wazir Jahan Karim. Oxford: Berg Publishers, 1995. 35-74. Print.

Karim, Wazir Jahan. *Women and Culture: Between Malay Adat and Islam.* Boulder: Westview Press, 1992. Print.

Kaos, Joseph, Jr. "Every 15 Minutes, a Muslim Couple Gets Divorced in Malaysia." *Muslim Observer.* Muslim Observer, 5 May 2011. Web. 9 Apr. 2016.

Kassim, Norma. *A Walk Through Life: Issues and Challenges Through the Eyes of a Muslim Woman.* Kuala Lumpur: NK & Associates, 2007. Print.

Kausar, Zeenath. *Social Ills in Malaysia: Causes and Remedies.* Kuala Lumpur: Internal Islamic University Malaysia Research Centre, 2005. Print.

Mahmood, Saba. *Politics of Piety: The Islamic Revival and the Feminist Subject.* Princeton: Princeton University Press, 2005. Print.

Ng, Eileen. "'Obedient Wives' Club: Malaysia Group Says Good Sex Is a Duty." *The Huffington Post.* The Huffington Post. 5 June, 2011. Web. 6 April, 2016.

"Number of Divorces Rises by 105pc." *The New Straits Times Online,* 12 Sept. 2011. Web. 9 April, 2016.

Omar, Roziah. "Negotiating Their Visibility: The Lives of Educated and Married Malay Women." *Women in Malaysia: Breaking Boundaries*. Eds. Roziah Omar and Azizah Hamzah. Kuala Lumpur: Utusan Publication and Distributors, 2003. 117-142. Print.

Omar, Roziah. *State, Islam and Malay Reproduction*. Canberra: Australian National University, 1996. Print.

Omar, Roziah. *The Malay Woman in the Body: Between Biology and Culture*. Kuala Lumpur: Penerbit Fajar Bakti, 1994. Print.

Ong, Aihwa and Michael G. Peletz, eds. *Bewitching Women, Pious Men: Gender and Body Politics in Southeast Asia*. Berkeley: University of California Press, 1995. Print.

Peletz, Michael G. *Islamic Modern: Religious Courts and Cultural Politics in Malaysia*. Princeton: Princeton University Press, 2002. Print.

Peletz, Michael. "Neither Reasonable nor Responsible: Contrasting Representations of Masculinity in a Malay Society." *Bewitching Women, Pious Men: Gender and Body Politics in Southeast Asia*. Eds. Aihwa Ong and Michael G. Peletz. Berkeley: University of California Press, 1995. 76-123. Print.

Peletz, Michael. *Reason and Passion: Representations of Gender in a Malay Society*. Berkeley: University of California Press, 1996. Print.

Peletz, Michael. *Reinscribing "Asian (Family) Values": Nation Building, Subject Making, and Judicial Process in Malaysia's Islamic Courts*. Notre Dame: Erasmus Institute, 2003. Print.

"Singled Out for Discrimination." *The Star*. 19 Feb. 2003, Petaling Jaya, ed.: 5-6. Print.

Sisters in Islam. N.p., n.d. Web. 6 Apr. 2016

Stivens, Maila K. "The Hope of the Nation: Moral Panics and the Construction of Teenagerhood in Contemporary Malaysia." *Coming of Age in South and Southeast Asia: Youth, Courtship and Sexuality*. Eds. Lenore Manderson and Pranee Liamputtong. Richmond: Routledge Curzon Press, 2002.188-206. Print.

Stivens, Maila K. *Matriliny and Modernity: Sexual Politics and Social Change in Rural Malaysia*. St. Leonards: Allen and Unwin, 1996. Print.

Stivens, Maila K. "Sex, Gender, and the Making of the New Malay Middle Classes." *Gender and Power in Affluent Asia*. Eds. Krishna Sen and Maila Stivens. London: Routledge, 1998.

87-126. Print.

Stivens, Maila K. "Theorising Gender, Power, and Modernity in Affluent Asia." *Gender and Power in Affluent Asia.* Eds. Krishna Sen and Maila Stivens. London: Routledge, 1998.1-34. Print.

Tan Beng Hui. "Women's Sexuality and the Discourse on Asian Values: Cross-Dressing in Malaysia." *Same-Sex Relations and Female Desires: Transgender Practices Across Cultures.* Eds. Evelyn Blackwood and Saskia E. Wieringa. New York: Columbia University Press, 1999. 281-307. Print.

"The 8 Things You Need To Know On Hudud Law In Kelantan." *My News Hub*, 20 Mar. 2015. Web. 7 April, 2016.

Weis, Lois, and Michelle Fine. *Working Method: Research and Social Justice.* New York: Routledge, 2004. Print.

5.

Between Blood and Milk, East and West

Muslim Adoptive Mothering in a Transnational Context

MARGARET AZIZA PAPPANO

THE MOTHER IS DEFINED in Western psychoanalytic theory by contiguity with the child: an originary, primal attachment is imagined, described by Freud as a pre-Oedipal stage. This stage is, according to Julia Kristeva, pre-linguistic, characterized by infantile dependency, a focus on body rhythms, and incomplete corporeal mapping, so as to fail to distinguish mother from self. Only once the child accedes to language and to symbolization in the Oedipal stage does he or she become aware of the mother as an other, a separate person. In Arabic-speaking contexts, the term *kebda*, "liver," is used to speak of the primal physical and emotional bond between mother and child, suggesting similar notions of corporeal continguity. What then of the child who is separated from the mother after birth? The child who is reared by another woman? Is the adoptive mother a mother in the same way? The mother is singular: a pole around whom the child revolves, the centre, the home. The Prophet is reported to have said, "Paradise lies under the feet of the mother." What then of the adopted child with two mothers, a birth mother and an adopted mother? Which one represents the gateway to paradise? The mother is also socially constructed as a non-sexual being: "the sexual act leading to procreation is one that is entirely sublimated," as Jamila Bargach observes (130). However, in the case of non-marital or "illegitimate birth" in a traditional Muslim society, the mother is seen primarily as a sexual being; indeed, she often becomes an outcast, and the child rather than standing for innocence stands for shame. The stigmatization of single motherhood in many Muslim-majority contexts is frequently associated with the orphaning of such children.

Hence, adoptive mothering in a Muslim context necessarily confronts and complicates traditional, socially embedded ideas of motherhood and childhood, and questions what is normally conceived of as a natural or biological bond. Adoption lays bare some of the most cherished assumptions concerning the mother and child. As David Eng notes, "Adoption is often bound up with questions of faltering maternity—of failed reproduction and proper mothering" (22). Although motherhood may have deep cultural and psychological resonance among Muslims, the mother-child relationship is not always well protected in Islamic-oriented states, since the *sharia* may be interpreted to privilege the paternal relationship over the maternal in many areas. For instance, in some countries, mothers receive custody only for younger children, but that custody can be displaced by the legal claims of the father when the child is older.[1] In adoptive relations, in contrast, the mother can suture the fractured primal bond by providing breast milk to the adoptive child: as I explore below, the substance of milk creates both the legal tie and the imagined biological contiguity of family members, which renders visible the mother's centrality to the family unit. Such milk relations may be transformative, challenging and complicating rigid definitions of blood kinship that are underwritten by patriarchal and patrilineal conceptions of legitimacy. Although Muslim adoptive mothers can play key roles in creating new kinship formations, the systemic inequities that underlie the orphaning, fostering, and adoption of children—in particular the stigmatizaion and financial challenges endemic to single mothering in Muslim communities—need to be foregrounded in Muslim adoption practices.

ADOPTION AND *KAFALAH*

None are their mothers save those who gave birth to them.
—Qur'an (58:2)

Western-style adoption—in which a child is taken from one family and subsumed into another, with consequent loss of natal identity, that is, his or her knowledge of and link with biological family—is usually prohibited by Islamic rulings, although recent studies indicate that "secret adoptions" do occur in Muslim-majority contexts.[2] Sura thirty-three of the Qur'an is commonly understood to provide explicit guidelines on the issue of adoption:

> God has not placed two hearts in the breast of any man.... Nor has he made those whom you claim as your sons your sons. Those are mere words of your mouth. But God speaks the truth and guides the way. Call them after their fathers. That is more equitable before God. And if you do not know their fathers, then they are your brethren in religion and your clients. (33: 4-5)

This sura was revealed in response to Muhammad's hesitation over marriage to Zainab bint Jahsh, a paternal cousin of his and also the wife of his own adopted son, Zayd. Subsequent to the revelation, Zayd divorced Zainab, whom he had already sought the prophet's permission to divorce, since the marriage was an unhappy one, and the Prophet married her after the proper waiting period (a period of three months to ensure that the former wife is not carrying the former husband's child). However, marriage to the wife of one's son was prohibited. Hence, this revelation radically redefined the relationship between adopted and "natural" children, creating new parameters of kinship in Islamic law. According to verse four, a distinction must be made between "your sons" and those "whom you claim as your sons," that is, your adopted sons. It further commands that the distinction between biological sons and other dependents must be registered by patronymic to provide clear evidence of genealogy. Henceforth, children are to maintain their birth names, even when subsumed into another family unit. There are also distinctions to be made in the division of inheritance. Children are to inherit from their birth parents, not from their "adoptive" parents, unless specific bequests are made.[3] The clear pronouncement in the Qur'an against a guardian appropriating an orphan's property in sura four and elsewhere suggests that this law was intended, at least partly, to protect orphans; yet in modern times, when orphans are often without personal property, alienation from inheritance in the adoptive family usually reinforces kinship distinctions and works to their disadvantage.

A captured slave, Zayd developed such love for Muhammad that when his birth family eventually found him, he refused to return to them, choosing to stay with Muhammad. Since this was several years before the occasion of the first revelation, such devotion has been taken to presage Muhammad's divine gift. After Zayd's show of devotion, Muhammad adopted him in what was then the customary manner in which Zayd bin Hâritha officially became Zayd bin Muhammad: that is, Zayd clearly forfeited his birth identity and became known as the son of Muhammad (Powers, *Zayd*, 23). Subsequent to the revelation of sura thirty-three, however, another ceremony was conducted. In this one, the Prophet reversed the proceedings, and Zayd returned to his former name, Zayd bin Hâritha, although he continued to be very close to Muhammad and was commonly known as "the Beloved of the Messenger of God" (Powers, *Zayd*, 31, 37-38). Although hostile commentators, especially early Christian polemicists, have snidely viewed this event as a theological convenience so that the Prophet could marry Zayd's wife without transgressing restrictions on kinship marriages—that is, marriage to the daughter-in-law—David S. Powers's more recent interpretation stresses instead the theological imperative of sonlessness necessary for Muhammad's status as the "seal of the prophets" or the last prophet. Since prophecy was viewed in the Abrahamic tradition as hereditary, it was necessary, he argues, that Muhammad be sonless, and, hence, Zayd's status had to be changed (*Muhammad*, 35-71). Indeed, sura thirty-three goes on to proclaim that "Muhammad is not the father of any man among you; rather he is the Messenger of God and the Seal of the prophets" (Qur'an 33:40). Since masculinity is frequently tied up with reproduction, lineage, and the production of sons, such a pronouncement emphasized the Prophet's difference from other men and his relation to a higher sphere.

The figure of Zayd has been sidelined in the Islamic tradition, but early sources portray him as a devoted follower of Muhammad and he is even, though somewhat erroneously, proclaimed to be the first Muslim after the Prophet. (He was the third person, but the first adult male to accept the faith.) Muhammad himself was an orphan, reared by his uncle, and there are many places in the Quran and *hadith* where support for orphans is enjoined on Muslims.[4] With sura thirty-three as a touchstone, care of orphaned children has developed differently in Muslim-majority contexts than in Western nations. Instead of "adoption," a form of guardianship called *"kafalah"* (or *kefala*) is practised, whereby a child may be nurtured and provided for financially just like a biological child, but his or her name is not changed, he or she is aware of her natal family (as far as possible), and he or she may receive different inheritance provisions than would a biological child. *Kafalah* is often compared to the Western practice of fostering, but unlike foster care, it usually carries a sense of permanency, and often (but not always) no state remuneration is involved.[5] In some ways, *kafalah* is more comparable to open adoption in the West, whereby even when a child is adopted, connection to his or her birth mother and sometimes birth family is maintained. This practice is considered a major advance in Western adoption because it allows the child access to a fuller sense of identity and helps to alleviate the experience of psychological trauma associated with loss of natal origins (Gritter). In this area of family law, Muslim practices generally have been far in advance of liberal Western policies, although this comparison has rarely been acknowledged.

Although the Muslim practice of maintaining a consciousness of lineage in a child's identity originated in a tribal context, it speaks to a concept of identity that has been identified as characteristic of non-Western states and may be relevant today for many Muslim-majority contexts. Admantia Pollis, for instance, describes a concept of "self-identity defined in terms of group membership," that is "traditionally determined by one's status and role in the family and village" (334). The child is conceived and learns to conceive of himself or herself as part of a kinship group over and above his or her sense of self as an individual. The difference between these two paradigms of identity often arises in human rights discourses, such as the discussions and dissent involved in the process of drafting the 1989 Convention on the Rights of the Child (UNCRC). When the United States tried to introduce a clause stating that a child should be free to choose his or her religion, the representatives from Bangladesh dissented, explaining that "in many

Islamic countries a child follows the religion of his parents and does not generally make a choice of his own" (Harris-Short 26). The child is not seen as an autonomous individual with personal choice but as a member of his or her kinship group who reflects its beliefs and follows its practices. Though slightly modified after some discussion, the clause about religious choice was included in the final version of the UNCRC, leading many Muslim-majority states to register official reservations in the signatory process.

Alternative conceptions of identity may also help to account for how orphaned children may be viewed differently in Muslim-majority contexts and, hence, help to explain the Muslim preference for *kafalah* arrangements over adoption. Western practices of transnational adoption have often involved the assimilation of a child from one family and/or one country into another, with a concomitant loss of natal origins and, thus, birth identity. Transnational adoption is practised overwhelmingly in the United States (which has received more transnational adoptees than all other nations combined) and its wealthy allies; the other major "receiving" countries are those of Western Europe, Canada, Australia, New Zealand. The "sending" countries, many of which were colonized by Western powers, are those in which adverse conditions—poverty, war, natural disaster, or sometimes severe social stigmatism against children of non-marital relationships—make it impossible for families to properly care for their children.[6] Many transnational adoption agencies from Western countries deemphasize issues of a child's identity—whether biological, religious, cultural, or racial—thus treating affluent Westerners as consumers and the infants as decontextualized commodities that can be transferred from place to place with little to no psychological repercussions. Many Westerners adopt children from places to which they have no cultural ties, do not speak the language, and can say little to nothing about the region's history. In fact, transnational adoption agencies promote and adoptive parents seem to seek out programs in which an adoptive parent can return quickly, spending just a few days in the "sending" country to obtain custody of the child.[7]

To date, most open adoptions in the West have involved domestic placements; transnational adoption continues to be haunted by the spectre of colonialism in which affluent whites appropriate powerless non-white bodies even if construed through the frame of "mission" or charity work. Adoptees from South Korea, who began to arrive in the U.S. in the late 1950s, are now adults and have spoken out about their feeling of alienation, loss, and fractured identity (Kim).[8] Until recently, the only model of adoption involved assimilation: the Korean child, for example, lost all sense of natal identity, his or her name, history, race. They were usually reared alongside white children, without any sense of their own racialized identity, even as they stood out as visibly different. Korean adoptees have been essential in challenging these normative practices and have demanded an awareness of the psychological costs of transnational adoption on adopted children. As a result, there have been some more thoughtful discussions in the transnational adoption world and some sophisticated studies and publications available aimed at creating a more ethical system. However, as transnational adoption continues to be a big and largely unregulated business, agencies continue to be demand-driven—that is, driven to find babies for families with money rather than to strive to find families for children who are in need of homes and support.[9]

Partly because of what is perceived as a religious prohibition of adoption and/or openly stated as a national policy, most Muslim-majority countries have remained out of the transnational adoption business. There are of course needy and homeless children in these countries, but different state policies have been developed to care for these children: some countries stress institutional care, whereas others seek to place orphaned children in family environments. Exceptionally, Morocco, a country that is almost 99 percent Muslim, opened its doors to transnational adoption agencies for several years, stipulating that potential adoptive parents must be Muslim.[10] In this process, Moroccan courts conferred *kafalah* rights on prospective parents, who then took the child to their own countries to be adopted according to their home country's national laws. Unfortunately some agencies, in an effort to sell this new program to a larger public, have decided that the relatively simple profession of faith called the *shahada* that is required for conversion to Islam need not deter non-Muslims from bringing home a Moroccan child. While paying lip service to the need to take conversion seriously, the agencies tend to emphasize the logistical ease of the process. According to Hopscotch Adoptions, to adopt from Morocco, parents "must be Muslim or willing to convert to Islam"; their website then immediately assures prospective parents that "the conversion appointment is completed on your first day of arrival." In England, the request of one couple seeking to adopt a second child from Morocco was rejected by their local social workers, who discovered that although the parents had seemingly converted in the process of adopting their first child, they had neglected to actually practice any form of Islam. *The London Times* article expresses sympathy towards the parents, quoting the mother as saying "Did they really expect me to be covered up, sitting on a prayer mat? When we'd converted to Islam so that we could adopt Samuel, there'd been no clause in the paperwork saying we had to put the Koran in our entrance" (Kaufman). Evoking the stereotypical image of an oppressed Muslim women, the English mother expects that public opinion will support her assessment of Islam's regressiveness. Such an attitude reflects the continuance of the entrenched belief in Western countries that the affluent lifestyle proffered to impoverished Third World children adequately compensates for their loss of identity and origin. Why should it matter that children loose their Moroccan and Muslim identity if they have a nice English home?

Kafalah seeks to preserve the child's lineage, ensuring that he or she maintains a sense of his or her origins and family. In Muslim-majority contexts, practices of *kafalah* can be informal, as an orphaned child is often cared for in the wider family network, which speaks to the concept of identity governed by group membership. If the child is placed with another family, he or she remains part of his or her natal bloodline, maintaining the familial birth name, even when reared in another family; the new family function as "trustees and caretakers of someone else's child," which in community or village settings can also be informal.[11] The UNCRC, however, mandates that certain formal procedures be followed in such childcare arrangements, which has led to conflict with states practice *kafalah* or depend on more informal arrangements. As Sonia Harris-Short observes, "in a society based on the model of the nuclear family, informal adoption within the extended family might not work. Care of the child would therefore be entrusted to strangers. Where, however, the extended family lies at the heart of the social organisation of a community and members of the extended family are willing and able to assume the care of a child, informal 'adoption' can often provide an appropriate solution" (44). Although *kafalah* does make distinctions between family members based on blood kinship, it also emerges from situations where "family" can pertain to a large and somewhat amorphous unit. In contrast, Western-style adoption, where the child's natal identity is frequently effaced in favour of that of the adoptive family, responds to the imperatives of a society governed by the closed unit of the nuclear family that seeks to eliminate difference within. Because of the perception (and practice) of traditional closed adoptions as the governing models in Western societies, Muslims in diasporic contexts have often been reluctant to adopt, according to videos such as the six-part series, "Please Can I Have a Mummy and Daddy," aired on the U.K.'s Islamic Channel. In this series, sheikhs from the Islamic Sharia Council in London encourage Muslim families to adopt the many Muslim children in the state care system, assuring them that it is more important to keep a child in the faith than to adhere to the letter of certain proscriptions, such as the preservation of an orphaned or abandoned child's family name.

UNKNOWN IDENTITIES

As long as the child possesses a known *nasab*, a familial lineage, the practice of *kafalah* appears to usefully function to foster an orphan's greater understanding of his or her identity and history. In the case of a foundling, or *laqît*, an abandoned child with no identifying markers, the issues are much more complex. Beth Baron observes that "orphans stand out in Islamic writings as deserving of special protection; abandoned babies, by contrast, were an anathema in Middle Eastern societies, evoking shame not sympathy" (13). Although it may be true that "a completely abandoned child is a rarity" (O'Halloran 383), it is apparently more and more common. In Pakistan, the Edhi Foundation has installed cribs (*jhoolas*) in their emergency centres across the country as an acknowledgement that abandoned infants are an unfortunate consequence of the hardships of contemporary times.

From the earliest centuries, the juridical schools of Islam have delved into the issue of foundling children and their care. There are rulings governing practicalities of discovery and protection as well as financial support. The four main Sunni schools agree that the community at large is responsible for the foundling's financial support and enjoin use of the public purse for that purpose (Pollack et al. 147). Issues of identity are, of course, often more complex than financial responsibility; however, the Islamic schools agreed that all foundlings must be given the presumption of free status. One reason for this presumption was to prevent the enslavement of foundlings by their rescuers. On the question of a foundling's religion, there was some difference of opinion. Although some schools took a "probabilistic approach," (i.e., if the child were found in a Christian neighbourhood, he or she is probably Christian), in general, "the determinative consideration, so long as there was no proof of the identity of the true parent, was the perceived best interest of the child" (Pollack, et al. 153). Likewise, there was some difference among the schools concerning proof of paternity; whereas the Maliki school requires specific forms of proof, the Hanafi school accepts a man's paternal claim if it is seen as beneficial to the child. Arguing that there is an historical concern in Islamic law with the principle "in the best interests of the child," Mohammad H. Fadel advocates a synthesis that acknowledges an adoptive father's duties and obligations without "fictive kinship" (Pollack et al. 155-157). Fadel's discussion points to the overwhelmingly paternalistic framework for establishing a child's sense of identity in Islamic legal sources; sources are far more concerned with establishing paternal than maternal lineage.

Kinship is the crux of the problem for orphaned children in many Muslim-majority contexts, where family ties govern so many parts of social life. For children of "unknown identity"—that is, those who are abandoned while infants with no indication of parentage, no verbal histories to their bodies—what sort of *nasab* can they be said to possess? The Prophet's pronouncement in a custody dispute that "the child belongs to the bed," has been commonly taken to indicate that childbirth in an Islamic context must take place within a framework of legal marriage. In the case of extra-marital childbirth, the child may, if the mother is married, take on her husband's *nasab* unless he specifically disavows the child as a product of adultery. If the mother is unmarried, the child, in the Hanafi tradition, may take on the *nasab* and inherit from the mother. However, in Morocco as well as in other countries, the child may take on the mother's family name only with the permission of her male relatives, which may not be forthcoming (Bargach 117). Furthermore, as Shabnam Ishaque points out, "referring to a child by the mother's family name would publicize the illegitimate birth of such a child" (406). The stigma of single motherhood in Muslim-majority contexts can be intense, making it near-impossible for mothers to nurture their own children; indeed, it is the paternal *nasab* that confers legitimacy and, hence, social acceptance on the child.[12]

Although juridical rulings and *hadith* carefully distinguish be-tween the responsibilities of the parents and the child who is the product of non-marital liaisons, in practice, the children too often bear the mark of shame.[13] Government documents, such as birth certificates and identity cards, can become the means through which abandoned children are marked, categorized, and hence stigmatized and ostracized. When the name of the father is left blank, the birth certificate is marked as that of an "illegitimate" child in Morocco and Lebanon. In Jordan, children of "unknown identities" receive a special national number on their identity card along with a fabricated name that signals "illegitimacy." The 2011 short film *ID:000* dramatizes the plight of these children, espe-cially when they leave the orphanage and try to make a life for themselves in the world. The film documents the social treatment of these individuals: their mothers are cursed, their honour is im-puted, and they are treated as outcasts. "My existence is wrong," says one. "There is no place for me." Without a lineage, without a claim of family, which is recognized as the "name of the father," there is no identity. "My mother made a mistake and now I have to pay the price," says another. The mother's body is figured as the site of crime; the father, the site of the law, legitimacy, and the coveted name. To fail to receive that legal name, one is forever aligned with the mother, as if eternally linked to that primal body and never fully a subject—an unknown identity: "They treat us like nobody, with no existence."

Those with unknown identities are seen as the product of a crime (adultery) and are consequently typecast as criminals. The social experts interviewed in *ID:000*, while evincing sympathy and concern, refer to the orphans' propensity to crime and to their disturbing effect on the order of Jordanian society. Their motivations to help the orphans focus on practical matters—vocational training, education, psychological services—more than on the society itself that has rendered the orphan an outcast or criminal. "When others convey to you that you are of no account because your parents are of no account, that, as they are invisible, they do not exist, you are suddenly aware that you are an orphan, and sometimes accountable for being so," Kristeva writes (21). The tendency to hold orphans accountable for their state of being is to make them the master of their own primal scene; unlike other children, the orphan is already there before his or her conception, a creature held responsible for the very history that begets him or her. To protect the sanctity of the family, such children are commonly displaced from it and disavowed so as to create the illusion of its inviolable borders and the impeccable status of the law (the father).

In Muslim-majority countries, children do become orphans for a variety of reasons other than non-marital unions: trauma to the family including war or poverty, death of one or more parents, imprisonment or remarriage of parents. The United States' invasions of Iraq and Afghanistan have created thousands of orphans. In Egypt, the majority of institutionalized children are those who are slightly older, perhaps old enough to know their name, and are found wandering the streets, presumably abandoned by their parents out of poverty, homelessness, or some other crisis. These children, deemed legitimate, remain in group homes until adulthood in the hopes that their parents find them (Sonbol; Rugh). In Jordan, too, children of a known *nasab* remain in institutional care with the understanding that their parents may one day wish to reclaim them. Only those of "unknown identity," usually very young children, may be placed with families in a *kafalah* arrangement. These systems reflect the belief that "in Islam, the bond between a natural parent and a child cannot be given away" (O'Halloran 393); however, even if theologically driven ideas privilege such "blood" bonds, children are, in practice, given away and left without family. In addition, through secret adoptions, *kafalah* arrangements, and as discussed below, *rida*, "milk relations," kinship is constantly being configured so as to render "family" more fluid—and mothers play central roles in these transformations.

MILK MOTHERS

There seems to be a vast gulf in attitudes towards orphans between Western countries and Muslim-majority ones: one in which natal identity is too easily "denied, repressed, and effaced" (Eng 14) and the other in which it may be so determinate so as to create indelible categories of insider and outsider for the orphaned child. However, there are changes in both directions taking place. The movement by many transnational adoptees and their families in Canada, the United States, and elsewhere to track down and establish connections with birth mothers and the promotion of programs encouraging the return of adoptees in South Korea have meant a renewed emphasis on the orphan's historicity (Dubinsky; Jones). Concomitantly, the encouragement on adoptive websites for Muslims to explore lactaction techniques suggests the desire to find means within Islam to create another space or parental bond between *kafalah* and kinship, between "unknown identity" and blood relations.

Between the seemingly inviolate relationship of blood, and the apparently less determinate one of guardianship in the Muslim imagination lies another form of relation, that of milk bonds, bonds that are created through breastfeeding. The Prophet himself had a milk mother, Halima Saadia, who was so attached to him that she continued to care for him after the suckling period. Some, like Omar Mokhtar El Kadi, see milk fostering as a solution to the problems besetting orphans of no known identity. Although the Qur'an is usually read to prohibit inheritance between the *kafil* (guardian) and child, unless specifically bequeathed in a will, the inheritance traditions surrounding milk fosterage are more murky, as some *hadith* suggest that women can inherit from nurslings. In addition, the precepts governing relationships of possible affinity (marriage) of milk relationships are similar to those of blood relationships. In other words, although the Qur'an is understood to permit marital relationships between siblings by *kafalah* or other relationships formed by incorporating a child through *kafalah* into the family, as though there were no kinship ties whatsoever at stake, it prohibits marital relationships of those related by nursing, and, for example, those who shared a milk mother. Although those in a *kafalah*-governed relationship may be enjoined to practice gender segregation upon puberty, those in a milk relationship are considered on the same terms as in a close blood kinship relationship. El Kadi suggests that with the help of drugs, modern medicine makes lactation possible in nearly every women, hence enabling such milk bonds to be created to suture the orphan into society and reestablish his biological ties to both an immediate family and an extended kin. In his optimistic reading, such milk relationships solve the problem of the fate of unknown children, granting them the possibility of receiving *nasab* from the milk family:

> A child who grows up in an orphanage encounters many difficulties in adult life such as his rejection at work or in marriage. But when people say that someone is the milk-son of someone and was raised in a house of good reputation, there is no doubt that his chances of securing employment or a wife will increase. Once he acquires the milk kinship allowed by Islam, he is freed from the stigma of being a foundling and can proclaim that such is his mother, father, grandfather, brother and sister in milk. (16)

Although the Sunni schools disagree about the number of requisite feedings needed to create the milk bond—some saying five, others only one—they concur that the feedings must take place before the child is two years of age (or in the Maliki tradition, two years and two months).[14] Even though this age limit may at first appear arbitrary, it does encourage a relationship based on milk to be established while a child is arguably just beginning to form memories and, hence, to develop a primary maternal bond with his or her adopted mother while still young. This is also the age to which in the Islamic tradition birth mothers are encouraged to feed their infants. However, as the recent study on breastfeeding in the Middle East shows, in general, breastfeeding in the region is in decline, as women often work outside the home and lack the time to commit themselves to the rigours (Batterjee). To an even greater extent, induced lactation, requiring extensive pumping and/or breast manipulation in addition to access to drugs, does, of course, limit its availability and, thus, may not serve as the panacea proposed by El Kadi.

Yet milk bonds do foreground the role that women can play in defining *mahram* relations and, thus, kinship bonds.[15] With induced lactation, the mother may be a widow, a virgin, un-married or married, procreative or infertile, old or young, even transgendered, which vastly expands and, hence, challenges the way that motherhood is commonly viewed in Muslim societies. Milk is imagined in ways similar to blood and, thus, endowed with some aspects of its sacred mystique. Although in many Muslim-majority contexts and traditions of Islamic law, men may control the way that blood is made legible by controlling the process of naming, women can control the passage of lactation fluids and, hence, create an alternative economy of kinship and become mothers to both biological and non-biological children. Anthropological studies have discovered a vast number of ways that the milk relationship has been manipulated. In Morocco, for instance, the wife is permitted to breastfeed someone only with the consent of her husband. One study found that the wom-en generally breastfed only members of the husband's kinship group, thus allowing him to cement ties of his family (Maher). Another study revealed that women in rural Turkey manipulated their breastfeeding so as to control the ways that marriages were arranged, making some individuals *mahram* and, thus, ineligible as marriage partners to others (MacClancy).

In recent years in Saudi Arabia, the Umm Al-Qura Philanthropic Society has created a program to provide stipends to women to breastfeed orphans. Noura Al-Asheikh, the director of Women's Issues at the Ministry of Social Affairs, suggests that the ministry prefers to encourage mothers with orphaned children in their care to breastfeed rather than to pay nurses to do so (Hawari). Otherwise, it happens that at the age of twelve, the children are often returned to the ministry and many have to go to shelters ("Kids"). To simply pay women to nurse orphans does little, she suggests, since mothers in Saudi Arabia often use surrogates for nursing their children. It is clear from Al-Asheikh's comments that nursing and the creation of affective ties are two distinct categories of maternal labour, although the former may facilitate the latter since the child will not have to be re-orphaned at puberty. Milk is represented as more fluid than blood and needs to be supplemented with affective ties to manufacture family bonds. Al-Asheikh describes the following scenario: "I was faced with a case where a woman took a baby in, and after he grew up, she discovered he has a retardation, but she refused to give him up ...To her the child was like her own, and she would not have given him up. That is the type of adoptive parent the organization is looking for" (qtd. in Hawari). The woman's tie with her son mimicked the Islamic conception of the biological tie in that it could not be alienated or given away, even under trying circumstances. Although women can be paid to nurse, it is the unpaid labour, the affective and usually unacknowledged maternal work, that actually creates a *nasab*.

A NEW *UMMAH*:
SINGLE AND ADOPTIVE MUSLIM MOTHERING

Transnational adoptive families often speak of the problem of "misrecognition" or "interracial surveillance" that haunts their daily life, as others ask, is he or she really their child? (Anagost 395; Katz and Hunt 52). Rather than being confronted by the inquiring gaze of others, the gaze from outside, as many transracial and transnational adoptive families are, Muslim adoptive families in the diaspora instead speak of the issue of internal scrutiny. Many of these Muslim adoptive families enunciate their fears of rejection by their extended families: will the adoptive child be "accepted" by their families? Will they approve of the decision to adopt, especially when it is commonly seen as prohibited in Islam? Adoption can make manifest the reconfiguration of the family unit, what is usually imagined through tradition, continuity, and sameness in the diaspora. One Muslim American mother, who adopted from

Morocco, maintained a blog documenting her and her husband's "adoption journey," a common activity of mainstream adoptive American families. Although clearly Muslim in orientation with typical discussion of *du'a* and prayer, the blog included a brief excerpt from an article by Nelson Handel from a mainstream adoptive website:

> We live in an era that forces us to reconceive our notions of traditional kinship. No longer dependent on genetics or breeding, family must now be defined as parents and children united in love and common self-interest. Perhaps it's the logical, postmodern extension of family, a collage approach that says the glue is more important than the bits being conjoined. (qtd. in "Family is Family")

The post was titled "Family is family," but did not contain other commentary. Although the blog featured regular comments by the extended family members who were following and supporting the couple's adoption, the gesture of including this excerpt implied that there was some need to justify the step outside of normative, biologically structured family patterns. This mother, though seemingly strongly linked to both her and her husband's Muslim families, positioned herself in relation to this discourse marked "postmodern," even as she breastfed the child to make him *mahram*. When kinship is reconfigured in this new era, Muslim identity is positioned as the unifying force, a sort of transcendent "*ummah*."

Another adoptive Muslim mother, Christina Tobias-Nahi of the Joint Council on International Children Services, writes about breastfeeding her first son in similar terms:

> I embarked on this fairly arduous task less to ensure his position in our family, but so that later in life I would not need to wear a head covering in front of him or observe some of the other gender protocols that could come into play when he would reach maturity ... So the decision to breastfeed in our family was more than just a nutritional good start but laid the groundwork for their cultural and religious upbringing. ("Nutrion Profile")

For her, the issue of providing a *nasab* to her son, or his acceptance by kin, is less significant than the maintenance of religious
values: in the diaspora, religious identity is rendered more primary
than lineage. As cultural identity can become attenuated and often
diluted in the immigrant experience, Muslim identity can become
more pronounced, especially in post-9/11 North America and
Europe, where to be Muslim is to be aberrantly and significantly
marked; notably, in Tobias-Naha's remarks, "culture" seems to
collapse into "religion." There is surprisingly little discussion about
how to maintain the adopted child's sense of distinct cultural and
natal identity on these websites: the foregrounding of an imagined
transcendent Muslim identity and personal associations with recent
immigrant experiences perhaps make these concerns seem less urgent. Although breastfeeding allows the child to be legally *mahram*
to family members, it more importantly signifies the maintenance of
Muslim values across national borders, transmitting the comforting
fiction that "we all believe in the same things" and positioning the
adoptive mother as the conduit of religious tradition.

I am not intending to critique these bloggers, who have provided
an important service by sharing their experiences with others. And
indeed, a Muslim mother's investment in the *ummah* as a source
of identity for an adoptive child has some validity, even as it fails
to account for that child's particular history. For example, while
(white) Western parents adopting children from Third World
countries often have to manufacture connections with others from
that country in highly artificial and usually unsatisfactory ways,
participation in a North American mosque community usually
involves interaction with immigrants from a wide variety of nations. Indeed, with immigration constituting such a large part of
the Muslim diasporic experience, feelings of cultural displacement
and alienation are close to the surface of family life. Ann Anagnost's
discussion of transnational adoption proposes that "restoring
history to the process of constructing the child's subjectivity may
even lead to powerful alliances for an antiracist politics that could
conceivably cut across historically constituted divisions of race and
class" (414). She suggests that viewing the transnationally adopted
child in relation to the immigrants attempting to enter the U.S. for
economic reasons may be one possible alliance. In many Muslim

diasporic adoptive families, it can be argued that such alliances are already in place in the family's recent history.

Nonetheless, I believe that Muslim adoptive mothers must confront many of the same issues that beset adoption more generally. As Peter Selman observes, "For every mother who 'becomes' a mother through adoption there is another who loses her child and so in one sense ceases to be a mother" (85). Attending to the conditions that create orphaned children and working to destigmatize the ways that orphans, adoption, non-marital children and single motherhood are viewed in the Muslim community is certainly a first step. The creation of homes for single mothers in Morocco and Tunisia is a positive development, for it has allowed some mothers to bring up their own children amid societies that can be antagonistic to such maternally headed family units (Copnall; Sbouaï). The journalist Sana Sbouaï writes about the dilemma of single mothers in Tunisia:

> [T]hese single mothers are ... often girls who fell in love and naively trusted their partners. Their average age is 24, are from urban and rural backgrounds, and one in five has some tertiary education. The child's father is often a man they had been seeing for some time: relationships lasting between one and three years, approaching marriage. If society didn't condemn their relationships, there would be nothing remarkable about them.

Often abandoned by the fathers and their own families, many single mothers are forced to fend for themselves and frequently lack resources and community support to care for their children.

As Amina Wadud points out, Islamic family law is predicated on men providing protection and material needs for wives and children. All other models, especially that of the female-headed household, "are deviant within a legal construction that is premised upon the patriarchal extended or nuclear family" (153). Noting the centrality of Hajar in the Muslim hajj ritual and her importance to Islamic geneaology, Wadud has called attention to the glaring elision of her experience in the historical formation of Islamic family law:

Islamic personal law is build upon a notion of family that does not include a woman thrown into the desert, forced to construct a health, happy life for her child and to fend for herself. Islamic law for family, as constructed and still maintained, is not only premised upon an ideal of an extended family network, it presumes that a woman will never, for any reason, become responsible for providing for and protecting herself and her offspring. Yet this reality happens more and more frequently the world over. (144)

Hajar, abandoned with Ishmael by a man she loved and trusted, runs between the hills of Marwa and Safa in the desert in search of water before God causes a well to miraculously appear, an event that is commemorated in the *Sa'y* in Hajj as pilgrims process seven times between two points representing the hills. Although Hajar is frequently revered as a figure of steadfast faith, Wadud suggests that we also should value her experience of single motherhood and attend to how she managed to help her child, the ancestor of the Prophet and the Arab people, to "achieve a life of prosperity." She notes that "the mechanisms available to her to achieve that prosperity are silenced in Islamic family law. That silence needs to be broken for the many women who face a similar dilemma" (152). Indeed, Hajar's trauma of abandonment by Abraham is not dissimilar to that of the single mothers of Tunisia discussed above. Islam provides important and resonant resources in the figures of Zayd and Hajar to inform discussions of alternative family arrangments, such as that of adoptive or single-mother families. It is imperative that we use these resources to displace the patriarchal, patrilineal model of family as the basis of Islamic law and the normative value systems of Muslims today.

NOTES

[1]Morgan Clarke's analysis of family law practice in Lebanon notes that men generally receive legal precedence for children in Sunni courts, at seven for a boy and nine for a girl, and in Shiite courts at two for a boy and seven for a girl (84 n.10).
[2]On secret adoption, see Bargach for Morocco, Clarke for Leba-

non, Baron for Egypt. I have also received information via word of mouth of secret adoptions in relation to Jordan.

[3]Islamic inheritance proscriptions allow for a third of one's estate to be given away in personal bequests.

[4]The Prophet's mother Aminah lived until he was five, but his father died before his birth.

[5]Kafalah rulings may be dissolved by law, but this does not appear to happen frequently, whereas many foster homes are considered temporary arrangements. In Saudi Arabia, the government does provide stipends to those who care for orphans as well as paying for the orphan's education.

[6]In addition, China was, until recently, a major "sending" country on account of its one-child policy, which was just terminated in 2015.

[7]My sense of these issues has been informed by reading the material posted on websites of international adoption agencies as well as posts by adoptive and prospective adoptive parents on discussion forums.

[8]Between 1953 and 2008, 162,665 children were adopted from South Korea, over two-thirds by people in the United States. For a good analysis of issues relating to adoption and adoptees from South Korea, see Eleana J. Kim's recent study.

[9]E. J. Graff's article "The Lie We Love" (2008) played an important role in exposing the myths of humanitarian rescue that underlie transnational adoption practices.

[10]In October of 2012 a new ruling placed restrictions on adoption from Morocco by non-residents.

[11]See Clarke (74) and Mattson (25) on such informal *kafalah* arrangements within kinship networks.

[12]For example, see Clarke's quotation of Shaykh Muhammad Kana'an of the Sunni religious court in Lebanon that "*nasab* comes from the father"(96).

[13]See the remarks by Baron indicating that a child of a non-marital union "was perceived to have 'tainted' blood" (14).

[14]There is some minority opinion that milk kinship can be established even in adulthood, as the recent rulings in Saudi Arabia demonstrate.

[15]The term "*mahram*" refers to relations of kinship through both

blood and marriage that would make it illicit for individuals to marry. Many Muslim women who observe gender segregation practices do not cover in the presence of those considered *mahram*.

WORKS CITED

Anagnost, Ann. "Scenes of Misrecognition: Maternal Citizenship in the Age of Transnational Adoption." *positions* 8.2 (2000): 389-421. Print.

Bargach, Jamila. *Orphans of Islam: Family, Abandonment, and Secret Adoption in Morocco*. New York: Rowman and Littlefield, 2002. Print.

Baron, Beth. "Orphans and Abandoned Children in Modern Egypt." *Between Missionaries and Dervishes: Interpreting Welfare and Relief in the Middle East*. Eds. Nefissa Naguib and Inger Marie Okkenhaug. Leiden: Brill, 2008. 12-34. Print.

Batterjee, Modia. *A Fading Art: Understanding Breast Feeding in the Middle East*. CreateSpace: 2010. Print.

Clarke, Morgan. *Islam and the New Kinship: Reproductive Technology and the Shariah in Lebanon*. New York: Berghahn Books, 2009. Print.

Copnall, James. "Helping Morocco's Outcast Single Mothers." BBC, 12 Jan. 2009. Web. 7 Apr. 2016.

Dubinsky, Karen. "Our Son of Three Mothers." *theglobeandmail.com*. The Globe and Mail, 14 Sept, 2014.Web. 7 Apr. 2016.

El Kadi, Omar Mokhtar. "Rights of Abandoned Children to Family Ties and Kinship." *Islam Today* 26 (2009): 89-116. Web. 7 Apr. 2016.

Eng, David L. "Transnational Adoption and Queer Diasporas." *Social Text* 21.3 (2003): 1-37. Print.

"Family is Family." *Baby Maghrib*. WordPress, n.d. Web. 7 Apr. 2016.

Gritter, James L. *The Spirit of Open Adoption*. Washington, DC: Child Welfare League of America, 1997. Print.

Harris-Short, Sonia. "Listening to the "Other": The *Convention on the Rights of the Child*." *Melbourne Journal of International Law* 2.2 (2001): 1-47. Print.

Hawari, Walaa. "Milk Kinship Can Be an Interesting Adoption

Tool." *Arab News*, 7 Sept. 2007 Web. 7 Apr. 2016.

Ishaque, Shabnam. "Islamic Principles on Adoption: Examining the Impact of Illegitimacy and Inheritance Related Concerns in Contest of a Child's Right to an Identity." *International Journal of Law, Policy and the Family* 22 (2008): 393-420. Print.

Jones, Maggie. "Why a Generation of Adoptees is Returning to South Korea." *The New York Times* y, 14 Jan. 2015. Web. 7 Apr. 2016.

Kaufman, Rachel. "Muslim Converts 'Not Islamic Enough' for Their Adopted Son to Have a Brother." *London Times*, 18 Oct.2008. Web. 7 Apr. 2016.

Katz, Jennifer, and Emily Hunt, "Adoptive Mothers Mothering." *Mothers, Mothering and Motherhood across Cultural Differences: A Reader*. Ed. Andrea O'Reilly. Bradford: Demeter, 2014. 41-64. Print.

"Kids of Unknown Parenthood are Accorded Full Citizenship Rights: Official." *Arab News*, 9 Dec. 2011. Web. 7 Apr. 2016.

Kim, J. Eleana. *Adopted Territory: Transnational Korean Adoptees and the Politics of Belonging*. Durham: Duke University Press, 2010. Print.

Kristeva, Julia. *Strangers to Ourselves*. Trans. Leon Roudiez. New York: Columbia University Press, 1991. Print.

MacClancy, Jeremy. "The Milk Tie." *The Anthropology of Food*. N.p., 2 Sept 2003. Web. 19 Jan. 2013.

Maher, V. "Possession and Dispossession: Maternity and Mortality in Morocco." *Interest and Emotion: Essays on the Subject of Family and Kinship*. Eds. H. Medick and D.W. Sabean. Cambridge: Cambridge University Press, 1984. 103-28. Print.

Mattson, Ingrid. "Adopting Children." *Islamic Horizons* Jan./Feb. 37.1 (2008): 22-28. Print.

"Morocco Adoption Agency: Muslim Families and Adoption." *Hopscotch Adoptions*. N.p., n.d. Web. 3 Jan. 2013.

O'Halloran, Kerry. *The Politics of Adoption: International Perspectives on Law, Policy, and Practice*. London: Springer, 2009. Print.

"Please Can I Have a Mummy and Daddy?" U.K. Islamic Channel. YouTube. 30 Mar. 2014. Web. 17 Sept. 2014.

Pollack, Daniel, Moshe Bleich, Charles J. Reid, and Mohammad H. Fadel. "Classical Religious Perspectives of Adoption Law."

Notre Dame Law Review 79.2 (2008): 101-158. Print.

Pollis, Admantia. "Cultural Relativism Revisited: Through a State Prism." *Human Rights Quarterly* 18 (1996): 316-344. Print.

Powers, David S. *Muhammad Is Not the Father of Any of Your Men: The Making of the Last Prophet*. Philadelphia: University of Pennsylvania Press, 2009. Print.

Powers, David S. *Zayd*. Philadelphia: University of Pennsylvania Press, 2014. Print.

Rugh, Andrea B. "Orphanages in Egypt: Contradictions or Affirmation in a Family-Oriented Society." *Children in the Muslim Middle East*. Ed. Elizabeth Warnock Fernea. Austin: University of Texas Press, 1995. 124-142. Print.

Sbouaï, Sana. "Life as a Single Mother in Tunisia." *Nawaat*. N.p., 18 June, 2013. Web. 21 Aug. 2015.

Selman, Peter. "Intercountry Adoption as Globalized Motherhood." *The Globalization of Motherhood: Deconstructions and Reconstructions of Biology and Care*. Eds. Wendy Chavkin and JaneMaree Maher. London: Routledge, 2101. 79-105. Print.

Shafakoj, Widad, David Deir, and Yazan Hazeem. *ID: 000. YouTube*. YouTube, 1 May 2012. Web. 3 January 2013.

Sonbol, Amira al-Azhary. "Adoption in Islamic Society: A Historical Survey," *Children in the Muslim Middle East*. Ed. Elizabeth Warnock Fernea. Austin: University of Texas Press, 1995. 45-67. Print.

The Study Quran: A New Translation and Commentary. Ed. and Trans. Seyyed Hossein Nasr. New York: HarperCollins, 2015. Print.

Tobias-Nahi, Christina. "Nutriton Profile." *Adoption Nutrition*. N.p., n.d. Web. 7 Apr. 2016.

Wadud, Amina. *Inside the Gender Jihad: Women's Reform in Islam*. Oxford: Oneworld: 2006. Print.

6.
"Sister Mothers"

Turkish American Muslim Mothers' and
Grandmothers' Networks in Diaspora

MARIA F. CURTIS

T HIS CHAPTER EXAMINES FEMININE NETWORKS of support
among Turkish women living in the United States in the
Hizmet movement, a social renewalist movement of pious
Turkish Muslims who follow the teachings of the Turkish Islamic
scholar Fethullah Gülen (Balcı and Miller 2-3). Gülen's followers
read in study circles, and his writings have inspired followers in
Turkey and beyond who find a blueprint for contemporary Islam in
his call for a renewed sense of pious living, emphasis on education,
and his insistence that Muslims must be active and serve others.
Although much has been written about the biographical details
of his life and teachings, far less is known about the daily lives of
those who aspire to live according to Gülen's principles. Among his
most enthusiastic followers are women who find inspiration in his
writings and speeches. I am interested in exploring the ways that
Turkish women's kinship models change and adapt in the United
States, and how the notion of service in the Gülen movement builds
networks of support for women and girls. It is left to the women
who read and apply his teachings in their daily lives to establish
what Muslim motherhood in non-Muslim majority places looks
like at the day-to-day level. It is in this space of extended diasporic
mothering that this chapter focuses.

Women in the *Hizmet* movement have had increased access
to education and are now choosing from a range of careers and
leadership roles. They transgress established Turkish religious and
secular gender roles by working outside the home in a "modern"
sense while still actively maintaining "traditional" duties at home

and those related to hospitality and caregiving, which is offered to extended family and neighbours. Turkish women in *Hizmet* come to the United States to study or to accompany their spouses or other family members, and they, sometimes, stay on longer than they planned to raise their children. As with the earlier Turkish immigrants who came before them to the United States after the disintegration of the Ottoman Empire (Şenyürekli), Turkish women today hold deep attachments to the cultures that they come from, and these attachments continue to inform their worldviews and offer them strength as they find their way in American society. Actively countering Islamophobia and nativist discourses, the Turkish American community organizes interfaith dialogue events to build bridges between various communities to help create an America in which their children feel truly at home. Outside formal interfaith events, women are often ambassadors of their faith because their modest Muslim clothing marks them as "other." They are held to more rigorous standards by non-Muslims with whom they interact in their children's schools and in public settings as their mothering is not only integral to their own families' well-being, but it is examined as an indication of the wellness of the Muslim community at large.

Shahnaz Khan has written about the ways that Muslim women's lives are "overdetermined" by the competing and often critical discourses (e.g., Orientalist, Islamic, secular, multiculturalist) that shape their lives, and how they effectively carve out "third spaces," in which they create social and religious spaces that make sense of life in diasporic settings (463). Similar to Khan's approach, I offer ethnographic snapshots from interviews in Houston, Texas.[1] In contrast to Shah's examination of Islamic mothering that focuses on the sexual control of daughters, my research looks at a variety of Turkish Muslim mothering strategies, which range from religious education, to inventive notions of co-operative childcare and co-mothering non-biological children, to fun and leisure activities, and to the celebration of food and festival.

Peter Van de Veer's work on "alternative cosmopolitanisms" helps open ways for discussing religious diasporic communities and their experiences (14-17). Scholars of contemporary Islam in diasporic settings (McGown; Metcalf; Slymovics; Van de Veer;

Werbner; Göle; Ammann) have examined Muslim space, public spheres, and communities that emerge from collective endeavours. Pnina Werbner's discussion of "fun spaces" is productive with regard to Gülen's women adherents, as they seek to build mutually supportive and culturally coherent Turkish experiences for their children in the U.S.

GÜLEN'S LEGACY FOR WOMEN AND GIRLS

Born in 1941, Gülen has been preaching on the importance of education since the 1960s, and since that time, one can see a firm position emerge with regard to his commitment to education for girls and women (Gülen, *Toward a Global Civilization*; Curtis, "Among the Heavenly Branches" and "The Women's Side of the Coin"). He has written about women as "rare gems" that add value to their families and homes, and about men and women as "two sides of a coin,"[2] indicating that society cannot flourish without women who are active in civic life. Gülen has a limited familiarity with the many strands of feminism and tends to regard it as a monolithic body of writing and as a threat to the well-being of women. His discomfort with feminism as a Western idea that divests women of traditional values is also mirrored in the discourse of Islamic or Muslim feminists who themselves struggle to reconcile the Qur'an with secular notions of feminism. While women in the Gülen movement do not typically self-identify as Islamic feminists, Margot Badran's definition of it may prove helpful:

> I have defined Islamic Feminism as a feminist discourse and practice that derives its understanding and mandate from the Qur'an and seeks rights and justice within the framework of the equality of women and men in the totality of their existence as part and parcel of the Qur'anic notion of equality of all human beings (*insan*). (*Feminism*, 324)

Gülen has written widely on the importance of mothers, which echoes pages of the Qur'an and the *hadith* and on the influence of his mother on his own spiritual development. He ultimately thanks her for providing him with his most basic orientation in the world as a Muslim through her acts of compassion. Although Gülen grew up in a family of imams influenced by the teachings of Nakshibandi Sufism, he credits his mother as being his first teacher of Islam and says that all mothers are, indeed, Islamic examples of faith in practice. He has also written that if women have to choose between wearing the scarf and education, then education is what they should choose. He asserts the idea that marriage should not be seen as an institution for simply producing children and that parents must focus on the conscientious caring and education of their children (Gülen, "Evlilik, Evcilik Oyunu Değildir"). He authored a very critical article in which he called Muslim men to task on the issue of spousal abuse. The article states that women not only have legal and religious recourse to defend themselves, but that they also have the right to *physically* defend themselves, and goes so far as to suggest that they enrol in self-defence courses (Kurucan). He maintains gender difference in Islam, as seen in the Qur'an, and recognizes and praises women for their religious devotion. However uneven Gülen's writings on women may be, it is clear that he holds women in very high regard, and the size-able group of women around the world who follow his teachings indicate that his words do certainly resonate with them.

Turkish women in *Hizmet* are rethinking the space between home and work and creating women-run institutions that enable women greater social participation, thereby negotiating a "muslim woman's third space" (Khan). These women embrace the idea that an ideal Muslim community is built through *temsil* or living by ex-ample (Özdalga 86). They hope their good works will both change misperceptions about Muslims as well as build strong interfaith networks and friendships. Gülen-inspired women share a unique sense of sisterhood that not only serves as emotional and spiritual support as they relocate and adjust to life in the United States, but also provides practical forms of support to allow women to study and work and become active participants in American society.

Diaspora in this context denotes Turks who retain a strong sense of Turkish identity, even after moving far from their homeland. Members of the Turkish Gülen community in the United States typically have highly skilled jobs and advanced degrees; their ex-periences differ markedly from those Turks in Europe, who have faced discrimination as guest workers. They are a community of conscious and a diaspora by choice rather than due to economic hardship. Counter to the notion that immigrants are successful once they have assimilated, it appears that Turkish women's notions of woman-to-woman support help them flourish at the personal level and at the level of the wider American community, as they rely on one another and on family members from Turkey who co-reside with them for long periods of time, primary their sisters, mothers, and mothers-in-law. Women relying on extended family members, particularly during childbearing years, is a pattern seen across Muslim countries (Waldman 319; Al-Faruqi 4-5).

TURKISH WOMEN IN SERVICE TO ALLAH: MOTHERING AND SISTERING AS SERVICE TO HUMANITY

Hizmet women are an amalgam of Turkish society: they blend traditional Islamic religious values from the Qur'an with an appreciation for secular notions of progress and democracy and broad access to education through formal university instruction. These different threads of thought come together through the spiritual development that takes place in women's Islamic study circles (*sohbetler*), academic seminars, and retreats. When Turkish women move between the United States and Turkey, they move and circulate among other groups of women in *Hizmet*, creating circles of knowledge and experience. Together, they constitute a veritable transnational sisterhood, one that models its efforts on Turkish cultural understandings of motherhood (*annelik*) and "elder sisterhood" (*ablalik*), as it is understood by those aiming to serve others. Turkish culture holds the position of an *abla*, an elder sister, in very high esteem, and women in *Hizmet* dedicate themselves to girls and women by taking on added responsibilities, approaching what I call adoptive-sister mothering, or "sister mothers." Research on Turkish Americans has shown that Turks in the American diaspora struggle with living far from their families (Şenyürekli). In mothering from a distance (Parrenas), Turkish American women find a myriad of ways to keep Turkish traditions alive, to adjust to American life, and to develop a Turkish American Muslim identity. Their style of mothering and the woman-to-woman support that they offer have a great impact beyond the Turkish community itself and create bridges of understanding between Turks and non-Turks as well as Muslims and non-Muslims.

"HOW DOES ONE BECOME AN ABLA?": *HIZMET* WOMEN AND ANATOLIAN UNDERSTANDINGS OF SISTERHOOD

Ablalar (older sisters) are responsible for determining the spiritual needs of various groups of women and girls in the Turkish American community, and throughout the year, they create a variety of programs for girls in different age groups to help them feel a sense of belonging and shared identity. Working in accordance with the Islamic principle of *shura*, where consultation in regular group leadership settings is prioritized, *ablalar* decide what issues are most pressing in the community and what forms of support and programing will help offer guidance to young girls, adolescent girls, and women of various ages. Some of their priorities are directed at the larger American community in the form of vibrant cultural festivals and outreach to inform Americans about Islam and the Muslim experience. Cooking classes, Turkish language classes, Turkish water marbling artwork (*ebru*), community dinners and picnics as well as large-scale festivals create a vibrant cultural scene where Turks make connections with various Central Asian Turkic-speaking groups to create a pan-Turkic speaking cultural community. In this chapter, I am most interested in the different forms of direct intra-community organizing between Turkish and Turkic-speaking Muslims that takes place among Gülen-inspired *Hizmet* women in the United States, and I rely primarily on fieldwork and observations in Houston, Texas, and Istanbul, Turkey, between 2007 and 2012. Houston is home to a very dynamic American Muslim community and a growing Turkish and Central Asian community.

The spiritual curriculum is established and is adapted by *ablalar* as people bring and send new educational materials back and forth from Turkey. Additionally, they utilize online materials and Turkish television programs via the Internet in preparing weekly Qur'an and Islamic study lessons. Young girls are encouraged to read stories in Turkish that focus on character education and then take online quizzes testing their understanding. An *abla's* religious authority is vested in her Islamic knowledge and participation in regular spiritual study circle groups (*sohbetler*), and in her willingness to help girls stay connected to Turkish culture. Ablalar often volunteer their time over weeks or a full year and remain in close contact with girls' mothers, giving reports on what they should practice and how they can improve their broader Islamic knowledge.

Turkish women take part in regular weekly discussion groups and tend to develop close relationships; they get to know more about the finer points of practising Islam and what makes sense for an American context. Although women may also join the regular Friday prayers, they can speak and ask questions in a more intimate and informal manner in a *sohbet* group. After weekly lessons wind down, conversations turn to issues related to family life and coping with one's daily problems. An *Abla* leading a regular discussion group is at once a spiritual guide as well as a stand-in family member, as she gives advice as best she can to other women about how to make well-suited decisions for themselves and their families while living away from Turkey.

It is quite natural that when people live in diaspora far from their own biological families they will both remain in contact with family members and also fill their new lives abroad with new relationships to offer comfort and support. In Houston in 2008 during an interview with a longtime resident of the U.S., a woman commented about the importance of support from *Abla* figures in the community. She said that living abroad in the United States caused her to feel that she needed two families: one cobbled together out of friends and acquaintances in the United States, in addition to her family back home in Turkey. She kept in regular contact with her own family in Turkey via telephone calls, Skype, and Facebook, although "technology cannot replace a family," she was quick to inform me. Not wanting to worry her family in Turkey too much with her difficulties adjusting to life in America, she explained that she "really needed" her *Abla*. *Ablalar* (plural of *abla*) in the United States understood the new difficulties she faced because they experienced them too. In the United States, many Americans had seemed interested in her Muslim identity and were welcoming of her in ways that had surprised her. Alternately, she felt some Americans wrongly categorized her as passive or subservient because she wore a scarf and modest clothing. The overdetermined social discourses that she was forced to face in Turkey were different than those that she faced in the United States; both discourses called on her to construct her Muslim identity in different ways. With respect to mothering her own children, her comments varied from the excitement of offering her kids the chance to be Muslim on something of a clean slate, in the sense that her daughters did not have to worry about the fear of veiling and going to school as she had in Turkey. On the other hand, she often worried about ingredients in food and wondered if her children might be eating foods that were not *halal* in school. She noted that her own sense of cultural marginality decreased, since there were "so many different kinds of people"; however, because the diversity was so different from what she was accustomed to, she felt at a loss to understand where people might be from and what their beliefs were. In this sense, having a strong Turkish community was beneficial: she felt that it gave her kids a sense of greater belonging to people they could easily identify with and it provided an anchor in the absence of her large extended family in Turkey.

An *Abla's* tasks revolve around organizing successful spiritual study circles and motivating group members. As girls become women, they feel a sense of wanting to help other girls in the cycle of support from one generation to the next, which is similar to the mutual aid model of support seen among other immigrant groups (Xie and Xia). Together, women create groups that uphold traditional Muslim values concerning modesty in dress and speech and place an emphasis on providing a high level of care to one's immediate family; these groups also enable women to work outside the home by providing childcare and children's programing. There is a keen awareness of subtle rites of passage—when babies become young girls, when girls become teenagers, when teenagers go to university, and when they might think about marriage. At each stage, *ablalar* of different age sets offer various forms of support to younger girls and women. In Turkey, elder women role models are always present and ready to offer advice. In the U.S. context, this traditional form of woman-to-woman support becomes more formalized with *Ablas* being assigned specific duties and tasks within specific periods of time. Sometimes in the U.S., an *Abla* may be assigned a role to perform for a year or more, then transition into another role later as the need emerges. Arriving at the threshold of marriage as a young woman who has a strong sense of Islamic values and personal modesty is of the upmost importance in this community.

Although the *Hizmet* community wants to serve the American community with acts of friendship and develop close ties with neighbours to demonstrate a tolerant, liberal understanding of Islam, they do worry about their children a great deal. Islamic values are imparted in weekly *Sohbet* study circles, and a host of programs offer girls an alternative girlhood, one that is not totally outside the American mainstream but at a safe distance so that a girl may retain her Islamic values and Turkish identity. To offer a Muslim alternative to the long Christmas break, the *Hizmet* community organizes winter-break camps where young children and teenagers take part in activities, such as watching films and arts and crafts, with instruction in reading the Qur'an and various other spiritual talks on a number of topics. The community acknowledges that children at different stages of development need different forms of care and nurturance, and fun and leisure must necessarily be woven into formative spiritual education if it is to be successful.

Similar programs are made for girls who stay in Houston for the summer instead of travelling back to Turkey. For those who are not able to return to Turkey, time at home in the summers can be disappointing and lonely. In the summer of 2012, a four-week Qur'an camp was organized by a group of *ablalar* for girls in elementary and middle school that overlapped with the month of Ramadan. The girls met every day from 9:30 a.m. to 4:00 p.m. and spent three hours a day studying Qur'an and *hadith* to learn correct pronunciation or *tecvit* (*tajwid*).[3] Additionally, they made gifts for their mothers during arts and crafts sessions. They were encouraged to fast for Ramadan, if they wanted to, but were served snacks and meals when hungry. Though fasting, the *ablalar* still organized carpooling on Saturdays and took the girls to museums and to an outdoor amusement park in 100-degree weather. When I asked one of the *Ablas* why she had taken the kids outdoors when fasting, she replied, "It was hard to do while fasting, but it is important for the girls to love Islam and to associate it with fun things; we cannot just have them sit inside all day and read Qur'an. We have to teach them to have a good balance and that Muslims can enjoy life, even while fasting." This attention to creating "fun spaces" (Werbner) and taking part in public life as Muslims (Göle and Ammann; Ammann) is an important characteristic of the pedagogy that *ablalar* use throughout their activities. They completed the Qur'an camp with a formal recital that only mothers, grandmothers, and siblings attended, in which each girl either recited a *surah*, or chapter, from the Qur'an, recited a poem in Turkish, or sang a hymn. The girls were encouraged to dress in colourful dresses, and some wore scarves, and others did not. The tone was celebratory and fun, and girls enjoyed themselves and the pageantry of the occasion. The grand finale was a song dedicated to mothers, with the girls emphatically thanking them for their nurturing and love. While fasting the *ablalar* served the girls an elaborate lunch while the mothers who were also fasting got caught up on back-to-school news and other updates about who had gone to Turkey for the summer. Afterwards, the *ablalar* stayed behind to rearrange tables and clean up, and they invited the kids to come back soon when the regular weekly lessons would resume after school started. The *ablalar* both taught the children and witnessed their development as family members would, while they also offered childcare so that the mothers could manage the responsibilities of added cooking and hosting for the month of Ramazan.[4]

With regard to recognizing Muslim woman-to-woman friendships and assistance as both charitable acts and activism, Gisela Webb reminds us that studies on Muslim women

> must include, and indeed unite, issues of theory and practice. This means that any analysis or theory of women's nature, role, rights, or problems must include attention to practical, immediate issues involved in actualizing the Qur'anic mandate of social justice and, concomitantly, that any considerations of "practical" solutions to problems and

injustices faced by women must have sound theological grounding in the Qur'anic worldview. (xi-xii)

To elaborate here, rather than producing studies of Muslim women based on simply "understanding and translating" their lives, or unwittingly adopting a colonial repugnance of the social conservativism associated with Islam, we should look for the epistemological models of opportunity that Muslim women find compelling today (Mahmoud 34). The *ablalik* considered here is one of the ways that piety is practised in the lives of devout women today. Whereas Webb and others have examined specific individuals and specific projects, *ablalik* is a general Turkish framework that engages taken-for-granted acts of female caregiving and endows it with a rich new set of social and religious meanings. I draw here from Saba Mahmoud's fascinating discussion of how liberals and progressives are uncomfortable with Islamic social conservatism yet often write from the position of understanding and translating for the sake of confronting intolerance, particularly after 9/11 (34-38). Similar to Webb, she seeks spaces of transformation and "that we may come to ask of politics a whole series of questions that seemed settled when we first embarked upon the inquiry" (39).

Nilüfer Göle wrote what is considered to have been the first work, *The Forbidden Modern*, on the newly emerging pious Turkish women who sought both a modern education and the choice to dress modestly in the larger Turkish public sphere. The women that Göle describes as marginal in her 1997 work have moved from the margins to a new political centre that is decidedly more Islamic. These new piety communities effectively created new feminine networks that, in some cases, mirrored Turkish constructions of family relatedness. Similar modern piety movements have been seen in other parts of the Muslim world, although their histories differ greatly from the Turkish example, and they have articulated some of the same themes around women reclaiming the rights afforded to them in the Qur'an and the *hadith* (see Abu-Lughod; Deeb; Göle and Ammann; Saktanber). Since the 1970s and 1980s when these renewed piety movements began to emerge, often in contrast to forms of secularization that were seen to have eroded core Islamic values, they have been labeled in a variety of ways

(Ahmed). Islamic feminists and believing women in Islam argue that the Qur'an has a feminine liberating voice that has been silenced after centuries of patriarchal jurisprudence (Wadud; Barlas). Scholars such as Leila Ahmed and Fatima Mernissi criticize patriarchy at both a religious and a social level (Barlas; Winter). Progressive Muslims have called for a revoicing of Islamic traditions in a contemporary timbre (Badran, "Between"; Othman). In different countries in the Muslim world, there are groups of "born-again" or "veiled-again" Muslims who seek to live in more visibly pious ways, beginning to take on more conservative modes of dress in a renewed way after having lived a more secular lifestyle (Haddad; Rozario; Van de Veer). The diversity of this literature demonstrates that a renewed sense of spiritual and social liberation, no longer mutually exclusive domains, is lived and understood among Muslim women worldwide.

What stands out about *Hizmet* women, both in Turkey and in the United States, is their determination to be extraordinary mothers to their own children, their zeal for academic achievement, and their willingness to co-mother others' children and to adopt sisters when they can. Those in the *Hizmet* movement create familial ties with others by using terms such as "*Abi*" (elder brother) and "*Abla.*" The idealization of traditional female support and caregiving are applied broadly both within, and notably, outside the nuclear and extended family. Within this is traditional Islamic motherhood framework (Upal 87), where women are seen as caring and nurturing, second only to Allah in compassion, yet applied in a non-traditional way outside nuclear families, and in many untraditional settings wherever *Hizmet* is around the world.

This service to not only one's own family but also to the greater human family is the essence of the Şemsinur Özdemir's narratives on Islamic women in Turkey. Although I was conducting interviews in Istanbul in 2008 and 2009 on notions of leadership among women in *Hizmet,* she advised me to look at those women taking part in the taken-for-granted forms of female caregiving and to examine that area as service to women rather than female leadership. Özdemir has written two books on the topic of active motherhood. *Mothers of Service* examines women doctors, Islamic scholars, and community leaders who were public in their faith in ways that inspired younger generations to live Islam and to embrace the difficulty of doing so in a rigidly secular context. Each chapter is dedicated to a unique woman who dedicated herself to helping others in different ways. Her other work *My Mother, My First Teacher* includes examples of how to raise children and offers guidance in specific circumstances as well as excerpts from interviews with women about how their mothers interacted with them. The book also offers examples from the Prophet Muhammad's behaviour that can be explained and taught to children, with information on how to address children at different ages and levels of development, and includes some sections on stepmothers.

Özdemir advised me to look to the caregiving work of women in order to understand the increased presence of pious Turkish women entering high levels of influence in the public sphere. She and other women whom I interviewed remarked that increased female caregiving directed at young girls in educational settings was directly related to the increased presence of women in successful career positions. Those that encounter *Hizmet* women in superficial ways may remark on what appears as a parallel gendered world, in which men and women live significant parts of their lives separately. *Hizmet* women see their lives in a different light, taking stock of all the instances in which they are free to make important life decisions in a truly woman-centred manner, in which formalized kinship notions, such as *ablalik*, ensure women will receive support if they seek it. The aspects of their lives that do not overlap with their husbands and fathers might be seen as zones of freedom rather than zones of invisibility. This is an important distinction because when women feel free to exercise decision making among a large network of women friends and *ablalar*, they are clearly not only resigned to decision making at the level of the nuclear family. More importantly, they may receive information and advice from study circles that challenge directly or indirectly the assumptions of their husbands and fathers.

Continuing the discussion on recognizing power in "home-spheres" and women's networks, anthropologist Jenny White's work has focused on women and their participation in Turkish vernacular politics and the growth of Islamism in Turkey. She describes women and their collective participation in building an urban political consensus in the same way that they had pooled resources together in rural village settings during harvest periods. White explores the term "*imece*" to describe their rural social order and how it works for a greater political cause while they take part in and rely on female friendship support networks. This is another Turkish framework for gendered collective labour that refers to shared work and harvesting in rural settings. Through physical, financial, and emotional nurturance, Turkish American women have taken Anatolian notions of sisterhood and enacted what Levitt and Glick Schiller have described as "migration simultaneity"—they have, simultaneously, settled in the United States because of the strength of their networks and resisted cultural assimilation due to the strength of their sense of ethnic identity. Their very distance from Turkey creates opportunities for them to rely on authentic Turkish modes of social exchange such as conceptions of *imece*, *annelik*, and *ablalik* (1002).

CO-OPERATIVE CHILDCARE

Ethnographic observations in a Turkish-run daycare centre and an all-woman run childcare co-operative in a Turkish community centre in Houston, Texas, offer fascinating examples of the ways that transnational communities selectively adapt to new social and cultural contexts. Narratives of women childcare providers, stay-at-home moms who create Turkish homescapes in diaspora, and grandmothers who lend a hand and fill in as mothers while their daughters work while abroad offer new insights into the dedication, strength, and intensive organization that produce a Turkish sense of what it means to be a Muslim mother in today's world, and a Turkish mother supporting her family in diaspora through strategic caregiving.

Turkish women often come to the United States to attend school and stay to work while they are in their childbearing years. Some women come as single college students, whereas some marry partners whom they meet in the United States; others come from Turkey to join their husbands who may have come earlier.

The *Hizmet* community in the United States encourages having children, as do all other Abrahamic traditions, and honours the notion of putting great care into raising children. Indeed the decree to "go forth and multiply" (Genesis 1:22, 9:1, 9:7) is found across all the Abrahamic traditions, as is the story of Adam and Eve. However, the version of Adam and Eve's fate is different in the Qur'an. According to the Qur'anic tradition, both Adam and Eve transgress and are punished for disobeying Allah. They are finally reunited with Allah and are taught to forgive others as Allah forgave them. Absent in the Islamic tradition is the notion of original sin, whereby all women share in Eve's guilt through painful menstruation and childbirth. From the Qur'an in *surah an-Nahl* (16:72), Muslims are told "And Allah has made for you mates from yourselves and made for you, out of them children and grandchildren" (Omran 31). In the spirit of "go forth and multiply" from the Old Testament, we see the same spirit in the *hadith* of the Prophet (as authenticated by Abu Dawoud): Muhammad is reported to have said, "Marry and multiply and I will make a display for you on the Day of Judgment" (Omran 31). Moreover, the Islamic tradition contends that children are the future caregivers of their parents and that both men and women have an innate curiosity and instinct for motherhood and fatherhood. The Qur'an also lays out a very clear list of responsibilities and duties for both parents and children (Omran 32-39). Often quoted among women in this community is the *hadith* that says when one kisses their children and is loving towards them, they earn the reward of eternal paradise and that paradise lies under the feet of mothers. Simply put, the idea is that the nurturance and selflessness that is a part of mothering is close to godliness, and that mothers will reap the rewards of their labour for eternity in the heaven. Indeed, the terms "*rahman*" (beneficent) and "*rahim*" (merciful), two of the terms most often used for Allah, are from the same root as the world for womb in Arabic. In this sense, Allah is a creator who is close to womblike in essence.

Turkish women who have young children in the United States aim to provide childcare in the manner that they would in Turkey. The children's books that Turkish women read to their children in the diaspora will likely exalt the role of the mother. A Turkish pious magazine for girls, *Gonca*, regularly features stories about the strength of mothers and their heroic acts of sacrifice. The pages overflow with poetry dedicated to mothers and fathers as well as to grandmothers and grandfathers. Although Turkish American children are likely to see their grandparents far less than they would if they were in Turkey, they are taught before they can talk just how much Turkish society values family closeness above all else. One can connect the themes found in the pages of *Gonca* magazine to the corresponding honour given to elders in Turkey and in the Turkish American diaspora.

If Turkish women are in school or working, they generally try to have family members come to the United States for a period of time to offer childcare assistance if feasible. Some families rely on assistance from the wife's sisters and parents as well as the parents of the husband. If family members are willing and able to, a couple may be able to offer long periods of uninterrupted caregiving to their children before they go to elementary school. A large number of Turkish grandmothers come to the United States and stay for as long as six months at a time. Enabling their daughters to work or study full time, they contribute to the family's well-being by offering childcare, housework, healthy traditional Turkish food, and, in some instances, plant gardens with seeds brought from Turkey to ensure that the family eats familiar types of food. Grandmothers take on responsibilities that make them second-time mothers to their grandchildren while the parents are working and studying full time. They preserve a sense of Turkish culinary tradition and abide by Islamic *halal* dietary laws and provide young children with uninterrupted Turkish language exposure. Their presence in homes in which both mother and father are studying or working facilitates a deeper observance of *Ramazan* and other key religious holidays.

When a couple can count on regular assistance from their parents while living in the diaspora, they may decide to have more children than they would have in Turkey. One grandmother who had stayed for six months to look after her daughter's fifth child in Houston, Texas waved her finger jokingly at her daughter on the eve of her return, saying, "That's enough! No more children for you!" This grandmother not only had helped take care of her five grandchildren but also looked after the children of two other nearby Turkish families as well. Those families had not been able to bring their parents over, so this grandmother extended a helping hand. She enjoyed having the large group of children under her care. She got to know her daughter's American neighbours who enjoyed the presence of a multigenerational family's home as a site where neighbourhood kids could play safely. She lamented that American families and neighbourliness seemed in decline and wondered how people were to take care of one another if they were not comfortable allowing their kids to play freely outside under the watch of others in a collective notion of childcare.

Grandparents visiting from Turkey carry a wide variety of food items—such as dried spices, sundried vegetables, olives, cheeses and dried meats, homemade pasta, *halal* ingredients for baking, including alcohol-free vanilla, dried *ufka* sheets for making savory breads, and home processed pickled vegetables and dried soup mixes. Grandparents also come with items such as hand knit sweaters, socks, and slippers for children and a wide variety of undershirts that keep the body at what is believed to be an ideal temperature for ensuring that one stays healthy. Turkish American parents understand that these notions of maintaining health will not be observed in American daycares, and the cooler temperatures with air conditioning are also understood as "cold" in the sense that Americans are not as caring as they would hope for. For some who live in the U.S. for extended periods of time, this becomes less important and their sense of maintaining wellness shifts.

Certain aspects of Turkish grandmother's and mother's mothering strategies can be seen as forms of preservation of traditions as well as resistance to acculturation. The emphasis on food is abundant in a Turkish American household. When Turkish grandmothers cannot be present in the Unites States, they send what items they can to instill an appreciation and remembrance of Turkish lifeways and foodways. Food is extremely important to the Turkish household, and well-balanced food is associated with wellness and health. Food becomes more important when family members leave Turkey, and those in diaspora miss foods from home that cannot be found abroad. Food is symbolic of home, of family and of nurturing.

MARIA F. CURTIS

COMMUNITY CHILDCARE INITIATIVES

A number of Turkish community members collaborated in launching a Turkish-run daycare in Houston. It was staffed by Turkish, Central Asian, and American teachers, and employed a Turkish cook who prepared a *halal* diet for all the children whether they were Muslim or not. In addition to the balanced food that the Turkish cook at the daycare prepared for meal times, she also prepared items that would normally be consumed as snacks in Turkey in the afternoon, and varieties of savoury breads and cakes. In the afternoon during naptime, she prepared the food in the daycare and served it to the other women; in her own way, she was mothering those who mothered others' children. The daycare also organized Mother's Day crafts and snacks, and offered gifts to the mothers of the children in their care. Food here takes on a significant role: it contributes to a sense of security and builds community. And although it is easy to discount the presentation of traditional, regional foods as "just food preparation," food, in fact, should be seen as a powerful form of solidarity building and community space making. Here, Turkish women created caring food chains that nourish not only their own families but also those children under their care and with whom they work (Curtis "Among the Heavenly Branches"; Allen and Sachs; Counihan and Van Esterik; Counihan and Kaplan; Inness; Karaosmanoğlu; Metcalf).

Although the Turkish-run daycare served all families in its residential Houston neighbourhood, collective childcare is also offered at the Turkish American Turquoise community centre in Houston. It was decided by the community at large that a building was needed for children so that mothers could continue to meet to organize volunteer activities and to take part in spiritual study circles. A prefabricated building was purchased, and it is now used as a site for childcare for young children and as a separate site for young girls who are studying the Qur'an with their *ablalar*. Women volunteer their time to keep the facility staffed and alternate in keeping the babysitting hours filled as well as in co-ordinating *halal* meals and snacks for the children and young girls in their care. Each room is equipped with Turkish-style couches that convert easily into full-sized beds for napping children or for guests who might need a place to rest. This area serves as the most crucial site for serving mothers with very young children who may have no family members to assist them as they learn to become mothers. It is a community priority to create spheres of care for people in different situations. Providing young inexperienced mothers with a short break so that they might interact with others helps prevent postpartum depression and isolation. When children are older, they might also then accompany their fathers in an adjacent area to play or have picnics, and when young boys get a bit bigger, they, too, will have access to programs mentioned here for girls, but the programs will be organized by *abiler* or "elder bothers." In this sense, the larger community, both men and women, shares in the community's responsibilities for caring for educating children.

The children's building is used on most Saturdays for Qur'an lessons for elementary-aged girls. Girls are paired in groups of five to six to study with an *Abla*. As young girls get older, they will likely begin to spend the weekends at a group of younger, single *Abla*'s house. Weekend activities include shared meals, movie nights, outings to local restaurant and malls, and special study group celebrations marking special occasions, such as the Prophet Muhammad's birthday. As the unmarried *ablalar* begins to move on to college dormitories or gets married, younger *ablalar* replace them and take on their responsibilities, and so the cycle continues. This cycle of girls becoming *ablalar* and then becoming mothers is important. Girls are taught to listen to and respect their elders and to see the potential for close friendships, not just within their own families but also across the community at large. Building on Anatolian kin and meta-kin models, Turkish American women in diaspora create dense care networks that reach girls and women of all age groups.

CONCLUSION

In the United States, Turkish Americans are continuing to build on the foundations of communities that have existed since the last days of the Ottoman Empire and the birth of the modern Republic of Turkey. Among the newer groups of Turks coming to the United States is the *Hizmet* movement, a group that emerged as a result of and in contrast to Turkey's strong secular past. Women in Turkey bring to the United States their deeply held Anatolian conceptions of woman-centred networks that both create traditional home spheres and support women who want to work outside the home. Scholars of immigration have noted the unique and vital ways that immigrant women support communities and families across diaspora. Turkish American women continue to find means to sustain their own cultural identity and to reach out to their non-Muslim neighbours. Sister mothering in the Turkish *Abla* tradition engenders Muslim women's sense of support and sense of self. More than resisting assimilation and acculturation, Anatolian *ablalar* and grandmothers in diaspora bring with them a secure sense of feminine space that not only benefits their own group,[5] but also contributes to notions of mothering and feminine well-being to all those with whom they interact. Turkish American women stand as an example of the ways that collective notions of motherhood, a cosmopolitan Islamic blending of *ablalik* set in motion in diaspora, only serve to expand and enrich our notions of what it means to create a society in which all members may find various forms of support and education at important junctures in their individual development. These feminine networks of support and the Islamic "fun spaces" that become public through festivals and food serve to rework the overwrought and overdetermined simplifications offered by the American media, and require Americans to rethink their misconceptions about Islam and Muslim women.

NOTES

[1] Interviews were conducted in both Turkish and English for this research. Translations for the Turkish responses during interviews were done by the researcher.

[2] This quote is taken from the front cover of a promotional booklet that summarizes Gülen's interfaith efforts. Not meant to be a book *per se*, it was distributed at various Turkish cultural centres and bears no title. It was printed by The Light, Inc. in Rutherford, New Jersey.

[3] *Tecvit* is Turkish for the Arabic *tajwid*.

[4] *Ramazan* in Turkish, *Ramadan* in Arabic: the holy month of the

Islamic year when observant Muslims fast from sunrise to sunset.
[5]On intergenerational identity construction in the wider Turkish
American community, see Kaya, Ilhan.

WORKS CITED

Abu-Lughod, Lila, ed. *Remaking Women: Feminism and Modernity in the Middle East.* Princeton: Princeton University Press, 1998. Print.

Ahmed, Leila. "Feminism and Feminist Movements in the Middle East, a Preliminary Exploration: Turkey, Egypt, Algeria, People's Democratic Republic of Yemen." *Women's Studies International Forum* 5.2 (1982): 153-168. Print.

Al-Faruqi, Lois Ibsen. "An Extended Family Model from Islamic Culture." *Journal of Comparative Family Studies* 9:2 (1978): 243-256. Print.

Allen, Patricia, and Carolyn Sachs, eds. "Women and Food Chains: The Gendered Politics of Food." *International Journal of Sociology of Agriculture and Food* 15 (2007): 1-23. Print.

Ammann, Ludwig. "Islam in Public." *Public Culture* 1 (2002): 277-279. Print.

Badran, Margot. "Between Secular and Islamic Feminism/s: Reflections on the Middle East and Beyond." *Journal of Middle East Women's Studies* 1 (2005): 6-28. Print.

Badran, Margot. *Feminism in Islam: Secular and Religious Convergences.* Oxford: OneWorld, 2009. Print.

Balcı, Tamer, and Christopher L. Miller, eds. *The Gülen Hizmet Movement: Circumspect Activism in Faith-Based Reform.* Newcastle upon Tyne: Cambridge Scholars, 2012. Print.

Barlas, Asma. *"Believing Women" in Islam: Unreading Patriarchal Interpretations of the Qur'an.* Austin: The University of Texas Press, 2002. Print.

Counihan, Carole, and Penny Van Esterik, eds. *Food and Culture: A Reader.* New York: Routledge, 1997. Print.

Counihan, Carole, and Steven L. Kaplan, eds. *Food and Gender: Identity and Power.* London: Routledge, 2004.

Curtis, Maria F. "Among the Heavenly Branches: Leadership and Authority among Women in the Gülen Hizmet Movement." *The*

Gülen Hizmet Movement: Circumspect Activism in Faith-Based Reform. Eds. Tamer Balcı and Christopher L. Miller. Newcastle upon Tyne: Cambridge Scholars, 2012. 119-154. Print.

Curtis, Maria F. "The Women's Side of the Coin: The Gülen Movement in America: A New Turkish American Community Taking Root." Presentation at the Islam in the Contemporary World: The Fethullah Gülen Movement in Thought and Practice Conference. Rice University, Houston, Texas. 2005.

Deeb, Laura. *An Enchanted Modern: Gender and Public Piety in Shi'i Lebanon.* Princeton: Princeton University Press, 2006. Print.

Göle, Nilüfer. *The Forbidden Modern: Civilization and Veiling.* Ann Arbor: The University of Michigan Press, 1997. Print.

Göle, Nilüfer, and Ludwig Ammann, eds. *Islam in Public: Turkey, Iran, Europe.* Istanbul: Bilgi Univeristy Press, 2006. Print.

Gülen, M. Fethullah. "Evlilik, Evcilik Oyunu Değildir." *Fethullah Gulen.* N.p., 16 Jan. 2009. Web. 21 Dec. 2011.

Gülen, M. Fethullah. "The Ideal Husband." *Muslims Today.* WordPress, 20 Oct. 2007. Web. 21 Dec. 2011.

Gülen, M. Fethullah. *Toward a Global Civilization of Love and Tolerance.* Somerset, NJ: The Light, 2004. Print.

Gülen, M. Fethullah. "Women Confined and Mistreated." *Fethullah Gulen.* N.p., n.d. Web. 23 Jan. 2012.

Haddad, Yvonne Y. "A Century of Islam in America." *Hamdard Islamicus* 22.4 (1997): Print.

Inness, Sherrie A. *Cooking Lessons: The Politics of Gender and Food.* Lanham: Rowman and Littlefield P, 2001. Print.

Levitt, Peggy, and Nina Glick Schiller. "Conceptualizing Simultaneity: A Transnational Social Field Perspective." *International Migration Review* 38.3 (2004): 1002-1039. Print.

Karaosmanoğlu, Defne. "Nostalgia Spaces of Consumption and Heterotopia." *Culture Unbound: Journal of Current Cultural Research* 2 (2010): 283–302. Print.

Kaya, Ilhan. "Identity across Generations: A Turkish American Case Study." *Middle East Journal* 63.4 (2009): 617-632. Print.

Khan, Shahnaz. "Muslim Women: Negotiations in the Third Space." *Signs: Journal of Women and Culture in Society* 23.2 (1998): 463-494. Print.

Kurucan, Ahmet. "Intra-Family Violence and Islam." *Today's*

Zaman. Zaman Gazetesi, 28 Oct. 2008. Web.

Mahmood, Saba. *Politics of Piety: The Islamic Revival and the Feminist Subject.* Princeton: Princeton University Press, 2005. Print.

McGown, Rima Berns. *Muslims in the Diaspora: The Somali Communities of London and Toronto.* Toronto: University of Toronto Press, 1999. Print.

Metcalf, Barbara Daly. *Making Muslim Space in North America and Europe.* Berkeley: University of California Press, 1996. Print.

Omran, Abdel Rahim. *Family Planning in the Legacy of Islam.* London: Routledge, 1992. Print.

Othman, Norani. "Muslim Women and the Challenge of Islamic Fundamentalism/Extremism: An Overview of Southeast Asian Women's Struggles for Human Rights and Gender Equality." *Women's Studies International Forum* 29.4 (2006): 339-353. Print.

Özdalga, Elisabeth. "Redeemer or Outsider? The Gülen Community in the Civilizing Process." *Muslim World* 95 (2005): 429-446. Print.

Özdalga, Elisabeth. "Three Women Teachers Tell Their Stories." *Turkish Islam and the Secular State: The Gülen Movement.* Eds. M. Hakan Yavuz and John L. Esposito. Syracuse: Syracuse University Press, 2003. 85-114. Print.

Özdemir, Şemsinur. *Hizmet Anneleri* [Mothers of Service]. Istanbul: Zaman Kitap, 2008. Print.

Özdemir, Şemsinur. *Annem İlk Öğretmenim* [My Mother, My first Teacher]. Istanbul: Gül Yayınları, 2008. Print.

Parrenas, Rhacel Salazar. "Mothering from a Distance: Emotions, Gender, and Intergenerational Relations in Filipino Transnational Families." *Feminist Studies* 27.2 (2001): 361-390. Print.

Popp, Maximilian. "Altruistic Society or Sect?: The Shadowy World of the Islamic Gülen Movement." *Der Speigel,* 6 Aug. 2012. Web.

Rozario, Santi. "On Being Australian and Being Muslim: Muslim Women as Defenders of Islamic Heritage." *Women's Studies International Forum* 21.6 (1988): 649-661. Print.

Saktanber, Ayşe. *Living Islam: Women, Religion, and the Politicization of Culture in Turkey.* London: I. B. Taurus, 2002. Print.

Şenyürekli, Ayşem R. "A Profile of Immigrant Women from Turkey in the United States." *International Journal of Turkish Studies* 12 (2006): 117-132. Print.

Şenyürekli, Ayşem R. "A Profile of Immigrant Women from Turkey in the United States, 1900-2000." *Turkish Migration to the United States: From Ottoman Times to the Present.* Eds. A. Deniz Balgamis and Kemal Karpat. Madison: The University of Wisconsin Press, 2008. Print.

Şenyürekli, Ayşem R. and Daniel F. Detzner. "Intergenerational Relationships in a Transnational Context: The Case of Turkish Families." *Family Relations* 57.4 (2008): 457-467. Print.

Slymovics, Susan. "The Muslim World Day Parade and 'Storefront' Mosques of New York City." *Making Muslim Space in North America and Europe.* Ed. Barbara Daly Metcalf. Berkeley: University of California Press, 1996. 204-216. Print.

The Study Quran: A New Translation and Commentary. Ed. and Trans. Seyyed Hossein Nasr. New York: HarperCollins, 2015. Print.

Upal, Hinna Mirza. "A Celebration of Mothering in the Qur'an." *Journal of the Motherhood Initiative for Research and Community Involvement* 7.1 (2005): 86-97. Print.

Van der Veer, Peter. "Transnational Religions: Hindu and Muslim Movements." *Journal for the Study of Religions and Ideologies* 7 (2004): 4-18. Print.

Webb, Gisela. "May Muslim Women Speak for Themselves, Please?" *Windows of Faith: Muslim Women Scholar-Activists in North America.* Ed. Gisela Webb. Syracuse: Syracuse University Press, 2000. xi-xix. Print.

Werbner, Pnina. "Fun Spaces: On Identity and Social Empowerment among British Pakistanis." *Theory, Culture, & Society* 13.4 (1996): 53-80. Print.

Waldman, Marilyn Robinson. "Reflections on Islamic Tradition, Women, and Family." *Muslim Families in North America.* Eds. Earle H. Waugh, Sharon McIrvin Abu-Laban, and Regula Burckhardt Qureshi. Edmonton: The University of Alberta Press, 1991. Print.

White, Jenny. *Islamist Mobilization in Turkey: A Study in Vernacular Politics.* Seattle: University of Washington Press, 2003. Print.

Winter, Bronwyn. "Fundamental Misunderstandings: Issues in

Feminist Approaches to Islamism." *Journal of Women's History* 13.1(2001): 9-41. Print.

Xie, Xiaolin and Yan Xia. "Co-residence in Chinese Immigrant Families." *Strengths and Challenges of New Immigrant Families: Implications for Research, Education, Policy, and Service.* Eds. Rochelle L. Dalla, John Defrain, Julie Johnson, and Douglass A. Abbott. Lanham, Maryland: Lexington Books, 2009. 309-328. Print.

III.
MUSLIM MOTHERING IN THE DIASPORA

7.
Muslim, Immigrant, and Francophone in Ontario

A Triple Minoritization or How to See Mothering as an Integrative Process

AURÉLIE LACASSAGNE

THE OBJECTIVE OF THIS CHAPTER is to begin exploring the realities of Francophone immigrant mothers in Sudbury, a bilingual (French and English), mid-sized, northeastern Ontario city. In particular, I seek to uncover the problems and challenges these women may face as they experience their triple minoritization: Muslim, immigrant and Francophone (a minority within the minority within the minority). I also examine whether or not being a mother helps these Muslim women to integrate into a community, in contrast to a traditional perception of motherhood that excludes. (Mothers are said to not have time to enjoy an active social life.) The hypothesis is that mothering and motherhood may prevent the isolation experienced by immigrant and Muslim women. Through in-depth interviews with some Muslim immigrant mothers, I look not only at their experiences of discrimination and racialization, of "otherness" and "otherization," but also at the possibility of openness and inclusion that mothering provides to bridge the potential cultural gap between these mothers and the community at large, especially with other Francophone mothers. In the last couple of decades, Sudbury has welcomed an increasing number of immigrants from Muslim backgrounds (apart from a few isolated cases who arrived earlier), yet the numbers are still very low: only a few hundred Muslim women live in Sudbury. Among them, there are some Francophone Muslim mothers arriving with their partners, who are, for the vast majority, students, and, for a handful of them, professionals (education and health sectors). The chapter contends that a common identity based on motherhood could be an element that practitioners working in community and educational organizations could use to build more welcoming communities. In other words, this paper investigates how Muslim and immigrant mothers can unite with other French-speaking mothers to be at the forefront of a truly diversified, multicultural and bilingual community. In the first part of this chapter, I will look at how the triple minoritization context is perceived and experienced by the interviewees. The second part examines the mothering practices of Muslim women and their potential influence on building Sudbury into a more inclusive and welcoming community.

SETTING UP THE CONTEXT: WHAT IS A MUSLIM MOTHER?

Drawing on the reflections of Shahnaz Khan, I take as a point of departure the category "Muslim," while being aware of the problems associated with that category, in particular its reifying effects. As Khan points out, both Oriental discourses and Islamist discourses "essentialize the ideal Muslim Woman and reduce her to the same symbols and icons" (469). The intent of this chapter is not only to avoid this trap but also to showcase the experiences of Muslim mothers who were expressly chosen in this study for their different perceptions, practices, self-identification, and relations to Islam. Most interviewees told me that they were glad to be able to express themselves and their feelings and experiences. Some stated that it was useful, a sort of relief compared to their experiences of isolation. Some were positively surprised a university professor could have an interest in what they have to say about their lives.

Another objective of this study is to show the diversity of Islam and how Muslims' heterogeneity is reflected in mothering and maternal thinking. Therefore, there is not one way of being a "Muslim mother." Muslim identities and practices are experienced within broader contexts. Not only do the cultural, social, political, and racialized figurations in which Muslim identities and practices are embedded matter in terms of integration, but there exists as well an individual level of integration: does the mother have a university degree or work experience? What were her parents' practices, and how have they affected her own mothering practices? These personal elements make every Muslim mother unique in the way that she perceives her religious practices and motherwork. "Motherwork" or "maternal work" is term that I borrow from Sara Ruddick's *Maternal Thinking*. It insists on the fact that mothering practices, experiences, and thinking are also forms of work. Although it is often non-paid work, this term serves to legitimize the efforts made by mothers in performing and doing mothering. Ruddick underscores three demands—protection, nurturance and training—that constitute maternal work (17, 65-123). Emphasizing mothering as work is especially important for immigrant women, as it can be used to debunk preconceived ideas about immigrant mothers not working and being financial burdens on the social system. An analysis of the interviews reveals that practising Muslim women seem particularly conscious that their mothering practices and experiences are, indeed, work in its entirety.

This section deals with Muslim mothers who are also living largely outside of their home countries in diasporic communities located in Ontario, Canada. Canada presents itself as a multicultural state. Multiculturalism is a state policy that portrays itself as multifaceted; among its characteristics is tolerance towards various religious and cultural practices both in the private and public spheres. This policy, implemented by Trudeau in 1971, has been strongly criticized on many grounds. For my purposes, the relevant criticisms are that multiculturalism reinforces patriarchy, strengthens difference, homogenizes religious and ethnic groups, racializes groups, and genders social relations (Bannerji, *Dark* and *Returning*; Thobani). In particular, multiculturalism tends to provincialize religious groups, what Bhabha calls the "*creation* of cultural diversity and a *containment* of cultural difference" (Bhabha's emphasis, 208). Muslims are often conflated into one imagined community by the majority in Canada as well as in other Western states, especially ones that have adopted multicultural policies; this conflation has escalated since 9/11 (Razack). The majority of people in these states expect certain images and behaviours from this group. Khan makes the same point:

Pluralist multicultural policies promoted by many First World countries such as Britain, Canada, and the United States have been a mixed blessing. In affording diverse communities much-needed respect, multicultural policies and practices allow members of communities to anchor their identities. This acceptance of difference is valid and crucial. Yet the multicultural paradigm assumes pre-given, static, and undifferentiated notions of communities that leave the myriad cultures within it unconnected to social and political history. (471)

In the case study at hand, the Muslim mothers are located in Sudbury, a northern Ontario city that has limited experiences with so-called diversity (outside of older waves of European immigrants). According to the census of 2006 (Canada, Statistics Canada), visible minorities represented 2.1 percent of Sudbury's population, compared to 22.8 percent in Ontario; immigrants who arrived between 2001 and 2006 represented 0.42 percent of Sudbury's population, compared to 4.9 percent for the province; 27.5 percent of Sudbury's respondents declared French as their mother tongue, compared to 4.9 percent province wide. Otherwise stated, Sudbury has remained largely a white community. It has to be remembered, however, that the Canadian obsession with shades of colour —what Bannerji calls the "political colour coding" (*Dark* 30) —has had certain complexities for immigrant groups. Italians, for instance, who arrived in Sudbury in large groups in the 1950s and 1960s were not considered "white," which suggests that the notion of colour and the dichotomy between "whites" and "people of color" exists only in the minds of people and serves to maintain the power ratios already in place. "Diversity" has been a term used to label newcomers perceived by the dominant group as non-white and to signify to them that they do not fully belong to the Canadian "nation." By promoting diversity, actors in position of power are actually excluding and keeping at the margins of society these "diverse" people. As Bannerji puts it, diversity "displaces these political and historical readings by presenting a complex interpretative code which encapsulates a few particularities of people's cultures, adding a touch of reality, and averts our gaze from power relations or differences which continue to organize the Canadian public life and culture" (*Dark* 51).

Because many Sudburians are rarely in close contact with Muslim mothers, they have developed perceptions of them mainly based on mass media portrayals: they are veiled; they are fanatics, brainwashed by radical Islamists; they are deprived of any agency and oppressed; they are poor; they are "women of colour"; they are inclined to violence, if not terrorism (Zine; Haque; Korteweg). The different moral panics that have surged in the last decade about Muslims women may be reinforced within a community that does not have daily contact with these women, contact that could allow a debunking of many myths. Of course, since 9/11, these misperceptions have been terribly reinforced (Jiwani; Sjoberg and Gentry). In a post 9/11 world, discourses about Muslims have been even more gendered, and gender stereotypes have been reinforced. In a community such as Sudbury—where only a small Muslim community lives, with very different practices and with almost no cohesion—this stereotyping is even worse in the experience of the Muslim mothers in question.

Another level of stigmatization applies to Muslim mothers. Not only do they suffer the stereotypes of Muslim women but, as mothers, they may be seen as responsible for the "terrorist" acts committed by their sons and daughters. (This stigma experienced by Muslim mothers comes from the populace [Gunaratnam] but is also strengthened by some subtle subtexts in "scientific" discourses focusing solely on psychological and/or sociological causes to explain terrorism). Yet the mothers whom I interviewed differ greatly from these stereotypes. Sabrina and Sarah do not veil; Khadija wears it rarely; Nadiyya, Noor, and Fatima[1] wear it daily. Sarah is white-skinned with blue eyes, so in the Canadian context, she is not automatically colour coded; appearance-wise, she can be perceived as a "true Canadian" by the majority (Bannerji, *Dark*). Some of them possess university degrees and are socially active; few are actually poor; and some perceive themselves definitely as actors of their own lives and in their communities. Two of them are single mothers and, thus, are not under the authority of any male at home. Most of them do not perceive themselves as oppressed.

Sarah, from France, does not define herself as Muslim but says that she has been educated in this religious culture, as her father was from North Africa (where she spent two years of her childhood), and her husband is from the same region. I decided to include her in this study because this family context partly informs her mothering practices. Although she does not claim a Muslim identity, her Arabic name makes people perceive her as such. Her fair skin and blue eyes include her in the Canadian "we," but as soon as she says her name, she falls in the "them" category. Sabrina defines herself as "Muslim by culture not by religion."[2] She went on to explain that "I am bi-cultural French and Muslim. It is hybrid, I take women's freedom, freedom of expression, women's rights movements from France; the importance of family and humility from Islam." She lived most of her life in Morocco and does not seem to reject its still pervasive French colonial culture. On the contrary, she values aspects of her colonial heritage as "positive." As she explained, "I have two cultures, I studied in a French lycée, I spoke French at home ... well always French with my dad, more often Arabic with my mum. There was no prayers, no Ramadan at home. My mum could go out without the authorization of my dad. It was very different in my ex-husband's family who was very traditional." Nadiyya, Noor, and Fatima practise Islam daily, and for the three of them, Islam represents their first identity. Khadija stated: "I am a believer, but I do not practise. I do not wear the veil, and it is rare for me to define myself as Muslim. I think it is not necessary to claim your religion everywhere." That type of statement could be interpreted in rather different ways: does the interviewee feel uncomfortable claiming her religious identity? Is not claiming it a strategy to better integrate or to "whiten" herself? Does this mean she is engaged in a secularizing process? If so, is it by choice or to "fit in"? In any case, it contradicts the wish of the Canadian state to have these people fit in an assigned mold. (There is, increasingly, an emphasis put on assimilation, even if the word is not pronounced and the vague term of "integration" is used). As multicultural policies exist to assign immigrants to specific places, they cannot pretend to belong to the Canadian "we," even if they wanted to. This attitude may also be explained by Sudbury itself, where Islam is largely unknown. Contrary to big cities such as Toronto and Ottawa, one rarely comes across women wearing a veil in Sudbury. Not wearing a veil may be a

172

strategy to fit in more easily, to not have to tolerate strange looks every minute.

ON BEING A FRANCOPHONE AND
AN IMMIGRANT MOTHER IN ONTARIO

Ontario is the province with the second largest Francophone population after Quebec, with about 600,000 French speakers. Canada is officially a bilingual state and therefore Francophones have constitutional rights at the federal level. The province of Ontario adopted the French Language Services Act in 1986 and, consequently, provides, often with difficulties, French services in designated areas. Francophones are a linguistic and cultural minority, but with special legal guarantees and services not enjoyed by other minorities. They do not fall under the "multicultural umbrella;" instead, they enjoy special historical and linguistic rights. It must also be noted that, historically, the Canadian state has tried to assimilate French speakers, who also had to live under discriminatory policies.

Sudbury occupies a very special location in the Ontarian Francophonie. Not only is it a city where a lot of French speakers are concentrated, but it is also where the Franco-Ontarian identity was defined in the 1970s. The very expression "Franco-Ontarian" turned into a political identity under the influence of a mainly cultural movement in Sudbury. This historic mini-social movement has had two consequences: firstly, Franco-Ontarian identity is deeply rooted in and associated with its culture, and, secondly, a distinction is now very well established in northern Ontario between what it is to be "Francophone" and to be "Franco-Ontarian." As I have explained elsewhere ("Le Contact"), until recently, there were tensions between the open-minded Franco-Ontarian identity (a Francophone only has to claim her Franco-Ontarian identity to be so) and the ethnic Franco-Ontarian identity (a Francophone has to be of Catholic, French settler, and peasant origin, and have been born and bred in Ontario). If the elites mostly seem to favour an open Franco-Ontarian identity, many "lay people" are still attached to an ethnic identity. Both Sarah and Khadija affirm that they view themselves as being part of the Franco-Ontarian community. Khadija stated that "It is my community of identification. It is within here I am integrated. We have to maintain it, because of its rich culture." Nadiyya, Noor, and Fatima said they are comfortable with being identified as Francophones; but Nadiyya and Noor do not feel comfortable with that identity. For them, French is just another language they were forced to learn. They see that language in an instrumental fashion but do not feel any attachment to it. They do not relate to any type of French culture. Again, this demonstrates the negative effects of "the discourse of diversity," which "wipes away its location in history, thus obscuring colonialism, capital and slavery" (Bannerji, *Dark* 51). These women are Francophones because of former colonial relations; they speak French because France colonized their birth countries and imposed French. After decolonization, many former colonies retained French as an official language (particularly for the education system). In some ways then, they are Francophone not by choice but because of a specific colonial past.

This problematic Francophone history is very important in order to understand the difficulties that Francophone Muslim immigrant mothers may encounter. As Francophones, they are treated as such by the Anglophone majority. Among the French-speaking community, they are partly admitted: they are "in" as Francophones, but they are different enough not to be fully included in the "we." Because of such exclusions, is it possible for a Muslim immigrant mother to be considered a Franco-Ontarian? Again, within some circles, the answer is in the affirmative. Within the community at large, the answer is in the negative. Not only are these mothers perceived as "others" because of their names, religious signs and/or skin color, but even as French speakers, they are "others" because of their accent.

Another problem commonly found among French-speaking immigrants in Sudbury is their inability to communicate in English. Although Sudbury is among the few Ontarian cities in which you can live mainly in French, it is impossible to fully enjoy all services and social life without speaking English. On one hand, this linguistic reality forces immigrants to integrate into the Francophone community, but, on the other, it also forces them to identify primarily with their linguistic identity before any of their other identities, which is problematic as this identity is inherited from a former colonial relationship. To the common question "Are you bilingual?," most of the mothers answered "yes"; they speak French and other native languages, but not necessarily French and English. As Tummala-Narra points out, "One specific area of separation that becomes salient for many immigrants is the loss of native language usage and the adaptation to a new language and style of emotional expression" (169). In this case, not only are the mothers expected to be the cultural carriers of native language(s) so that the connections with the mother country and the extended family overseas are not broken, but they are also expected to make sure that their children remain proficient in French and, more importantly, that they build a new proficiency in English, which is the dominant language of Canada. For practising Muslim mothers interviewed, proficiency in Arabic is also viewed as paramount, as it is the sacred language of the Qur'an. Mothers are expected to make sure their children master both official languages of Canada, Arabic, and other native family languages. The mothering work is multiplied just on that ground.

For instance, Sabrina does not speak English at all, and she recognizes that this has complicated her adjustment to life in Sudbury. One of her objectives is, therefore, to learn it. As a mother, she has made sure that her children learn English. When they were in the Moroccan school system, they learned French. And although Arabic was the compulsory second language, her children took English as a second language. (As Canadian citizens, they were able to exercise a special opt out option not open to most Moroccans). Consequently, her children understand some Arabic but are not as fluent as she is. It was a motherly choice bearing in mind the "socialization for acceptance" aspect of mothering or "the primary social groups with which a mother is identified, whether by force, kinship, or choice, demand that she raise her children in a manner acceptable for them" (Ruddick 17). But this demand often appears very challenging. Particularly, Ruddick emphasizes the issues of inauthenticity when the mother "repudiate[s] [her] own perceptions and values" because of the "fear of the gaze of others" (112). For Sabrina, it must have required a lot of courage and authenticity, for that matter, to make such a choice and to go against Moroccan society, her husband, and his family. Again, the concept of motherwork helps reveal how much more maternal work these Muslim mothers have to do and how much more maternal thinking is required when one is located in this multi-minority situation. For Sarah, the socialization of her child is not seen as problematic except on the linguistic issue. As Sarah explained it, "As I speak only a few words of Arabic, I push my husband to speak Arabic a bit to our daughter so that she can have the two languages." Sarah is also keen on saying that she defines herself increasingly as Franco-Ontarian but admits she has problems with pure-laine[3]: "I feel a bit strange; it is blurred. I feel I always need to justify myself. I am identified as an "other"; I always have to do more effort." She added that "I prefer to be part of the Franco-Ontarian minority, but when I am with newcomers, I feel more of an immigrant. It is upsetting. People always think I am the French—la Française—of the gang!"

To conclude this section, these three intertwined contexts of minoritization represent many "alienating positions" (Khan 488) within which mothers must circulate, create their own space, and find ways to survive and flourish. Their work of translation, in Bhabha's sense, is a triple task: "[b]y translation I first all mean a process by which, in order to objectify cultural meaning, there always has to be a process of alienation and of secondariness *in relation to itself*. In that sense there is no 'in itself' and 'for itself' within cultures because they are always subject to intrinsic forms of translation" (emphasis in original, 210). The situation of these mothers exemplifies the "third space" that Bhabha discusses and shows rather well the hybridization processes work. As Bhabha states, "This third space displaces the histories that constitute it, and sets up new structures of authority, new political initiatives, which are inadequately understood through received wisdom" (211). In other words, the women interviewed are constantly trying to negotiate their place and identities in the community; these processes are displacing, ambivalent, and alienating, and, above, they all require a lot of labour. What is striking is to see how these contexts shape their maternal thinking and Muslim mothering practices.

MOTHERHOOD, MOTHERING PRACTICES, AND
MATERNAL THINKING: SOME VOICES

On Becoming a Mother

Becoming a mother not in one's home country represents a series of challenges. Close relatives, especially female relatives, may not be there to accompany the mother on this journey; moreover, the medical practices may differ (Lacassagne, "Où sont"). As Tummala-Narra points out, "The process of becoming a mother in an adopted land presents specific challenges in identity formation of immigrant mothers" (167). From the interviews, it became clear that the process of becoming a mother was foundational for many choices the women made. For example, Khadija had a child in her home country. She moved to Canada and left him behind because she wanted first to "understand the education system, Sudbury culture, and learn English." Only after she had her second child a few years later, was the elder child brought to Canada. It is also interesting to note that this elder child has Muslim roots from both parents and also from life experiences within a Muslim North African community, whereas the youngest child has a less diverse exposure to what it might mean to be Muslim, mediated only through his mother's experiences. Sabrina's story is also relevant here as her migratory patterns follow her pregnancies. She was pregnant in Canada, but she went back home when her father became sick. A child was born prematurely, so she stayed for a while in her country of origin before returning to Canada. Upon her return, she became pregnant, but her husband did not want another child, whereas she wanted four, so she left again to Morocco, where her second child was born. She came back a third time to Canada, and she experienced problems with her husband as he "wanted both the Western woman and the traditional woman."

Most interviewees stated that it was hard to become mothers so far away from their relatives. Yet Nadiyya and Fatima pointed out that the presence of few immigrant mothers from the same community was very helpful. They also said that becoming a mother was for them a sacred duty; for them, there exists a primordial link between motherhood and Islam. Being a good woman largely means being a good wife and a good mother. They both expressed that if a woman does not have children, she is neither a good wife nor a good woman. In Sarah's case, she remembers having a wonderful experience with her midwife; she had the help and support she wanted within the health system. But she recognized that since she became a mother, she has had less time to be involved in social and cultural activities and does less volunteer work. Her social activities are now linked to children's organizations. Noor preferred to have her baby at home in "a more traditional fashion."

Some of the interviewees' statements are also striking in the context of the Western "mothering discourse," which puts forward the idea that a mother is "the sole caregiver of children" and has to "sacrifice her own needs for those of a child," especially her career (Chaze 61). This discourse works as a pervasive ideology, and "[i]n many societies, the ideology of motherhood is oppressive to women. It defines maternal work as a consuming identity requiring sacrifices of health, pleasure, and ambitions unnecessary for the well-being of children" (Ruddick 29). This discourse has been strongly criticized by many scholars for being patriarchal and unachievable. Yet some of the interviewees seem to adhere to such a discourse, and this position may not be foreign to their views of Islam. The mothering duties of protecting, nurturing and socializing are Islamic duties for these Muslim women. But two difficulties may emerge. Firstly, socialization may be required in two different directions: socialization to the Islamic teachings (a shared duty with the males of the family) and socialization to the host society. Secondly, these mothers, as immigrants, may not enjoy the family support that they might have had in their country of origin, where other parents, male and female, also assume these duties (Chaze). Thus, it is not so much an adhesion to the hegemonic mothering discourse, but it is more of a trap. They refuse the model of the wonder woman and wonder mother. They do not pursue a career; they strictly conceive their lives around being a good Muslim mother. They ensure that their children are raised as good Muslims; they learn to respect the teachings, learn and say their daily prayers, respect the different bans, and wear appropriate clothes. But it does require extra maternal work and thinking because as long as they live in Canada, a minimal balance has to be found between this socialization and the social requirements of the host society.

Two of the interviewees actually stated that when the children are teenagers, they will go back to their country of origin—a point I will come back to later. Only Noor, during the interview, seemed to be ambivalent: at the same time as she defended what is usually termed "a traditional discourse," she also seemed interested in thinking and behaving as a "Western mother." In fact, she would like to go to university to get an education, but her husband thinks she does not need to and should stay home. Noor also made it clear that she wanted to have children, but she thinks motherhood has now prevented her from realizing her university dream. "I feel I trapped myself," she said. She talked about feeling guilty about even thinking these thoughts. Yet Noor's feelings are not related to her being Muslim; these feelings are shared by many immigrant mothers as well as by privileged Western-born mothers who experience being a mother and having a career as heavy burdens. Access to the labour market and a well-paid job have long been considered by scholars as more difficult for migrant mothers, even if the contemporary global economic structure may be changing that reality (Glass, Petrzelka and Mannon).

Mothering Practices

I decided to follow Ruddick's categorization of motherwork because her conceptual apparatus allows the unfolding of the complexities related to mothering and, at the same time, offers a useful and workable categorization of maternal work. It includes (1) developing preservative love that encompasses the mother's extreme "commitment to protect" her child but also many contradictory feelings stemming from that commitment—"[w]hat we are pleased to call "mother-love" is intermixed with hate, sorrow, impatience, resentment, and despair" (Ruddick 68-69); (2) fostering growth that "nurture[s] a child's developing spirit" (Ruddick 82) with all the complexities this involves; and (3) encouraging socialization for acceptance and the social training a child needs to survive and to be happy in the world that she lives in. The two main issues of this maternal work are about deciding what social values to transmit and finding the place or legitimacy of the mother to perform that work "rather than teachers, priests, Fathers" (Ruddick 103). Indeed, it was striking to see that the narratives given by the interviewees were related to these mothering practices. For four mothers, preservative love constituted an important part of their personal stories, as they migrated to escape social conditions that directly challenged their children's survival. They also pointed out the importance of being able to live in Canada, "a country with a good health system," which they viewed in a positive light because this system was expected to increase the chances of their children's physical survival. Two of them actually acknowledged a motivational perspective behind their migration decision that was designed to allow these children to flourish physically in their newly adopted communities. Nadiyya, Fatima, and Noor offered a clear discourse on preservative love as unconditional love, framed as a duty for a "good Muslim mother." Sabrina also explained that she returned to Canada to protect her daughter: "In 2005, I decided to return to Canada. What motivated me was the rise of Islamism. The capital was being transformed. I was verbally abused several times—'Whore, cover your face'—I realized that for my own sake and even more for my daughter, it was better to go back to Canada." Sabrina's country had experienced a wave of liberalization with the arrival of a younger king; this domestic development coupled with an international rise of Islamic fundamentalism made that type of rarely heard statement increasingly common.

In terms of fostering growth and the nurturing of the "child's developing spirit" (Ruddick 82), the effects of the various practices of Islam were very apparent. For Sarah, whose husband practises Islam, it is complicated. For instance she said, "Sometimes my husband tries to talk to me about that. He does not want our daughter to eat pork, so we don't. But if I am alone with my daughter, at home or outside, I give her pork!" As for Sabrina who does not practise Islam said that she consciously raises her daughter and son as "feminists." She mentioned that they have close relations and talk about sexuality. In contrast, as briefly mentioned above, two of the practising Muslim interviewees stated that they plan to go back to their home countries before the children become teenagers because they do not think that

Canadian society reflects the values that they want to transmit. One of them talked about how Canadian society was too "promiscuous." They also mentioned the importance of maintaining the Arabic language and of Islamic teachings in the education for their children. They do not think Canada can provide either of those things adequately.

Ruddick defines socialization for acceptance as "training a child to be the kind of person whom others accept and whom the mothers themselves can actively appreciate" (104). In terms of religious socialization—for Sarah, Sabrina, and Khadija—if Islam is somehow to be present in their children's life, they conceive it as only within the private sphere. Indeed, multiculturalism has reinforced patriarchy and has empowered male so-called representatives of different religions to act as they wish in the public sphere (Bannerji, *Dark* 48). If one is perceived as belonging to the constructed category "Muslim," one has to behave as such. Multiculturalism homogenizes religious (as well as ethnic and racialized) groups, thus emptying the term "diversity" of any meaning. According to Bannerji, multiculturalism was an apparatus that rearranged questions of social justice, of unemployment and racism, into issues of cultural diversity and that focused on symbols of religion, and, thus, immigrants were ethnicized and culturalized (*Dark*).

The socialization of their children is aligned with an assimilationist stance on religion. Sabrina's ex-husband registered the children in a Catholic school. She thinks that in certain respects the school is too strict. She recalled that "One day my daughter wore shorts at school and the principal phoned home and asked to speak with their dad. I was appalled and angry. I wanted to go and talk with the principal, but my daughter asked me to leave it there. It is amazing when I think back at it. We immigrated because we thought we would have the freedom to wear anything we wanted!" This powerful statement highlights the extent to which relations to religion influence the mothers' constructed view of what ought to be socialization for acceptance.

This "socialization for acceptance" aspect of mothering is also reflected in the navigation of the different social institutions of the host society that mothers constantly undertake. As O'Reilly and

Ruddick remind us: "We should see certain institutions as inseparable from the experiences—or more precisely the practices—of
mothering. Schools, clinics, welfare offices, dentists, public librar-
ies—these are some of the institutions of motherhood on which
mothers depend" (20). But in Sudbury, this navigation happens in
a social context involving the triple minoritization of these Muslim mothers. The three practising Muslim mothers pick up their
children daily at their schools. My own children attend the same
school and have interacted with them on a number of occasions.
However, I have noticed that these mothers rarely interact with any
other mothers or school personnel. Their isolation was reinforced
for me when they told me that they had never gone to any cultural
events of the Franco-Ontarian community, except the African
Cabaret organized by the *Contact Interculturel Francophone de
Sudbury* (CIFS), the French service provider for immigrants. But as
Nadiyya pointed out: "It was just for the kids because they asked
for it; I do not like this organization; we do not need them." She
sounded very suspicious of any type of social agency, especially
immigrant service providers. This aversion may be due to a general
suspicion about social organizations because of possible experiences in their home countries or it may be a rejection of being
categorized as "immigrant," a way to show that she can manage
her family's life without any help. For health issues, they prefer
to go to Toronto to see doctors from their ethnic community, so
they have no experience with the health system in Sudbury. Sarah
is the one mother that seems to enjoy this navigation and did not
underline having problems in "surviv[ing] in institutions, [and in]
negotiat[ing] a place within them" (O'Reilly and Ruddick 20). It is
significant that she is from France and appears white. As already
mentioned, the Canadian nation and its relation to immigrants
is highly colour coded; if one is not perceived as "white," one
cannot be fully part of the Canadian "we." Moreover, coming
from France, she possesses an accent (when speaking French) that
automatically makes Francophone locals respectful, as it is seen as
the "best" and the "pure" accent. To conclude this section, maternal practices are both shaped by and shape maternal thinking.
As Bonifacio explains, "maternal thinking ... is a crucial element
in the migration experience of many migrant women" (162). The

voices heard in this chapter highlight that the triple minoritization context makes maternal thinking even more complex.

CONCLUSION: COULD MOTHERING EXPERIENCES FACILITATE INTEGRATION?

In a chapter reflecting on Ruddick's work, Jean Keller writes, "Yet as a mother, she knew that she and other mothers faced even greater marginalization as mothers than as women" (173). This comment by Keller pushed me to write this chapter. It contradicted my own experience and my preconceived ideas about motherhood being a positive factor in facilitating integration into an established society. I could see why motherhood could be a factor in marginalization, but I felt that for an immigrant mother, it could also have the opposite integrating effect. Originally, I had intended in this research to organize a focus group with Muslim immigrant mothers and "established" Franco-Ontarian mothers to discuss the idea of an "intercultural parent group" at school. Unfortunately, I could not organize it, but I later talked about this idea with the interviewees, and they all agreed that it would be a great idea. The executive director of CIFS also believes that implementing this idea could be useful as it might "help some women to get out of their isolation" (Tummala-Narra). I believe that a process that focuses on the self-awareness and agency of these Muslim mothers could help them avoid the traps of triple minoritization, which includes feelings of isolation, racialization from the state and, perhaps, social institutions, and potential discrimination. As Maria Josepha Yax-Fraser underscores "[t]he work women do as mothers, their changing values, intentions and practices relating to rearing and socializing children, has largely gone unnoticed by policy makers and academics when gauging the success and failure of newcomer' integration" (252). It is my sincere hope that this small exploratory research has planted the seeds of resistance, consciousness, and mobilization among Sudburian mothers and that the difficult navigations, redefinitions of maternal work and thinking undertaken by these immigrant Muslim mothers will be recognized as an effort to integrate into Canadian society at large.

NOTES

[1]All first names were changed to respect the anonymity of the participants.
[2]All interview excerpts were translated from French to English by the author.
[3]A French expression mainly used by Quebeckers but also other Canadian French-speakers who define their identity in ethnic terms—they are the descendants of the French settlers. This identity excludes Francophone immigrants from the "we."

WORKS CITED

Bannerji, Himani, ed. *The Dark Side of the Nation*. Toronto: Canadian Scholars' Press, 2000. Print.

Bannerji, Himani. *Returning the Gaze*. Toronto: Sister Vision Press, 1993. Print.

Bhabha, Homi. "The Third Space." *Identity: Community, Culture, Difference*. Ed. Jonathan Rutherford. London: Lawrence and Wishart, 1990. 26-33. Print.

Bonifacio, Glenda, and Lynna Anne Tibe. "Migration and Maternalism: (Re)Configuring Ruddick's Maternal Thinking." *Maternal Thinking. Philosophy, Politics, Practice*. Ed. Andrea O'Reilly. Bradford, Ontario: Demeter Press, 2009. 160-172. Print.

Chaze, Ferzana. "Child Welfare Intervention in Visible Minority Immigrant Families." *Journal of the Association for Research on Mothering* 11.2 (2009): 56-65. Print.

Glass, Christy, Peggy Petrzelka, and Susan Mannon. "Mothers, Migrants and Markets." *Journal of the Motherhood Initiative for Research and Community Involvement* 2.2 (2011): 129-145. Print.

Gunaratnam, Yasmin. "Roadworks: British Bangladeshi Mothers, Temporality and Intimate Citizenship in East London." *European Journal of Women's Studies* 20.3 (2013): 249-263. Print.

Haque, Eve. "Homegrown, Muslim and Other: Tolerance, Secularism and the Limits of Multiculturalism." *Social Identities* 16.1 (2010): 79-101. Print.

Jiwani, Yasmin. *Discourses of Denial: Mediations of Race, Gender, and Violence*. Vancouver: University of British Columbia Press, 2006. Print.

Keller, Jean. "Rethinking Ruddick's Birthgiver/Adoptive Mother Distinction." *Maternal Thinking. Philosophy, Politics, Practice*. Ed. Andrea O'Reilly. Toronto: Demeter P, 2009. 173-187. Print.

Khan, Shahnaz. "Muslim Women: Negotiations in the Third Space." *Signs* 23.2 (1998): 463-494.

Korteweg, Anna. "The Sharia Debate in Ontario. Gender, Islam, and Representations of Muslim Women's Agency." *Gender & Society* 22.4 (2008): 434-454. Print.

Lacassagne, Aurélie. "Le Contact Interculturel Francophone de Sudbury (CIFS): Francophones avant tout! Exemple d'un inter-culturalisme réussi." *Reflets* 16.2 (2010): 202-213. Print.

Lacassagne, Aurélie. "Où sont les sages-femmes? Le choc culturel d'une femme immigrés en Ontario face aux pratiques de santé concernant la maternité." *Mothering Canada: Interdisciplinary Voices / La maternité au Canada : voix interdisciplinaires*. Ed. Shawna Geissler et al. Bradford: Demeter Press, 2010. 33-41. Print.

O'Reilly, Andrea and Sara Ruddick. "A Conversation About Maternal Thinking." *Maternal Thinking. Philosophy, Politics, Practice*. Ed. Andrea O'Reilly. Toronto: Demeter Press, 2009. 14-38. Print.

Razack, Sherene. *Casting Out. The Eviction of Muslims from Western Law & Politics*. Toronto: University of Toronto Press, 2008. Print.

Ruddick, Sara. *Maternal Thinking. Towards a Politics of Peace*. Boston: Beacon Press, 1989. Print.

Sjoberg, Laura and Caron Gentry, eds. *Mothers, Monsters, Whores*. London: Zed Books, 2007. Print.

Thobani, Sunera. *Exalted Subjects*. Toronto: University of Toronto Press, 2007. Print.

Tummala-Narra, Pratyusha. "Mothering in a Foreign Land." *The American Journal of Psychoanalysis* 64.2 (2004): 167-82. Print.

Canada. Statistics Canada. "Greater Sudbury." *Community Profiles*. Government of Canada, 2006. Web. 28 Sept. 2011.

Yax-Fraser, Maria Josepha. "We Compromise on a Daily Basis. The Choices and Processes of Cross-Cultural Mothering." *Jour-*

nal of the Motherhood Initiative for Research and Community Involvement 2.2 (2011): 251-264. Print.

Zine, Jasmin. "Unveiled Sentiments: Gendered Islamophobia and Experience of Veiling among Mulsim Girls in a Canadian Islamic School." *Equity & Experience in Education* 39 (2006): 239-252. Print.

8.

Managing the Family, Combatting Violence

Faith as Resource and Promise of the Good Life in Case Studies of Migrant Muslim Mothers in Germany

ULRIKE LINGEN-ALI

I N GERMAN PUBLIC DISCOURSES, Muslim parenting practices are nearly exclusively associated with perceptions of migrant Turkish and Arab communities. The corresponding stereotypes and ascriptions include male patriarchal behaviour, restrictive rules for girls and women, forced marriage, and honour killings. The role of Muslim mothers within these patterns is either excluded, reduced to passiveness and weakness, or related to invisible, though powerful, manipulation and control. However, the (self-)definitions and perceptions by the people concerned are mostly disregarded (Kelek; Sarrazin).

"Muslim mothering" as a category is difficult to define. With respect to Stuart Hall's notions of the fluidity, fragmentation, and multiplicity of cultures and identities, it should be questioned if there is a theoretical and practical concept at all that might be named "Muslim mothering." But there is good reason to make use of the term, both in reaction to the before mentioned presumptions and because of the excluded self-perceptions of those who identify themselves as Muslim mothers. Within this chapter, I employ an anti-essentialist approach, refer to those mothers who identify themselves as Muslim women regardless how far their belief has influence on their mothering practices.

Although Muslim mothering as a topic has become current, there is a lack of literature within the German context. Existing literature and studies focus on migrant mothers (Kaya; BMFSFJ, "Mütter mit Migrationshintergrund) or migrant families (BMFS-FJ, "Familien mit Migrationshintergrund"; Fischer and Springer;

187

Geisen, Studer and Yildiz). Although the discourse on family and Islam is basically reduced to religious publications and websites, there is a huge amount of publications on "Women in Islam" (Lingen-Ali, "Agency," 56).

At this point, clarification of the term "migration background" is indispensable. In 2014, approximately 16.4 million people in Germany had a migrant background. This part of the population includes all people who have immigrated into the territory of today's Federal Republic of Germany after 1949, all foreigners born in Germany, and all people who have at least one parent who immigrated into the country or was born as a foreigner in Germany. Thus, also German nationals born in Germany may have a migration background. Based on results of the 2014 micro-census, the population group with migration background represented 20.3 percent of the total population.

As one of the main institutions, the Federal Office for Migration and Refugees (BAMF), provides information, publications, figures and statistics on migration, integration, and asylum in Germany. Furthermore, it examines the constitutional rights of refugees against persecution and conducts all asylum procedures in Germany; it issues—if protection is considered unnecessary—the deportation warning and/or order. The BAMF is responsible for developing and implementing the national integration program, conducting applied and policy-related migration research, and promoting voluntary return. Migration policy in Germany focuses on controlling migration, which is to be achieved by different tasks: restriction of illegal immigration; developing responsible and balanced perspectives for legal immigration; creating integration as condition and restriction for further migration in order to contribute to a prosperous community; and ensuring security for the people in Germany and Europe (Federal Office for Migration and Refugees; BMI).

Migrant one-parent families form—in correspondence with the share of migrants in the overall population in Germany—more than 20 percent of the total number of one-parent families. Based on interviews with migrant single or lone mothers in Germany, conducted within the framework of a research project on migrant one-parent families in Germany,[1] I will explore the self-perceptions of mothers who are ascribed as Muslim or identify themselves as such. The interviews reveal a great variety of issues, among them vocational and housing situations, experiences of violence, images of proper education, perceptions by family members and the broader Muslim and/or migrant community, questions of responsibility regarding caring and parenting practices, and the interaction and relationship between the mother and her children.

In this paper, I focus on two Muslim mothers, Hülya and Sahar.[2] How do they evaluate their modes of mothering? How do they mark themselves as Muslim and do they link these categories with each other? And how significant is their religion in relation to family concepts? Since experiences of violence—various shapes and intensities—play a major role within the interviewees' narrations, I will explore how the women cope and which strategies they employ to combat violence.

HÜLYA: "I PRAYED. I WAS PATIENT. I DON'T NEED A PSYCHOTHERAPIST."

Hülya is thirty-five years old; she is of Turkish origin but was born in Germany and has three children, the older ones—who are teenagers—with her first husband and a toddler with her second husband. Both husbands are Turkish nationals. She got divorced from her first husband after more than ten years. She married again in Turkey, and when her second husband came to Germany, he turned out to be despotic, controlling and restrictive towards Hülya and her children. He used to control the family members and their lives: the food in the kitchen, the amount that was eaten, and the clothes that were bought as well as relationships with friends and family.

When Hülya was pregnant with her third child, the second husband, and father of the unborn, sexually abused her teenage daughter Dana, his stepdaughter. Dana was afraid to tell her mother what had happened to her several times, mostly when her mother was in hospital for a longer term because of a critical pregnancy. After being violently attacked and threatened by her stepfather, Dana escaped from home, and the *Jugendamt*—the office for children, youth and family affairs—got involved. In the course of these events, Hülya separated from her husband, and after he was expelled from the house, Dana shared with her mother what she had gone through.

Nonetheless, Hülya believes she is responsible for what happened to her and her children, and she feels guilt about her assumed inability to give them a relaxed and safe life. The children, however, have forgiven her and give her words of comfort. Hülya links her reflections about her relationship with her children with her own experiences of sexual violence by her father when she was a young girl. Her mother did not protect her, and she expresses the hardness and complexity of these incidents.

Hülya now lives together with her three children and her mother, and she says: "However the child behaves, a mother never renounces her child." She is proud of her children, their personal developments and their success at school, just as she is proud of herself and her own achievements and decisions. Hülya summarizes: "I'm so proud. Firstly, I am proud of myself, how I brought up my children and that I chose the right way with the divorce. I have done something right, and I do not regret, I am proud that I have these children."

In order to protect her children, she has promised them that she will never marry again. For her, parenting without a partner has turned out to be the better option and a real alternative to a life of continuous violence and threats. Accordingly, she defines the mother's role as more relevant and comprehensive: "The father's role is quite different, and mothering is something else. The mother cares about everything of the children, she is always there, but the father is not like a mother. That's why I've said, it's better this way for my children than growing up in a family with only disputes and arguments. And I didn't regret it."

Hülya decidedly defines herself as Muslim woman and continuously combines her believe with religion-associated values, such as destiny, fate, devotion, modesty, patience, gratitude, and bearing. At the same time, she presents her religious framework as allowing her to voice clear concerns and demands. When talking about the omnipotence of God, in the meantime she presents reflections on herself: "He can tell me, for example, right now, 'I wish for her a good life.' And then I'll get a good life. Or: 'Right now, I want her to suffer, later I want her to be rewarded for her patience, she waited, she never complained about life, she always believed in me, and now I reward her.'" These reflections refer to a strong conviction that she, indeed, deserves to be rewarded and that she has good reason to expect rich compensation. Her expectations are closely linked with her wishes and desires. She says, "Someday my life will be as I have wished for. Just peace for my life. I don't wish for a luxurious life. I wish a life with my family, with my children, happy. Since childhood I am patient to be happy, I have this desire to be happy." She continues and speaks about her longing for a companion: "The one thing that I'm missing, I'm thirty-five, I've no one with me, who shares my life. This is what I really miss. I believe in Allah. I am Muslim."

Although Hülya does not mention any doubts in God's almightiness and his ability to direct her fortunes, she also stresses people's ability and, even more so, duty to make use of their brainpower: "Some things, okay, he gives to you, but he also gave you a brain to think. ... I mean, the dear God shows you something, he gives you something. But you also have to think about the right and wrong in your life. You can decide by yourself which way you want to go. I chose the way that I thought to be right, but it was wrong." This perspective, which corresponds to Islamic theology, seems to guide her and to help her put her life in a comprehensible order. On a practical level, for example, she independently took the decision not to follow certain Islamic rules, although she regrets this decision from a religious perspective: "I'm not one who is veiled. Unfortunately, I do not pray. I say, unfortunately. I would like to." Though partly excluding religious doings from her daily life, she also calls on religious statements to explain rather complex circumstances: "I was recommended to do therapy, to get psychological counselling. I won't do that. Until now, I didn't need a psychotherapist. I never had the need to ask for help. I always got myself going, I always said, Allah was with me. I prayed. I was patient. I knew that he is always with me, and this faith helped me to go on. Thank God. I don't need a psychotherapist."

Does Hülya link her understandings of mothering and education principles with her approach to religion? She does not explicitly refer to this question, but her narration sheds light on stereotypical perceptions of the "Muslim mother." Hülya's frequently expressed wish to protect her children is reflected in her continuous fear of leaving her daughter alone with her friends' families, and overnight stays are not accepted by Hülya, although she assumes that she should allow her daughter more freedom, as she says. Hülya's daughter Dana shared in the interview, commenting on her mother's narration from time to time and adding her own remarks.

> Dana: *There are limits for children at every place. Everything is fine, as long as you know how to deal with your children. But if you say: "I leave my child alone, I don't want to discuss this with her, do what you want," then this is not a real family life.*
> Hülya: *It is good that you are able to think this way.*
> Dana: *I always think this way.*
> Hülya: *A couple of months ago it was very hard with her. She could never understand me. As I said before, now she understands me, thank God, and what I mean with this [prohibition of] staying overnight with friends and why I am afraid. And that there need to be limits, otherwise it doesn't work. There is no family life without limits.*
> Dana: *Yes, if there are no limits you feel that people don't care about one another.*
> Hülya: *But you are very important for me. I need to protect you.*

It is noteworthy how mother and daughter, with their various experiences of violence and vulnerability, are able to speak with each other and articulate their feelings and assessments. Their interaction can be interpreted with reference to Martha Nussbaum's approach to identify the crucial elements of a "good human life". Nussbaum's "list of capabilities" – real opportunities based on personal and social circumstances – includes the capability to form a conception of the good and to engage in critical reflection about the planning of one's life ("practical reason") and the capability to live with and toward others, to recognize and show concern for other humans, to engage in various forms of social interaction and to be able to imagine the situation of another ("affiliation").

The short dialogue between the two is also important concerning its—not explicitly announced but indirectly stressed—links with Hülya's migration context: Hülya is of Turkish origin, and her religion, performed or not, is Islam. As mentioned earlier, the public perception of Turkish and/or Islamic families in Germany is (still) influenced by Orientalist stereotypes of a "backward and patriarchal system of family honour" (Sarrazin). The fact that Dana is not allowed to stay overnight with her friends might be explained within this context as "typical" Islamic means to "protect her chastity."

But Hülya's statements refer to a rather different interpretation: she does not even mention "Turkish," "Islamic," or migrations links and does not care about community rules or dominant social perceptions of her as a "Turkish" or "Muslim" mother. Instead, her order to refrain from overnight stays is only connected with her and her daughter's experiences of sexual violence, and, thus, Hülya is basically seeking protection for her daughter. In this respect, the indirect impact of the migration context—the ascription of the prohibition of overnight stays as "Muslim" or "Turkish" attribute—is imposed from outside (Lingen-Ali, "Islam").

SAHAR: "I DON'T ASK ANYONE. I DON'T EVEN ASK MY MAN."

Whereas Hülya tries to integrate her concepts of motherhood and being Muslim—stressing at times the one, at times the other concept—Sahar seems to locate both concepts within discourses of "othering."[3] She is thirty-seven years old, of Arab origin, and lives in a German city, with her extended family living in the same neighbourhood. She has two children, a boy with her former and second husband[4] and a daughter with her companion— whom she meets from time to time but decidedly does not want to live with. Her ex-husband has never cared about her and their son; for Sahar, however, her children are her priority, and her partner has to accept that fact. In her description, she gives to her children everything she did not get when she was young: time, attention, interest. "I talk a lot with them," she says, "I am a friend for my children. They tell me everything. My son tells me everything. I can rarely see that, especially with boys."

The son's father appears to be the opposite of Sahar: he does not show any interest in his child and does not care about developing an affectionate relationship. Instead, he demands that his son take the initiative to call him on the telephone, which is strictly rejected by Sahar:

> *How can I say to a child, "call your dad," whom he never or rarely saw and who doesn't show any interest. My son is very disappointed by him because he always says, "yes, I will come." Last summer, he wanted to come; he didn't. Christmas, he didn't come. This Easter, he didn't come, and this summer neither. Now he promised New Year's Eve. And that's soon.*

Sahar understands her son's disappointment, and it might be read that her son's feelings strongly correspond with her own sentiments: "My son doesn't want to get to know his father, who left him several years ago. If you have an interest in your son, then show it."

The father's role was accepted by her friend and companion, who "changed his diapers, fed him, took care of him, was a father for him." These concrete fathering practices led Sahar to question the patriarchal relevance and clarity of patrilineal ancestry: "I mean, nobody asks who the biological father is, only what you give to the child, and not who has born it." However, Sahar still perceives herself as the only parenting part: "I am both for them, mother and father. Look, for the time that they are awake, I must read for them, then I have to make crafts with them, I do so much with them, I don't let them alone. But half past eight, nine o'clock it's finish. There are four hours left for me until midnight, and then I want to have a rest."

Although Sahar defines herself as a Muslim woman, she does not stop mentioning her experiences with Christian life, which have had a great impact on her. This imbalance seems to be problematic for her on a theological level. She says:

> *I was a couple of times in a mosque, but I don't understand it. I sit there like a stupid person, and when he's reading*

Quran, I don't understand. It doesn't make sense to me,
you know. I understand the words but not the sense, be-
cause no one really explained to me Islam. I always taught
myself, I dealt much more with the Bible and Christianity,
to be honest.

But against these obstacles, Sahar decided to learn intensively about Islam in order to provide her children sustainable knowledge—a proceeding that is not only led by altruistic and parental motives: "I learn now [about Islam] and teach it to my children, then at least my children can say, 'Mom taught us what she knows.'" Her desire to teach her children is basically legitimized by parental motives as an advantage for her children, although she furthermore expects some reputation from them.

Another proceeding connected with religious motives is explicitly linked with Sahar's well-being and refers to her marriage arrangement. Sahar explains:

I have married again, an Iraqi, but only the Islamic way, not
civil marriage. You never know, really. We live separately
but we have contact with each other. He comes, sees his
daughter, I go to him, like that. He is not from my kin,
but I don't need to marry an Arab to be happy. The mar-
riage is Islamic. Why, I always think, I'm just a woman.
Sometimes you need, ehm, sex. Before doing that with a
stranger, well, I don't like something like that. Although
we are separated, but at least I go to someone who I know
and who is close to me. In our way it's halal, not a sin.
And then I have also my peace. He knows that. [He says,]
"Ah, you only come because you want something." [I say,]
"Yes, I'm a woman." At least, I admit it. I don't lie. But
it's good like that, before going to strange people, I mean,
I like it with him, so, why not.

With this arrangement, based on Islamic legitimation, Sahar finds a way to have a sexual relation within a certain—religion-based legal—framework. It enables her to experience safeness and stability, with, at the same time, the greatest possible independence.

Although Sahar's decision obviously provides her with advantages, she also mentions resulting conflicts. Her decision to marry "the Iraqi," as she continuously calls him during the interview, was accompanied by heavy objections by her family. She was partially estranged from her family because he belongs to a differing Islamic sect. "Because we are Sunni, and he is Shiite, and they have this conflict. That was hell on earth, none of them talked to me for three years."

Another difficulty for her relates to the different understandings of religion between her and her partner. Whereas Sahar likes to celebrate Christmas as a traditional, cultural feast, her partner accuses her of being more Christian than Muslim—an issue that occupies Sahar's thoughts.

> He always says, "Are you Christian or Muslim?" I say, "Why do you ask, I am Muslim." He says, "No, a Muslim doesn't have a Christmas tree." And I say, only to sedate him, "That's only decoration." I have celebrated Christmas for so many years. I don't know it otherwise.

Sahar admits that she understands his concerns, but she acquiesces to his claims only within the course of their being together. As soon as she is on her own, she reacts, behaves, and decides according to her own mind. However, there seem to be unsolved issues between both, which leaves Sahar feeling dissatisfied: "I would like to go swimming. Before, my hobby was swimming. But for a couple of years I have worn the headscarf, because of love for my man. Stupidity, really." It is remarkable that she not only can identify and name the deficiencies of her relationship but can also express them clearly vis-à-vis the interview. Discussing undesirable arrangements and conditions while, at the same time, striving for independence and autonomy—hence the integration of contradictions into the biographic narration—refers to a high degree of self-reflexivity.

However, Sahar employs binaries and clear divides in order to develop her own approach. Her parenting practices are not like "theirs," meaning the Arab community, and she clearly divides between "German" and "Arab" behaviour: "I deal with them [her children] like the Germans do: house arrest, forbidding Play Station, this goes down well, because they understand 'Oh, mama forbids the best thing, oh, that cannot be.'" The son has to tidy his room, carry the garbage downstairs, clean the living room, all according to a weekly cleaning plan. She says: "With us, with us Arabs, it is not like that, that a boy has to tidy his room. 'This is mummy's and sister's job.' But not with me." The binary division between "them" and "me" is also applied to the children and other members of the extended family: "When I see how they [the boys of the family] talk with their mothers, I swear, they do nothing. 'You are a woman. Boys don't do things like that.' They sit there, 'Bring me this, bring me that!'" Her son once tried to copy this attitude: "'Mom, bring me water!' And with such a voice! So I went to him: 'Where are your feet? Where are your hands? So get up and get your water yourself. If you are ill and you can't get up I will be happy to serve you. But not like that.' And then he noticed: 'Oh, I can't deal with her like that.'"

Sahar presents her interpretation of her experiences and refers again to the before mentioned binary between Arab and German approaches, but she goes further and adds another aspect, which is linked to her lone parenting status:

> When he goes to his father he can do as a foreigner. There he can do what he wants. But not with me. I am not a bad mother; the child has everything. I offer him everything, but with limits. This is better for his schooling, for his future. Because as a foreigner's child, it is always hard in Germany, everywhere. Because many foreigners, indeed, behave badly, but all are lumped together, and it is not like that.

Sahar's context and experience provide her with the option to dissociate herself from her community of origin within the frameworks of education, childcare and family communication. At the same time, she identifies herself as part of this community, as a foreigner in Germany. Her statements can be interpreted as a request towards the German majority to be perceived by a perspective of diversity and intersectionality, and not merely as a foreigner.

Despite several obstacles, adversities, and experiences of violence, Sahar's evaluation of her life is rather positive: "I am very satisfied with my children, I have no problems, thank God. Now, I have everything what I wish for, although I had to cope with a lot of things to get that, but I have two healthy kids. I have my own life. I live the way I want, obey no one. These discoveries are late, but you learn by your experiences."

She stresses her independence and puts it in a certain context:

I don't ask anyone, only superficially, to show some interest. But everything concerning my life I decide on my own, I don't ask anyone. I don't even ask my man. Because, as long as he is away, he also does everything without asking me. I have to decide everything on my own, and it's only me who decides. And this is why we argue a lot, because especially with the Muslims it is like that, they want the woman to ask the man. And I can't do that anymore, because I've learnt it like that. Really, it's not on purpose. My husband also says, "You are a great woman, but you always decide on your own." Life brought me to this, automatically, that I always decide on my own. I ask and answer myself, and if I consider something as right, I'll do it like this.

Thus, Sahar not only challenges religious and gender concepts but also integrates her individual experiences that have formed her character into her approaches towards these concepts. At the same time, she does not present herself as an object of her own biography but as an active, self-confident subject.

MIGRANT MOTHERING AND EXPERIENCES OF VIOLENCE

Sahar and Hülya are different people with different backgrounds and biographies; they do not know each other and will probably never meet. But they share a similar parental situation as single mothers and identify themselves as Muslim women. Moreover, they both have experienced various forms of violence and have searched for strategies to combat and resist. At least partly, they present themselves as successful with regard to developing a better life for themselves and their children, including the end of domestic violence. In this matter, their faith seems to be one of the supporting strategies to bear these violent experiences. Without negating the ambivalences, it can be said that their belief provides a sustainable resource, which is not limited to the mothers but also has deep effects on the children and their education.

It is important to mention that in the cases of Hülya and Sahar, Islam is not enforced or imposed by their husbands. On the contrary, both seem to have an intrinsic motivation to shape their belief. Both women do not question their religion and never consider Islam as part of their problems. Their narrations do not match with public discourses stressing the before mentioned "violent aspects of Islam" (Ali). Even more so, experiences of violence are never linked with religious motives; their narrations, thus, differ from the common perception of the German public, which recurrently connect migration and violence with religion, precisely Islam.

This presumption of an entanglement or even mutual dependences among migration, Islam and violence—and here a gender dimension needs to be integrated—should be questioned: recent studies indicate that gender-based violence is still an unresolved issue, and not at all limited to migrant communities (Baobaid and Hamed; European Union Agency for Fundamental Rights; Hagemann-White; BMFFSJ, "Zwangsverheiratung"). As a result, there is an urgent need for effective prevention programs in Germany.[5] The public adherence of stereotypical and common images of Muslim women and the denial of unheard voices like those of Hülya and Sahar might be why these prevention programs fail: prevention concepts should not present Islam as cause of violence but as a powerful resource of resilience.

Since programs with such an approach are missing in Germany, a brief look into one specific concept in Canada might provide some insights. The Muslim Resource Centre for Social Support and Integration (MRCSSI), based in London, Ontario, is an association aiming at preventing violence and empowering Muslim women and children with regard to migration contexts. Providing a safe place for families and individuals, the centre seeks to "establish social support networks for the diverse London Muslim community in dealing with issues of integration, family conflict, domestic violence, and children in conflict with the law" (MRCSSI). The centre engages local Muslim and Arab community leaders as well as social services and justice agencies. They all work together against complex family conflict and violence issues that result from migration-related stress factors, including cultural issues and pre-migration trauma. Thus, one main principle is co-operation with—and not exclusion of—Islamic leaders. This approach rejects the simplifying model of Islam as basic problem and, instead, focuses on the complexity of the stressors. Other principles are as follows: a very close network of social, religious, political and educational actors, which intensively works together and aims at meeting the needs of the people concerned; academic expertise through research and mentoring; and engaging the Muslim community, based on the idea that by raising awareness within the community (i.e., on gender-based violence), support will develop intrinsically within the community. The centre seeks alternatives for dispute resolution, meaning that disputes and conflicts are not negated, ignored, or degraded. Instead, members of the centre analyze the various causes for conflicts and develop strategies of action.

One part of the MRCSSI activities is the "Reclaim Honour Project," an approach to redefining the concept of honour in an empowering way. The centre's guidelines say that, "We find strength in our communities. This means we view our communities as capable, skilled, knowledgeable and filled with potential. We capitalize on community strengths to address existing challenges" (MRCSSI).

The contents of the MRCSSI approach may be perceived as a possible response to the narrations of Sahar and Hülya. It could potentially provide a network of support for Hülya and could function as counselling service for Sahar and a buffer zone between her and her family of origin. Thus, the centre reflects the capabilities and needs of Muslim mothers.

CONCLUSION

Speaking about violence in Muslim and migrant communities is still an unresolved problem (WHO), a problem that remains unresolved in German culture as well. But especially within the Muslim context, scholars, activists, and practitioners in Germany face a lack of literature and a lack of helpful strategies.

The existence of criminal acts such as violence in the name of so-called family honour and forced marriage should not be ignored. But they should also not be reduced to simplified and one-dimensional explanations (i.e., that they are caused by Islam). Instead, there are women's voices who clearly stress their conviction that Islam is not responsible for these crimes. It is needed to include these voices and to develop policies that reduce the very risk of such acts of violence. The community-based approach of the MRCSSI seems to be effective and helpful. The concept refers to the idea of a strong linkage between the individual and the (migrant, religious or ethno-cultural) community. Yet it can be assumed that there are individuals who have disassociated themselves from these communities—be it on purpose, as deliberate strategy, or caused by the community itself. These considerations should be involved in the development of implementation projects. One needs to ask: who are the main actors? Who needs to be included? Which factors may produce a higher susceptibility to violence? And last but not least the views of the people concerned need to be included. What do the people concerned say? What help do they need? Which support is effective? We could learn much and reach many by including and implementing the views of Muslim women themselves.

NOTES

[1]Migrant One-Parent Families in Lower Saxony, Germany (Alleinerziehende Migrantinnen und Migranten in Niedersachsen – ALMIN), research project of Carl von Ossietzky University of Oldenburg 2012-2016, funded by the State of Lower Saxony, Germany (http://www.almin-projekt.de, see also Potts and Lingen-Ali).

[2]Names are pseudonyms. In order to protect anonymity other biographical data were also changed. Interviews were conducted in 2013 and translated from German to English by the author.

[3]"Othering is defined as a process in which, through discursive practices, different subjects are formed, hegemonic subjects - that is, subjects in powerful social positions as well as those subjugated to these powerful conditions." (Thomas-Olalde and Velho 27)

[4]Sahar was forced by her family to marry when she was a teenager. The marriage, which included rape and beatings, lasted one month, then Sahar managed to escape. She found support in a women's shelter and lived with a German foster family until she reached full age. Although for a while the contact with her family of origin was interrupted, Sahar allowed (and maybe wished for) the redevelopment of spatial proximity. This closeness does not include the emotional or attitudinal level.

[5]The corresponding policy aims at restriction, regimentation and punishment, more than empowerment and support. Legal reforms in Germany to counter forced marriage, for instance, refer to the duration of marriage, which should consist for at least three years in order to provide the legal basis to grant a resident permit for the foreign spouse. Thus, the dependencies within a dysfunctional marriage will potentially be extended. In general, women and girls facing violence, regardless of the migration background, may access counselling centres (some of them explicitly for migrants) and offices for families and/or women as well as women's shelters. However, there are some local projects aiming at empowering Muslim and/or migrant women and girls as part of prevention programs, but a greater framework and concept is still lacking.

WORKS CITED

Ali, Ayaan Hirsi. *Reformiert euch! Warum der Islam sich ändern muss*. München: Albrecht Knaus Verlag, 2015. Print.

Baobaid, Mohammed, and Gahad Hamed. *Addressing Domestic Violence in Canadian Muslim Communities: A Training Manual for Muslim Communities and Ontario Service Providers*. London, Ontario: Muslim Resource Centre for Social Support and Integration, 2010. Print.

Bundesministerium des Inneren (BMI). *Aufenthaltsrecht, Migrations und Integrations politik in Deutschland*. Berlin, 2014. Print.

Bundesministerium für Familie, Senioren, Frauen und Jugend (BMFFSJ). *Familien mit Migrationshintergrund: Analysen zur Lebenssituation, Erwerbsbeteiligung und Vereinbarkeit von Familie und Beruf*. 2nd ed. Berlin, 2014. Print.

Bundesministerium für Familie, Senioren, Frauen und Jugend

(BMFFSJ). *Mütter mit Migrationshintergrund—Familienleben und Erwerbstätigkeit.* Monitor Familienforschung. Berlin, 2013. Print.

Bundesministerium für Familie, Senioren, Frauen und Jugend (BMFFSJ). *Zwangsverheiratung in Deutschland.* Baden-Baden: Nomos Verlag, 2007. Print.

European Union Agency for Fundamental Rights/FRA. *Violence Against Women: An EU-wide Survey. Main Results.* Luxembourg: Publications Office of the European Union, 2014. Print.

Federal Office for Migration and Refugees. *Migration, Integration, Asylum Political Developments in Germany 2014.* Annual Policy Report by the German National Contact Point for the European Migration Network. Nürnberg, 2015. Print.

Fischer, Veronika, and Monika Springer, eds. *Handbuch Migration und Familie.* Schwalbach/Taunus: Wochenschau Verlag, 2011. Print.

Geisen, Thomas, Tobias Studer, and Erol Yildiz, eds. *Migration, Familie und Gesellschaft. Beiträge zu Theorie, Kultur und Politik.* Wiesbaden: Springer VS, 2014. Print.

Hagemann-White, Carol. "Violence against Women in the European Context: Histories, Prevalences, Theories." *Thinking Differently. A Reader in European Women's Studies.* Eds. Rosi Braidotti, and Gabriele Griffin. London: Zed Books, 2002. 239-251. Print.

Hall, Stuart. "Who Needs 'Identity'"? *Questions of Cultural Identity.* Ed. Paul du Gay. London, Thousand Oaks, New Delhi: Sage, 1996. 1-17. Print.

Kaya, Asiye. *Mutter-Tochter-Beziehungen in der Migration. Biographische Erfahrungen im alevitischen und sunnitischen Kontext.* Wiesbaden: Springer VS, 2009. Print.

Kelek, Necla. *Die fremde Braut. Ein Bericht aus dem Inneren des türkischen Lebens in Deutschland.* Köln: Kiepenheuer & Witsch. 2005. Print.

Lingen-Ali, Ulrike. *Agency im Kontext. Eine transkulturelle, biografische Untersuchung zu frauenpolitischen Akteurinnen in Palästina und Deutschland.* Münster: Lit-Verlag, 2013. Print.

Lingen-Ali, Ulrike. "Islam als Zuordnungs und Differenzkategorie. Antimuslimische Ressentiments im Bereich von Bildung und Sozialer Arbeit." *Sozial Extra* No. 9.10 (2012): 24-27. Print.

Muslim Resource Center for Social Support and Integration

(MRCSSI). MRCSSI, 2015. Web. 22. Sept. 2015.

Nussbaum, Martha. *Women and Human Development. The Capabilities Approach.* Cambridge: Cambridge University Press, 2000. Print.

Potts, Lydia, and Ulrike Lingen-Ali. "Alleinerziehende Migrantinnen und Migranten in Deutschland. Lebenspraxen zwischen Ausgrenzung und Handlungsfähigkeit." *Migration und Soziale Arbeit* No. 2 (2013): 132-140. Print.

Sarrazin, Thilo. *Deutschland schafft sich ab. Wie wir unser Land aufs Spiel setzen.* München: DVA, 2012. Print.

Thomas-Olalde, Oscar, and Astrid Velho. "Othering and its Effects—Exploring the Concept." *Writing Postcolonial Histories of Intercultural Education.* Eds. Heike Niedrig and Christian Ydesen. Frankfurt: Peter Lang Verlag, 2011. 27-51. Print.

World Health Organization (WHO). *Global and Regional Estimates of Violence against Women: Prevalence and Health Effects of Intimate Partner Violence and Non-Partner Sexual Violence.* Geneva: WHO, 2013. Print.

9.
A Poetic Inquiry

Muslim Mothering and Islamophobia

MEHRA SHIRAZI

FTER 9/11, IMAGES OF the Middle Eastern or Muslim "other" have been highly visible in the Western world. Whereas Muslims across the world have faced personal and systemic acts of violence, the American Muslim community has been portrayed as inherently violent and all too often only accentuated in conversations on radicalization and terrorism. With the ongoing "War on Terror," a range of Orientalist imaginaries have further (re)produced binaries positioning the "West" in resistance and opposition to the "East." This body of discourse, drawn from colonial narratives, further formulates the relations of supremacy-inferiority, where white supremacy is implied through the relationship between power and representation in Orientalist discourses.

Today, Islamophobia is no longer a concept to be disputed or questioned but, more importantly, to be understood. Among the forces that shape racially motivated violence are ideologies and images that mark the "other." Islamophobia is understood to be far more than just a phobia or fear; it is an ideology, imagined and rooted within the neo-orientalist social and global patterns of thought and meaning about Muslims and Islam (Esposito and Sheehi). Reiterating the old dichotomy between barbarism and civilization, Islam and modernity, Islam and democracy, Islam and human rights, Sheehi remarks how these stories are told through mainstream media and "function as ideological fulcrums" for state discourses and discriminatory policies towards Muslims (219). To understand such discourse, writes Sheehi, "is to understand the structured thought of the ideological justification of U.S. policies" (219). Sheehi conceptualizes Islamophobia as an ideological formation within the context of the American empire, in which the American public is an important component within this discourse; this ideological formation about Muslims and Islam tends to be translated into a sustained domestic policy of racial profiling and Muslim baiting (225).

Jasmine Zine uses the term "gendered Islamophobia" to explain the discourse of representing Islam as inherently gender oppressive and Muslim women as miserably oppressed by the religion ("Anti-Islamophobia," 117). As Christina Ho points out, "anti Muslim racism is articulated in a paternalistic nationalism that seeks to protect women, whether they are Muslim women forced to wear the veil or non-Muslim women as victims of sexual assault by Muslim men. This paternalism draws on a long history of colonial feminism, which for centuries has used the discourse of women's rights to condemn inferior cultures" (290). As Ho demonstrates, such negative representations of Islam are "part of a broader history of colonial feminism" that validates "Western supremacy" through arguing that colonial societies oppressed "their women" and were, thus, incapable of self-governance (296). This characterization, deploying the old trope of colonial feminism, served to justify the war on Afghanistan, as it was presented as a campaign to liberate women from the Taliban. Anthropologist Lila Abu Lughod indicates that since 2001, defending the rights of Muslim women has been used as justification for military interventions. According to Abu Lughod, stereotyping Muslim women "distracts us from the thornier problem that our own politics and actions in the world help create the conditions in which distant others live" (784).

Gendered and Orientalist representations of the Muslim and Arab or Middle Eastern "other" have been highly visible in the Western world in both official discourses and mainstream media. Muslims and Arabs specifically have been vilified in images, cartoons, film, and television long before 9/11. In the aftermath of 9/11, (re)constructed Orientalist imagery has saturated the representation of Muslims in media and popular culture. The dehumanizing images portrayed by the media have led to legitimized fear and hatred

A POETIC INQUIRY

against Muslims and Islam. Depictions of fanatical terrorists and passive veiled women are rendered to suggest Eastern backwardness and the need for Western emancipation as the primary markers of the Muslim world.

Chandra Mohanty's work is useful here. She examines how popular constructions of oppressed "other" women are created by reference to Western women, who are represented as educated, modern, and equipped with the freedom to make their own decisions (65). In her critique of Western feminism, Mohanty argues that Western feminist discourses construct Third World women as an "already constituted, coherent group with identical interests and desires, regardless of class, ethnic or racial locations, or contradictions" (167).

Narratives of protection and liberation of Muslim women have not only relied on images of women defined by their attire but also on racializing violence against women, with the mainstream media discourses situating patriarchy "over there" and as an inherent part of "their traditional cultures." For example, the cover of the November 2001 edition of *Time* magazine featured Afghan women with their burqas removed with the following caption: "Liberation: Women in Kabul showed their faces in public for the first time in years" (Gibbs 32). This popular image is a suggestive example of the way in which Orientalist discourse is reproduced to demand intervention. The picture was followed by a photo essay on the future of Afghanistan and Afghan women titled "Lifting the Veil" that declared that military intervention had freed Afghan women, with the removal of the burqa providing the evidence of this liberation (Lacayo 47). Such compelling images of Afghan women lifting the veil reassured the Western public, ignoring the fact that the women's human rights abuses not only continued but also increased under the American-backed government (Ayotte and Husain).

Muslim women's visibility functions as signifiers that are socially constructed to embody Islamophobic meanings and understandings (Zine, "Muslim" 400). Islamophobia, therefore, exists in a process of "identification and recognition" that results in such meanings and understandings being unquestioned and accepted as "natural and normative" of Muslims and Islam (Allen 280).

THE POETIC INQUIRY

Ivan Brady describes how a poetic perspective

> moves us to draw comparisons from our own immersions
> in life in relation to those of others ... it begs compari-
> sons between being now and being then, between being
> one and being other, between being here and being
> there, and it thereby situates itself in our experience as
> fundamental to knowing other people, their histories,
> and the environmental complications of being in-place
> today. (1003)

The poems presented here focus on the experiences of three Muslim
mothers living in the United States. My intention is to provide a
richer understanding of the daily lives of the participants as their
voices communicate the lived realities of diasporic communities.
I specifically examined Islamophobia as it targets these mothers
and their families. Poetic representation of data allowed the voices
of three Muslim mothers to be heard on their own terms and as
Brady describes, a "poetic stance" must originate "with the truth
of raw experience, with life as lived and seen from the inside, from
the role of the participant" (1003).

Interviews in the form of open-ended questions lasted approximately two hours in length. The interviews were conducted
one-on-one in a location of each participant's choosing. Only one
interview was conducted over the phone. My first participant did
not want the interview audio recorded, so I took hand written
notes. To maintain consistency, I decided to take hand written or
typed notes for all subsequent interviews as well.

Documented standardized methods used to "condense" participants' transcripts into poems have been previously described
(Furman; Leitz, and Langer 24-34). I searched through the interview
text to choose recurring, meaningful, and significant phrases to
create a poem. In this case, phrases and/or words from the "found
poetry" technique were used to extract poetry from interview
transcripts. Transcripts were subsequently reread and revisited to
reveal individual narratives. I chose to relate participant feelings,

life events, and experiences of trauma, imaginations, and hopes about mothering and Islamophobia through participant-voiced poems that appeared central to their narratives.

Finally, the data were sorted and organized into recurring themes. I constructed "found poems" from the transcripts and restricted myself to the words and phrases used originally by participants in the interviews. Recurring themes were used to "find the poetry" by remaining genuine to the flow and meaning of participants narratives and by focusing on what appeared to be central in their experiences (Clarke et al. 927). Several weeks later, participants were given the opportunity to review the found poems for occurring themes and accuracy in meaning and representation.

Based on the themes, three categories were identified: 1) Experience: Things Changed after 9/11; 2) Mothering, Trauma and Islamophobia; and 3) Resilience and Hope. In the next sections, I will share the found poems with a short synopsis of what was revealed. In all cases, pseudonyms are used, and some details were altered to protect the women's identities.

EXPERIENCE: THINGS CHANGED AFTER 9/11

When asked about the impact of Islamophobia in their lives, the women initially identified a range of emotions that were complex and profound, including feelings, such as shock, fear, vulnerability, anger, and anxiety. Most Islamophobic incidents centred on the expression and display of verbal abuse directed at the Muslim women. For many, their dress code, hijab, or other recognizable features of being "Muslim" appeared to be the thing that prompted racist reactions.

The first found poem is based on the narrative of Maysoon, a young Palestinian American and mother of two young boys. Maysoon was born and raised in the United States. She is the daughter of immigrant parents and works full time in the field of social services. Maysoon reflected on the impact of belonging (or not belonging) and the existence of a structural form of racial discrimination, which results in increased harassment on a daily bases.

My life has changed
I feel uncomfortable and unsafe
I feel the stares
I feel the hate
It's awful because this is the only country I really know

I was born and raised here
I'm too proud to let go
Why I'm telling you this
It's important to understand
That this isn't easy

It's unrealistic
It's hard to imagine
To suffer so much discrimination
Under the guise of liberation
I was born and raised here!

The second poem is based on the narratives of Samira, an Iraqi-American and mother to a young daughter. Highly educated, Samira is a survivor of 2003 U.S. invasion of Iraq and holds a graduate degree from a university in Iraq. She had experienced significant trauma in her life, growing up in a war -torn country. After migrating to the United States with her partner and elderly parents, she decided to return to school. Her current aspiration is to investigate gender-based violent crimes against non-Muslim minorities in Iraq as an act of genocide.

Samira described the impact of Islamophobia on her family, specially her elderly mother. Samira's account reveals the pervasive impact of being reminded of her family's "otherness" and the ways in which structural barriers create and recreate intersectional discrimination.

My mother used to hide under her cover
Two silver braids called
Tigris and Euphrates rivers
My mother screams in silence and bitterness
I am not a terrorist

I am a Muslim woman
My mother's face is Babylon gardens
And a story of lover
Plays with my daughter
How to say the truth without error
But her tears fall like rain in the summer
My mother screams in silence and bitterness
I am not a terrorist
I am a grandmother

My mother like others
Wants to buy bread for dinner
The cashier monitors her hands
My mother screams in silence and bitterness
I am not a thief
I am a lady with honour
This is the daily story of a Muslim woman
Who wants to keep her cover

The third poem is based on the accounts of Mariam, a Somali American mother of four. She came to the United States as a refugee at the age of eight. She is a school teacher and a social justice activist. As an activist, Mariam discussed how Islamophobia is a form of gender violence that robs Muslin women of their agency, and how her religious identity expressed through the headscarf makes her an easy target for violence.

My name puts up flags in airports
They call it random screening
But it is not random, is it.

I take the bus home
 I feel the deep stares directed at my hijab
Judging me, calling me in their heads and sometimes loud
"Mrs Osama Bin Laden"
"Go back to where you came from"
"Go back to Afghanistan"
I have to think twice next time I get on the bus

I don't think there is a way to
Keep me from feeling afraid
My fear feeds the empire

MOTHERING, TRAUMA, AND ISLAMOPHOBIA

All three women provided important insights into the subtle and complex nature of racism and xenophobia in their children's lives, and how it generates a complex layer to mothering.

Maysoon expressed how as a Muslim mother, she was placed into a unique position where she had to protect her children from anti-Muslim bigotry. She recognized how living with this type of fear and confusion made her deeply aware of the intersecting oppressions, not only in her life but in the lives of other Muslims and marginalized groups. She shared a story of how a friend of hers was recovering from injuries after being beaten on the streets; such attacks, Maysoon remarked, justify her fear. Maysoon voiced the heavy emotional and mental responsibility required to support her children's ability to deconstruct repressive and Orientalist narratives about Arabs and Muslims.

Making their breakfast in the morning
Kissing them, embracing them
I tell them they can be anything they want to be
Don't let anyone tell you who and how you should be
No one is born to hate
One must learn to hate
And if they can learn to hate
They can be taught to love
Be anything you desire, proud and loud,
You are the Bahr [sea].

Samira's narrative depicts how the growth of Islamophobia rapidly changed, as first Afghanistan and then Iraq were invaded and occupied. She described her experiences of war and violence during the U.S. invasion of Iraq. She provided detailed information about her uprooting and dislocation and the effects of such trauma on her life as a mother. Samira shared her feelings of anxiety haunted by flashbacks and memories of her traumatic experiences.

For Samira, here memories of homeland are a way of processing traumas and rewriting of home and belonging.

> Inside my brain
> The sound was so loud
>
> Resurrect from the ash
> A child lost his hand in the war
>
> Resurrect from the rifted heart
> Mother eating in the trash
> Nominate my name to spring death
> The sound was loud
>
> Dogs ate bodies
> Today my prayer is to see less than twelve people shot dead
> Carry my home in a backpack
> Do I belong?
> Will I ever return?

Mariam's narrative reflects her strength and communicates the challenge expressed by Muslim mothers who experienced and fought anti-Muslim racism to be recognized as people deserving of respect and dignity.

> Bigotry is real
> Threats of violence are real
> The world is going mad
> We struggle against racism
> We struggle against Islamophobia
> Our voices need to be heard
>
> To cope with a tragedy you never knew
> To deal with the hate
> A tragedy that happened before you were even born
> I wonder if you can thrive in such a world that wants to
> punish you?

The world is going mad
And my children see the burning Qurans,
And hear you when you say "Every Muslim is a terrorist"

We stand up tall
Keep pushing forward
Rise up high
The haters will not reach you
Our voices must be heard
I exhale with tears in my eyes!

RESILIENCE AND HOPE

All three women articulated the feeling that mothering was a source of resilience. They spoke about not only the challenges that they faced but also their strategies of resistance to oppressive circumstances. The mothers see themselves as active agents in their children's lives. In her narrative Maysoon sees her passion for her job as a social worker inspired by her love for her children and their future.

Why do I care?
My children, our Muslim children are listening and watching
My children appreciate my work,
They listen, they struggle
It's tough, being attacked because of your faith,
It's tough being bullied
It's tough being arrested
It's tough when a mosque is ravaged
It breaks you down emotionally
It feeds the empire
But I do it for them over and over again

In Samira's experience, being a mother protected her from succumbing to social isolation and disengagement as a consequence of her experiences of trauma. Her narrative calls for resistance and hope. It reaffirms her faith in the power of her voice to reach out, to empower, and to encourage.

I spent my life living in a war zone
I witnessed four wars, one economic embargo, and one huge civil war
I was displaced from my country after I lost everything that I worked hard to earn

I still feel scared from loud sounds, which make me remember all the war sounds
I still look behind me, each time I feel someone walk near me
I still feel scared from dogs that ate human bodies in my country
I still remember how many times I vomited after I saw that

With all these memories, I still hold hope in each cell of my blood
Hope to create a better life for my daughter
Hope means everything for disposable bodies

Mariam's narrative portrays her resiliency and her continual emphasis on the power of the collective. She refuses the relentless politics of violence and fear. She contemplates a new meaning of hope in life and in the love that she has for her children.

I refuse to believe that all hope is gone
I refuse to believe that humanity is gone
I refuse to believe that our conscience is dead

As long as there is hope
My children need to be raised
To break the chains of impossibility for a new day
We are not meant to live in hatred and despair
So violent is our world today
We will give way to love
We are warriors

Love breaths
And life speaks
Alhamdulilah.

REFLECTION

Islamophobia functions as a colonial legacy and is based on "otherness," marginalization, and a growing concern about Muslims living in the West. In mainstream media, Muslim and Arab women are further stigmatized and presented as passive and oppressed. Furthermore, such rhetoric uses the language of women's liberation, in what Krista Hunt refers to as "embedded feminism." The co-opting of feminist discourse is used to justify military action in Arab and Muslim majority countries.

The inclusion of marginalized identities and experiences complicate colonialist frameworks and decentre dominant narratives. This chapter, based on a poetic inquiry of interview data, provides an alternative method of presenting and analyzing written transcripts, which allowed me to reconstruct and represent the written transcript. The poems offer a glimpse into the lived realities of diasporic communities: they highlight how Islamophobia exploits the image of Muslim mothers and has significant impact on their everyday lives. The Anti-Muslim racism that currently shapes the images of Muslim mothers sees them as helpless victims in the way in which their identities are both perceived and defined. Consequently, the harmful impact of Islamophobia is not restricted to those individuals but rather extends to their families and the larger Muslim community.

The poetic form permits the portrayal of experiences of injustice and discrimination as well as of the fears, challenges, and hopes of these Muslim mothers. It also provides an embodied voice to the lived experiences of women who have been demonized, marginalized and silenced in their own country. Taken together, the narratives demonstrate the complexity of Muslim mothers' experiences and directly contest the stereotypic thinking that characterizes Islamophobia.

WORKS CITED

Abu-Lughod, Lila. "Do Muslim Women Really Need Saving?: Anthropological Reflections on Cultural Relativism and Its Others." *American Anthropologist* 104.3 (2002): 783-790. Print.

Allen, Chris. "Opposing Islamification or Promoting Islamophobia? Understanding the English Defence League." *Patterns of
Prejudice* 45.4 (2011): 279-294. Print.

Ayotte, K., and Mary Husain. "Securing Afghan Women: *Neo-
colonialism, Epistemic Violence, and the Rhetoric of the Veil.*"
NWSA Journal 17.3 (2005): 112-133. Print.

Brady, Ivan. "Poetics for A Planet: Discourse on Some Problems
of Being-in-Place." *Handbook of Qualitative Research*. Eds.
Norman K. Denzin and Yvonna S. Lincoln. 3rd ed. Thousand
Oaks: Sage, 2005. 979–1026. Print.

Clarke, Juanne, Angela Febbraro, Maria Hatzipantelis, and Geof-
frey Nelson. "Poetry and Prose: Telling the Stories of Formerly
Homeless Mentally Ill People." *Qualitative Inquiry* 11.6: (2005):
913-932. Print.

Esposito, John L., and Ibrahim Kalin. *Islamophobia: The Challenge
of Pluralism in the 21st Century*. New York: Oxford University
Press, 2011. Print.

Furman, Rich, Cynthia Lietz, and Carol L. Langer. "The Research
Poem in International Social Work: Innovations in Qualitative
Methodology International." *Journal of Qualitative Methods*
3.5 (2006): 24-34. Print.

Gibbs, Nancy. "Blood and Joy." *Time*, 26 Nov. 2001: 30–32. Print.

Hunt, Krista. "'Embedded Feminism' and the War on Terror."
*(En)Gendering the War on Terror: War Stories and Camouflaged
Politics*. Eds. Krista Hunt and Kim Rygiel. Aldershot: Ashgate,
2006. 51-71. Print.

Ho, Christina. "Muslim Women's New Defenders: Women's Rights,
Nationalism and Islamophobia in Contemporary Australia."
Women's Studies International Forum 30.4 (2007): 290-298.
Web. 15 Feb. 2012.

Mohanty, Chandra. "Under Western Eyes: Feminist Scholarship and
Colonial Discourse." *Feminist Review* 30.1 (1988): 61-88. Print.

Sheehi, Stephen. *Islamophobia: The Ideological Campaign against
Muslims*. Atlanta: Clarity Press, 2011. Print.

Lacayo, Richard. "About Face for Afghan Women." *Time*, 24
December 3, 2001: 46-47. Print. Print.

Zine, Jasmine. "Anti-Islamophobia Education as Transformative
Pedagogy: Reflections from the Educational Front Lines." *The*

American Journal of Islamic Social Sciences 3.21 (2004): 110-119. Print.

Zine, Jasmine. "Muslim Youth in Canadian Schools: Education and the Politics of Religious Identity". *Anthropology and Education Quarterly* 32.4 (2001): 399-423. Print.

IV.
REPRODUCTION AND MATERNITY
IN MUSLIM SOCITIES

10.
Social and Religious Constructions of Motherhood in Indonesia

Negotiating Expectations of Childbearing, Family Size, and Governmental Policies

NINA NURMILA

THIS CHAPTER AIMS TO EXPLORE the social and religious construction of motherhood among Muslims in Indonesia by presenting several case studies of Indonesian Muslim women, which focus on their perceptions of mothering roles and how the social and religious constructions of motherhood affect their decisions in assuming their mothering roles. Although social pressure in Indonesia seems to negatively affect some women's feeling about being mothers, Islamic teaching stated in the Qur'an appears not to put pressure on mothering roles. In fact, the Qur'an acknowledges the physical hardships of pregnancy and breastfeeding and provides resource to help to counter societal pressures. In Indonesia, mothering is generally expected for married women only, whereas unmarried women are not expected to have children outside of wedlock. If unmarried women become pregnant, they can become victims of social gossip and isolation.

In order to present the case studies, I will firstly explain the changing social and political context of Indonesia. Located in Southeast Asia, Indonesia consists of 17,504 islands, with the five main islands of Kalimantan, Sumatra, Sulawesi, Java, Papua, and other smaller islands, such as Bali, Nusa Tenggara Timur, and Nusa Tenggara Barat. Indonesia is the most populated country in the world after China and India. Indonesia has a multicultural and multi-religious population. In Java, for example, there are at least three ethnicities: Sundanese, Batavian, and Javanese, each with their own native languages and unique cultural traditions. Islam is the majority religion in the country: about 86 percent of the population is Muslim. Protestants make up six percent of the population, Buddhists three-and-a-half percent, Roman Catholics three percent, and Hindus two percent. The rest are unidentified, which could include animists or atheists.

I will divide the Indonesian context into two periods in relation to the changing attitudes toward marriage which is related with the state of women's education: prior to the 1970s and after the 1970s. Prior to the 1970s, Indonesia had a very low level of female education. This was mainly because of the country's long period of colonization. The Indonesian archipelago was colonized by the Dutch for about three and a half centuries and then was colonized by Japan for about three and a half years. During the colonial era, the land and people of the Netherland Indies (now Indonesia) were exploited and mostly lived in very poor conditions. Only a very small number of the elite Netherland Indies people had access to education. Even though there were several women who fought for women's rights for education—such as Kartini (1879-1904) in Central Java, Dewi Sartika (1884-1947) in West Java, and Rahmah el-Yunusiyah (1900-1969) in West Sumatra—the majority of women were uneducated.

Even though Indonesia gained its independence in 1945, the country was in an unstable economic and political situation, especially right after independence when it was under the leadership of Soekarno (1945-1966). In this early stage of post-independence, Indonesia still had to struggle against the Dutch, who still wanted to continue colonizing Indonesia. As a result, the economy was not developed. In addition, in this era, most people were still poor and uneducated, especially women. This low level of education among both men and women had made the process of Indonesian development slower.

Prior to the 1970s, marriage in Indonesia was traditionally regarded as parents' business. Parents usually arranged their children's marriage at an early age, even without the knowledge and consent of the couple (Geertz; Koentjaraningrat; Jaspan and Hill). Many Muslim parents chose their daughters' partners because they were worried that their daughters would not choose the right partner and might marry a womanizer (Blackburn and Bessel). They were also afraid that their daughters might be involved in sexual misconduct and become pregnant before their marriage. Therefore, many Muslim parents prevented this by marrying off their daughters before they reached puberty (Jones). In addition, most parents, at that time, saw marriage as a passage to adulthood, in which after the marriage, their daughters would be free to choose either to stay or continue their parentally arranged marriages (Geertz).

Parentally arranged marriages at young ages were vulnerable to divorce due to immaturity and incompatibility (Jones; Firth; Heaton et al). Geertz reported that in the 1950s in Java, about 50 percent of all marriages ended in divorce, which mostly occurred in the first parentally arranged marriage. Some of these divorces even occurred before the marriage was consummated, especially in some areas in West Java such as Serang, where there was a tradition of *kawin gantung* (suspended marriage). *Kawin gantung* is marriage between a couple arranged by their parents at the age of seven to ten years old, but the marriage is usually consummated four to six years later (Blackburn and Bessel).

Prior to the 1970s, there was no written marriage law that could protect marital relationships. Many women were vulnerable to unilateral divorce,[1] abandonment, and arbitrary polygamy.[2] In response to this vulnerable position of women, some Indonesian women's organizations—such as Istri Sedar, Aisyiyah Muhammadiyah, Muslimat Nahdlatul Ulama—fought for better women's rights in marital relationships. However, women's positions, in general, did not improve much (Nurmila, *Women*).

In contrast, after the 1970s, the Indonesian situation began to improve. The New Order government (1966-1998), under the leadership of Soeharto, began its development program in 1969. Since the early 1970s, Indonesia has witnessed massive growth in educational facilities, especially in Java, resulting in expansion of both male and female education. Increased education has correlated with an increase of marriage age: from about sixteen to twenty years old in the 1980s, seventeen to twenty-five years old in the 1990s and seventeen to thirty-nine years old in 2000.[3] Consequently, there has been a change in attitudes to early marriage. Prior to the 1970s, especially in the 1950s, most parents would have been embarrassed to have a sixteen-year-old unmarried daughter; therefore, they would have quickly arranged her marriage because of the fear that the girl would be called a spinster. In contrast, after the 1970s, especially in the early twenty-first century, women who marry at an early age are ridiculed and receive negative comments (Smith-Hefner).

In addition, the educational expansions provided men and women with the opportunity to interact with one another, which has led them to choose whom to marry, in contrast to parentally arranged marriages. This personal choice marriage at a more mature age has contributed to a drop in the divorce rate, whereas parentally arranged marriage at an early age was vulnerable to divorce, even though some marriages did work well (Hull; Jones; "Population and the Family" and "Modernization and Divorce"; Wolf). This falling divorce rate is also connected to socio-economic developments. Better economic conditions can reduce poverty-related causes of divorce (Jones, "Population and the Family" and "Modernization and divorce"). The clear benefit of education— such as employment opportunities, economic security, and social status— have made many parents prefer to support their daughters' education, even if they have to send them away from home to continue their studies. The falling divorce rate after the 1970s can also be attributed to the enactment of the 1974 Marriage Law, which requires that divorce take place at the religious court, which makes decisions regarding personal affairs issues, such as marriage, divorce, and inheritance. Prior to the enactment of the Marriage Law, a husband could simply pronounce his divorce, sometimes without the wife's knowledge. After the enactment of the Marriage Law, couples were compelled to take their divorce cases to the religious court and pay legal expenses. The law stipulated that a couple wishing to obtain a divorce should attend at least three hearings before the divorce can take place: the first hearing aims at reconciliation; the second is to find out the result of the reconciliation effort; and if reconciliation is unsuccessful, the third hearing legalizes the divorce procedure (Jones, *Marriage and Divorce*). This requirement that the divorce should take place at the religious court allows some time for the couple to rethink the divorce, which may lead to reconciliation and also gives more room for women to exercise their right to ask for divorce when they are unhappy with the marriage.[4]

To reduce population growth, the New Order government imposed birth control programs beginning in the early 1970s. The results of these programs are seen in unfavourable attitudes towards high birth rates and in the decreasing number of children that women have from one generation to another, with the ideal number established as two children per married couple. This two-child government campaign seems to have been successful. For instance, my grandmother had thirteen children who were born between the 1940s and 1950s, prior to the New Order government. My mother, on the other hand, has six children who were born between the late 1960s and the late 1970s, at the beginning of the New Order government. My siblings and I have two to three children each, who were born between the early 1990s and 2010, nearly at the end of the New Order government and at the inception of the post-New Order period, which is called the Reform era.[5] Some parents who have had more than three children after the 1980s often receive unfavourable comments from neighbours or from government employees when they seek medical or social services.

SOCIAL CONSTRUCTIONS OF MOTHERHOOD IN INDONESIA

In Indonesia, women are generally expected to marry after they reach maturation age.[6] Soon after getting married, they are expected and even pressured to have children. They are also expected to take care of and educate their children. The pressure to have children after getting married can be observed from the questions often asked by neighbours or acquaintances to women at different stages of their lives. The question usually asked to seventeen- and eighteen- year-old-girls after the 1970s was "Where do you study?" This may be based on the assumption that, ideally, girls are still studying at senior high school. This question is usually asked until the age of twenty-four or twenty-five, when people assume that at that age, girls may still be completing their undergraduate studies, if the girls come from educated and middle-upper class families. The following questions are usually asked to women over twenty-five years old: "Are you single or married?" If the woman answers, "I am single," the next question asked would usually be, "When are you getting married?" This question might be annoying and intrusive, especially if the woman has no idea yet regarding when she is going to get married. If the woman answers, "I am married," the next question would be, "Have you had any children?" If she answers, "no," the inquirer may suggest many remedies on how to have children, including tips on what food, medicine, and herbs to have. If she answers, "yes," the next question could be one of the following: "How many children do you have?"; "Is your child male or female?"; "How old is he or she?"; or "When are you going to have another child?"

All of the above questions are commonly asked, even by strangers. For many Indonesians, these questions are not seen as rude or intrusive but as normal questions, often used as conversation starters with strangers. However, for some women, the questions can be unwelcome. I myself tend to see these questions as an intrusion into my privacy. In fact, these questions affected me negatively and could have changed my initial plan to postpone my first pregnancy.

After women have children, most Indonesians think that it is the natural duty for women to take care and educate their children. This social construction of motherhood can be seen, for instance, in the government development planning during the Soeharto period and various state laws, such as the 1974 Marriage Law, and many writings in the media that emphasized women's role as wife and mother. For example, the first three stages of Indonesian five-year development planning (1969 to 1984) constructed women as wives and mothers, as supporters of their husbands, and as educators of their children; the last three stages of the New Order five-year development planning (1984 to 1999) constructed women as having a double role: as housewives and, at the same time, as workers employed outside the home who contribute economically to their households and Indonesian development in general (Nurmila, "Indonesian Muslim"; Bappenas). As a wife, a woman is expected to take care of all her husband's physical, sexual, and emotional needs. As a mother, she is expected to take care of and educate her children. An article of the 1974 Marriage Law states that "a husband is the leader of the family, while a wife is a housewife," whereas another states that "a husband has to protect his wife and give her all living expenses of the household based on his capability" and that "a wife has to manage all the household affairs well" (Republik Indonesia). Managing household affairs has been interpreted to include many things, such as making the house neat, clean and comfortable, preparing a nutritious and healthy menu for the family, and managing family finances (Perempuan).

Similarly, Acik Mdy, a writer in online media, also suggests that a housewife has to be ready to work twenty-four hours a day and seven days a week: she must be ready at all times to manage all the household's affairs—such as taking care of and educating her children, managing household finance, and being involved in family decision making processes, including buying a house and deciding on her children's education. Others believe that women have three roles: mother, wife, and society member. As a mother, she is expected to educate her children and know her children's needs at every stage of their development. As a wife, she is expected to create a harmonious environment, look presentable, and be able to motivate her husband to do positive things, such as to work hard to earn a living. As a society member, she is expected to participate in her society, such as attending and organizing religious and social gatherings (Noor). This construction of women's role as mother and wife was also spread by the non-political women's organizations of *Dharma Wanita* and PKK (*Pembinaan Kesejahteraan Keluarga*/Family Welfare Guidance) founded by the New Order government. Most Indonesian women do not show any objection to this construction and try to fit its expectations of being a good mother and wife, except for a minority of Indonesian feminists, such as Julia Suryakusuma, Sita Aripurnami, and Sylvia Tiwon. Suryakusuma, in her master's thesis argues that the New Order construction of motherhood which, she called *state ibuism* (state motherhood), tends to be oriented towards the urban upper-middle class and ignores the realities of poor rural women, who must work to earn a living because of their husbands' desertion or unemployment. In addition, Aripurnami disagrees with the New Order's message spread in the *sinetron* (a television show), which tends to emphasize women's domestic roles and implicitly tells women that no matter how busy they are in the public sphere, they still have to be responsible for taking care of their children, doing household chores, and serving their husbands. The insistence that *ibu* (mother) is the core of women's nature, according to Tiwon, denies a woman's social identity as a person in her own right.

Despite social pressures for women to have children, there is a minority of urban, educated women who express their decisions not to have children; this decision is still very unusual in Indonesia and has only occured in the last five years of the Reform era. In the weekly female magazine *Femina*, in an article titled "Berdua saja cukup" ("Just Two of Us Is Enough"), there are stories of various women who have decided against having children for a number of social, political, and environmental reasons. For example, Ayu Utami, a forty-three-year-old writer, writes that she decided not to have children because the world is too heavily populated; she feels that having children may not be environmentally friendly. Eva, a thirty-two-year-old engineer, holds similar views to Ayu; she is concerned with the lack of food and resources, the dwindling of natural resources, and environmental destruction. Andhini, a thirty-year-old journalist, explains that her decision not to have children is motivated by her desire to achieve and enjoy various things, such as travelling around the world. She believes that if she were to have children, she would have to focus on taking care of them, and it would be financially difficult to pay for travelling. Also, Hera Diani, a thirty-five-year-old a journalist, sees having children as a liability. She fears that that she would not be able to juggle her work and her roles as a wife and a mother at the same time in a Jakarta context, where there are very few daycares available and heavy traffic jams most of the time, making getting from place to place very difficult (Jayalaksana). The opinions expressed in the article show how education, women's employment, and the more individualistic nature of urban life have influenced women's decision not to have children or to be mothers. This decision not to be a mother, however, is still not readily accepted by the majority of Indonesians, who idealize the nuclear family.

RELIGIOUS CONSTRUCTIONS OF MOTHERHOOD

Although Indonesian social constructions seem to obligate women to be mothers, which may negatively affect women's mothering roles, the Qur'an provides a sympathetic and supportive discussion of mothering roles. This can be seen, for example, in a number of different verses. The Qur'an acknowledges the physical hardships of carrying, bearing and rearing children. This is stated in the following two Qur'anic verses:

> And We have enjoined on people (to be good) to their parents: in travail upon travail did their mother bear them, and in years twain was their weaning: (hear the command). Show gratitude to Me and to your parents: to Me is (your final) goal. (31:14)
>
> We have enjoined on people kindness to their parents: in pain did their mother bear them, and in pain did she give them birth. The carrying of the (children) to their weaning is (a period of) thirty months. At length, when they reach the age of full strength and attain forty years, they say, "O my Lord! Grant me that I may be grateful for your favor which You have bestowed upon me, and upon both my parents, and that I may work righteousness such as You mayest approve; and be gracious to me in my issue. Truly have I turned to You and truly do I bow (to You) in Islam. (46:15)

The Qur'an acknowledges the pain of childbirth, shown specifically in the case of Mary's giving birth to the prophet Isa: "And the pains of childbirth drove her to the trunk of a palm tree: she cried (in her anguish): 'Ah! Would that I had died before this! Would that I had been a thing forgotten and out of sight!'" (19:23).

A Qur'anic chapter in *Al-Baqarah* (2:233) states that it is optional for a mother to breastfeed for a period of two years. This two year period of breastfeeding is often interpreted to be the ideal interval for a mother before having another child. The verse is also interpreted as obligating fathers (`alalmawludi) to help their wife or ex-wife breastfeeding the children. The Qur'an uses the suggestive verb (*fi`lul mudhari`*), not the instructive verb (*fi`lul amri*), in its directives on breastfeeding, but uses the word *'ala*, which means giving a burden, in *obligating* fathers to financially support breastfeeding mothers.

Unfortunately, many Indonesian Muslims seem to be unaware of these Qur'anic teachings, which are friendly to women and supportive of mothers. Instead, they seem to be influenced more by the Indonesian cultural constructions of motherhood that expect women to have two children soon after getting married. Such attitudes are seen in the following case studies.

MOTHERING IN INDONESIA

The following case studies are based on my interviews with several Indonesian women who were my roommates during my pilgrimage to Saudi Arabia.[7] Due to space limitations, I only present two cases of my interviewees and my own case study.

Case Study One: A Single Parent with Five Children

Sri, who is fifty-two years old, told me that she got married at the age of twenty, when she was in Pendidikan Guru Agama/PGA (a school to become a religious teacher). Sri told me that it was an arranged marriage, and she was not asked for her consent. Sri did not resist the marriage, but she postponed the consummation of the marriage for two years until she completed her secondary school. The postponement of her marriage consumation can be seen as a negotiation between Sri (who wanted to continue her education), her husband, and her parents, who were afraid Sri would become a spinster if she did not get married. After the consummation of their marriage, Sri and her husband, Amir, who was twenty-eight years old at the time of their marriage, had five children, two female and three male, who were each born a year apart. At the time of the interview, in December 2011, the ages of the five children ranged from twenty-three to twenty-seven years old. Sri was married in 1979, when most marriages in Indonesia were still arranged by parents, which might be one of the reasons why Sri accepted the arranged marriage. Sri's age at the time of her marriage was considered as an "appropriate" because the New Order government had tried to increase the age of marriage by campaigning that the ideal age of marriage was twenty for women and twenty-five for men, even though in the late 1970s most women, especially in rural areas, married in their mid-to-late teens. Sri told me that she believes that having children is something that she took for granted. In fact, most married women expected to be pregnant soon after getting married to fulfill existing social expectations that married women would become mothers. Sri told me that she did not plan on how many children she would have or when she would like to have them, a common tradition for Indonesian married women who were mostly unaware of their reproductive rights at that time. After having three children, she tried to use contraception pills without her husband's knowledge for fear of her husband's disapproval of her use of contraception, but they did not work. This shows that she tried to fit herself within the new government construction of the ideal nuclear family with two children, as she considered that having three children was more than what was expected. She did not try an IUD (intra uterine device) because she followed the pronouncements of the Indonesian Ulama Council, who declared the use of IUDs to be forbidden, except if inserted by female health staff or doctors.[8]

Amir, Sri's husband, was a government civil servant and a teacher at a secondary school. Sri told me that her husband was helpful in taking care of their children—something that is a bit rare in Indonesia, where taking care of the children is considered the woman's job. Unfortunately, Amir died in 1989 after being sick for about a week, when their youngest child was one year old. Sri was shocked to be left alone with their five small children, since she was a housewife who relied on her husband economically. The ideal roles of husband as the family breadwinner and wife as housewife as promoted in the Marriage Law do not anticipate the possibility of something going wrong; the law ignores the fact that some husbands are unemployed and/or not responsible for the economic well-being of their families.

After her husband died, Sri began to work as a tailor in a boutique, where she was given permission to go home during lunchtime to feed her children. She took care of and educated her children. She told me that she did not have any intention of marrying another man, even though several men had offered her marriage proposals. Even though she lived in poverty, she did her best for her children's education. She used the money from her husband's pension as a civil servant to support her children's education. In addition, she also worked as a private religious teacher after finishing her work as a tailor. It was the rich parents of one of her students who paid for Sri's pilgrimage to Saudi Arabia. At the time, Sri was considered an educated woman, who was able to teach religion and who had the skill to sew, which helped her to be economically independent. Now all of her children have a minimum of a diploma degree; three of them are married and have children.

It is not easy to be a single parent like Sri who supports and raises her five children alone, but she is determined not to marry another man. I have written elsewhere of similar case studies of single mothers who prefer not to marry another man when they can live on their employment earnings and the pensions of their late husbands (Nurmila, "When There Is"). For these women, marrying another man can mean the loss of the monthly income from the pension of their late husbands and the loss of the freedom to be an independent woman who does not have to serve her husband. For uneducated women, however, this is not possible, as they have no skills or a late husband with a good pension. Some of these women may have to marry another man just to have someone to support them economically.

Case Study Two: Having Many Children in the New Order Period

The following case study portrays another segment of Indonesian society: poor and uneducated rural women who tend to get married at an early age, as in the case of Aisyah who got married by choice, which was still unusual, as at that time, marriage was regularly arranged by parents.

Aisyah, a fifty-three-year-old woman, told me that she got married at the age of fourteen in the early 1970s. Her husband, Hamdan, was eighteen years old when they got married. Aisyah claimed that her age was falsified to sixteen, whereas Hamdan's age was changed to twenty-one. Aisyah told me that it was not an arranged marriage. Hamdan knew Aisyah when he worked as tailor in his brother's house, which was close to her house. Hamdan often saw Aisyah and then expressed his interest in marrying her after they knew each other for about two years. Aisyah only studied until grade four of primary school, and Hamdan only completed grade six of primary school.

Aisyah told me that she already had her menstruation at that time of her marriage, but she did not become pregnant until about a year after her marriage. When Aisyah was asked by her neighbours whether or not she had gotten pregnant after her marriage—the typical questions that neighbours asked newlywed women—she tried to ignore the questions. Her first baby girl was born in August 1975, her second baby girl was born in June 1978, and her third baby boy was born in 1980. By having children, she had fulfilled her cultural role to be a mother. After having three children, Aisyah tried to use the contraception pill, but it was unsuccessful. This is similar to Sri's case, who also tried to conform to the government's expectation of having a small family with two children. Therefore, both Sri and Aisyah considered that it was more than enough to have three children, but they were both unsuccessful in using contraception to prevent other pregnancies. Aisyah had the fourth baby girl in 1983. She, then, tried to use injections as her contraception, but it was unsuccessful again, and she had the fifth baby boy in 1986. She no longer tried to use contraception and had another three female babies, who were born in 1988, 1989 and 1991.

Aisyah told me that she often received negative comments about having too many children from her neighbours and government staff, especially when she or her children needed medical services. The doctors and nurses were always shocked when she told them that she has eight children. "How could you have so many children?" or "Don't you use any contraception?" were some of the questions that Aisyah typically received, which shows the success of the New Order government in restricting the number of children that Indonesian women should have. She tried to be calm in response to such comments, even though, sometimes, she angrily responded to the comments by saying, "I am the one who takes care and feeds my children, not you!" Or sometimes she said, "I have tried to use pills and injections, but none of them work well for me."

As an uneducated and low-income earner with so many children, Aisyah and Hamdan lived in very poor conditions. They helped each other deal with economic hardship and raised many children. To add additional income to what her husband earned as a tailor, Aisyah made and sold snacks, such as fried bananas, whereas her husband did not hesitate to take care of her children when he was home from work. There was time when Aisyah, after having three children, asked permission from her husband to work as a domestic worker in Saudi Arabia to improve their economic condition, but her husband did not give her permission. To alleviate their poverty, Hamdan and Aisyah then decided to move from Surabaya to Jakarta, Indonesia's capital city, where most people migrate to try for a better life. With the help of a friend, Hamdan and Aisyah set up a second-hand shop. Initially, they rented the shop, and, eventually, their economic condition improved. They could afford to buy two shops and two houses in Bekasi, near Jakarta. In 2008, they sold one of their houses to pay for their pilgrimage to Saudi Arabia, where I met them as my roommates in Medina. With the gradual improvement in their finances, they tried to educate their children. Five of her children graduated from senior high school, and three of them graduated from only junior high school, one of whom is their first daughter. The oldest girl had to stop studying after she graduated from her junior high school so that she could help take care of her younger siblings. Aisyah seemed to regret that her first daughter stopped studying after grade nine because she was a bright student, the best in her class.

The above case study shows how the pressure to have children after getting married was compounded by the questions from Aisyah's neighbours questions on whether or not she was pregnant. These questions, however, changed into negative comments when Aisyah had eight children, which were considered too many within in the context of the New Order's instruction to have only two children. In Indonesia, not having children for married women can be a disaster. It can be used as justification for a man to marry another woman, as stated in the Marriage Law, and it can be the object of gossip among neighbours, who may suggest that the woman is infertile (Bennett). As an Indonesian Muslim myself, I experienced the same pressures to have children soon after I got married, which was disturbing, but I ignored the social pressure after I had the first son in order to follow the religious suggestion to breastfeed up to two years. This will be elaborated below.

Case Study Three: From Social Pressure to a Choice

In this last case study, I will share my own experience of mothering. I became a mother due to social pressure when my first child was born in 1995. Because of my education, however, I could turn the pressure into a choice when I decided to have my second child, who was born in 2004. I got married in April 1994 when I was twenty-five, whereas my husband was twenty-six; I was considered old to be getting married because the ideal marriage age, as constructed by the New Order government, was twenty years old for women. It was not an arranged marriage because the tradition had changed since the early 1980s, but it was not really by choice in terms of timing. At that time, I was excited to have been selected to receive a scholarship to complete my MA degree in Australia. However, my mother insisted that I get married before I went abroad. She said, "I know that I do not need to ask you to study because you always want to study, but I am sorry that I have to ask you to get married before it is too late." I tried to avoid the pressure, but my mother insisted that I was required to get married first if I wanted to study abroad. I understood my mother's feeling of being pressured socially to marry off her daughter, since I had gained my first university degree and had reached the age of twenty-five. This was far older than the minimum age stipulated in the 1974 Marriage Law: sixteen years for females and nineteen years for males.

I could perfectly understand my mother's fear that my higher education and older age could possibly make me a spinster, a fear for most Indonesian mothers. I often heard my mother's story about how she was married in 1967 at the age of twenty-two, which was considered a very late age of marriage because, at that time, most girls were being married off by the age of seventeen. My mother was considered quite extraordinary in the late 1960s: she was an activist and an intelligent university student. This might have prevented her from having an ordinary husband, since many men tend to choose younger women with lower education levels. She finally married my father who was her classmate at the same university where she studied. Her experience of getting married at the late age made her worried if this was also experienced by her daughters. Therefore, my marriage relieved my mother's fear and social pressure of having a spinster daughter. However, the social pressure moved to me to have a child soon after I got married. When I met my friends or acquaintances, I was always asked, "Are you pregnant already?" When I answered, "Not yet," I felt that those who asked the questions seemed to wonder why I was not pregnant and might assume that I might be infertile. Some of them usually suggested tips for a quick pregnancy. I actually planned to postpone my first pregnancy until I finished my master's degree abroad. However, annoyed by the social pressure, I just let myself become pregnant.

In addition, I was socially constructed to see the wife's role as serving her husband, not the opposite. To avoid morning sickness during the first five months of my pregnancy, the doctor suggested I drink sweet hot tea before I got up slowly from my bed. However, I was not brave enough to ask for my husband's help in providing me with hot tea. I then preferred to drink medicine to prevent morning sickness, but the side effect was that I was very sleepy while I had to attend English classes in preparation for going abroad. I was supposed to go abroad in January 1995, but my baby was due in February. I was apprehensive and was not confident about giving birth abroad, so I postponed my departure abroad for one semester and gave birth in the clinic near my parents' home.

Influenced by Indonesian constructions of the good wife and mother, I tried to do my best to meet these ideals. I did all the housework, such as cooking, washing dishes, ironing, and giving bottle milk to my baby at night when my husband and my baby joined me to live in Australia three months after I had moved there. As a result, I suffered from lack of sleep and energy; I did not have enough time to study well. Consequently, I did not receive very good grades in the first semester. Knowing that my studies were in jeopardy, I talk to my husband about my study burdens. My husband was willing to help me, but he was not used to the work, so I took several days to teach him how to do housework because in Indonesia men are not expected or taught to do domestic works. He could finally do almost all of the housework and childcare, except cooking and ironing, which I could handle. With enough sleep, energy and time to study, I successfully completed my master's degree on time with better grades, which made it easier to receive a scholarship to pursue my PhD in Australia.

After I returned to Indonesia in mid-1997, my husband encouraged me to have our second child, but I was determined not to have another child until I felt that we were economically secure. The Indonesian economic crisis that began just after we returned to Indonesia forced me to take several additional jobs in addition to teaching at my university. Therefore, I felt that being home with the baby would be very hard to achieve in such difficult economic conditions. However, in response to my husband's constant insistence on having another child, I promised that I would be willing to have another baby if I could have another scholarship to do my PhD abroad; I thought it would be easier for me to breastfeed my baby abroad because I would be less mobile and more economically stable. The scholarship I received in Australia was enough to cover my family's daily expenses, which was different from the monthly salary that I received as a lecturer in Indonesia, which only covered part of our daily expenses at that time. I realized that the limited salary in Indonesia, which forced me to take several other jobs, would prevent me from being home with the baby, if I had the baby in Indonesia. In contrast, I had more control over my time when I did my PhD in Australia because my responsibility was to read and write a thesis, which I thought I could do at home with my baby close to me, or I could leave my baby at the university's daycare, where I could visit him to breastfeed regularly while on campus.

Like Hera Diani, a journalist who was determined not to have children, I tended to see having a baby as a liability that is attached to women. Therefore, if I had to have another baby, I wanted to ensure that it would not be too difficult for me to assume a mothering role. If I had to have a second baby, I wanted to follow the Qur'anic suggestion to breastfeed my baby for two years because I did not have a chance to do so for my first baby. I had to leave my first baby to go abroad because my sponsor did not permit me to go abroad for the first time with the baby, which I regretted because I had to stop breastfeeding after only four months. I did have a baby in the middle of my PhD, based on my choice to follow the

Qur'anic suggestion to breastfeed for about two years. Breastfeeding while studying in Australia was not without difficulties, but I found it easier to manage than it would have been being employed in Indonesia, which still has very limited facilities and support for breastfeeding mothers. Unlike in Australia, which provides places to breastfeed in most public facilities, in Indonesia such facilities are very rare even in a big city such as Jakarta. Daycare in the work place or near the workplace was almost non-existent. It is only recently that some women have initiated private daycares in their communities to cater to the needs of working mothers, but the number is still very small. Having a daycare is still regarded as a Western privilege and, thus, unsuitable for Indonesian culture, in which mothers are expected to be home to look after the baby, which ignores the reality that many women now participate in the public sphere.

CONCLUSION

This chapter has shown that in the post-New Order period educated urban women who have careers tend to plan and determine whether or not they will have children and when they will have them. Yet to some extent, Indonesian Muslim women who live in both rural and urban areas tend to live based on Indonesian culture rather than on the Qur'anic injunctions governing childbirth and mothering. During the New Order period, there was a tendency for Indonesians to see the maximum number of children per couple as three, with the ideal number being two. In campaigning for birth control to reduce the Indonesian population, the New Order government "negotiated" with the Indonesian Ulama Council to issue a *fatwa* (religious opinion) that said it is acceptable to use contraception as a family planning program, which was prohibited prior to the 1970s. As a result of this government campaign, beginning in the 1970s, some Muslims gradually accepted a limitation on the number of children they had, even though there are still some Muslims who consider it prohibited to limit the number of children or to use contraception. During the New Order period, those who had more than three children received unfavourable comments from neighbours or governments staff when they needed their services. This can be seen, for example, in the cases of Sri and Aisyah, when they tried to use contraception after they had three children but were unsuccessful and received negative comments.

Most Indonesian women generally prefer pills and injections as their contraception methods because they are easy to use, but they seem not to know the hormonal effects that this form of contraception can have on their breast milk and menstruation schedules. Only a small minority of men are involved in using contraception. Using contraception is still regarded as a women's responsibility and, therefore, is mainly imposed on women. Using contraception requires agency and knowledge. Women have to be powerful in saying no to have sex with their husbands before they use any contraception. Many Indonesian Muslim women believe that after they are married, they belong to their husbands so they have to be submissive and have to ask permission from their husband before using contraception. Some husbands do prohibit their wives to have contraception; therefore, some wives, such as Sri and Aisyah, use the contraception secretly, without their husband's knowledge for fear that it would be prohibited.

However, there are some progressive Muslim feminists who promote the idea that having a sex is also women's right. This means that women have the right to enjoy sex when they want it and have the right to reject their husbands politely when they do not want it (Mas'udi; Qibtiyah). Similarly, Indonesian Muslim feminists also argue that having children is a women's *right*, not an obligation. This means that women have the rights to decide whether or not to have children and when to have them. Muslim feminists base their opinion, for example, on the Qur'an chapter *Asy-Syura* (42:38), which suggests that a husband and wife consult each other in making decisions, including consulting each other on whether or not to bear children and when as well as on how many they want to have. Although there are two commonly cited *hadith* that encourage Muslims to have children (one *hadith* states, "Get married and have many children because I will be proud of your greater number than any other people," and another states, "Marry women whom you love and you can have many children"), Muslim feminists recognize that the Qur'an does not necessarily see having children as something positive. For example, the Qur'an chapter

Al-Anfal states that having children is a trial (*fitnah*): "And know that your possessions and your children are but a trial and that surely with Allah is a mighty reward" (8:28). Muslim feminists combine the above Qur'anic verse with the *hadith* that states, "If people pass away, all their deeds cannot be brought to the hereafter except three things: their charity, their beneficial knowledge and their children who pray for them." The result of this combination is either to have righteous children who can pray for their parents or not to have children at all, which, again, highlights that having children is a choice, not an obligation.

Unfortunately, more work still needs to be done to counter the existing belief that women belong to their husbands when they are married. In addition, we need more campaigns for women's reproductive rights and more education on the various forms of contraception, for both men and women, to empower women to make informed decisions in relation to having or not having children. We also need more campaigns to encourage the government to provide better facilities and support for breastfeeding mothers in the workplace and more flexibility for women when taking their maternity leaves.

NOTES

[1]Unilateral divorce takes place without the knowledge or consultation of the wife. For example, a man wants to marry another woman, but the woman does not want to be involved in a polygamous marriage and insists that the man divorce his wife first before marrying her. Therefore, the man, fulfilling the request of the woman whom he wants to marry, just says, "I divorce my wife." This was believed to be a valid divorce prior to the enactment of the 1974 Marriage Law.

[2]Arbitrary polygamy is when a man marries another woman without the knowledge of his existing wife. He does not divorce his first wife, merely neglects her and the children, and does not support her financially after his second marriage.

[3]However, among uneducated and low-income families, the incidence of early marriage between fourteen and sixteen year of age might still occur even now. Many of the parents from these

families still see marriage as a solution to reduce their burden of feeding their daughters. Unfortunately, this early marriage is often a disguise for child trafficking and, therefore, the daughters from these families are vulnerable to violence, even when they stay in their marriages.

[4]However, the common phenomenon of women exercising their rights for divorce only began to occur in the last ten years, during the Reform Era, when women tended to be more economically independent and less stigmatized as divorced women.

[5]The Reform era began after the end of Soeharto's authoritarian government in 1998. During the Reform era, many of the government regulations and laws were changed to avoid a centralistic system of government and to limit the term of presidency to a maximum of ten years.

[6]Girls are considered physically matured (*baligh*) after they have their menarche. However, the ideal age of marriage is changing as described above. Prior to the 1970s, most girls were expected to get married by the age of seventeen, but after the 1970s, the ideal age of marriage increased to between eighteen and twenty-five years old. The 1974 Marriage Law stipulates that the minimum age of marriage for women is sixteen and for men is nineteen. There have been amendments proposed to increase the minimum age of marriage for women to eighteen because another law, the Law on the Protection of Child, defines childhood to be up to eighteen years old. However, up until now, the amendment of the Marriage Law has not occurred, and the proposal to increase the minimum age of marriage to eighteen for women through judicial review was rejected by the Constitutional Court.

[7]In Mecca, I was in one big room with six other women, whereas in Medina I had only one female roommate.

[8]The use of contraception was controversial issue among Indonesian Muslims because the Ulama Council prohibited it prior to the 1970s. In 1975, President Soeharto helped to found the Indonesian Ulama Council (Majlis Ulama Indonesia) and used this council to legitimize the use of contraception to support the government program of controlling the population. As a result, many Muslim women participated in birth control programs by using contraception. The use of IUD was initially prohibited by

the council in 1972 because it exposed the female *aurat* (female parts of body that have to be covered), but this was changed in 1983 when the council issued a *fatwa* to allow the use of IUDs inserted by female health staff or a female doctor. If there is no female staff, it is acceptable for it to be inserted by a male doctor, with the requirement that the wife is accompanied by her husband.

WORKS CITED

Aripurnami, Sita. "Feminist Comment on the Sinetron Presentation of Indonesian Women." *Fantasizing the Feminine in Indonesia.* Ed. Laurie J. Sears. Durham: Duke University Press, 1996. 249–258. Print.

Bappenas. "Bab XIX Peranan Wanita, Anak dan Remaja dan Pemuda [Chapter XIX The Roles of Women, Children and Youth]."*Kementerian PPN / Bappenas.*Bappenas, 2012.Web. 10 Jan. 2012.

Bennett, L. R. "Sexual Morality and the Silencing of Sexual Health within Indonesian Infertility Care." *Sex and Sexualities in Indonesia: Sexual Politics, Health, Diversity and Representations.* Eds. Linda Rae Bennett and Sharyn Graham Davies. London: Routledge, 2015. 148-166. Print.

Blackburn, Susan, and Sharon Bessell. "Marriageable Age: Political Debates on Early Marriage in Twentieth-Century Indonesia." *Indonesia* 63 (April 1997):107–41. Print.

Dunia Perempuan. "Peranan dan Tugas Perempuan [Women's Roles and Duties]." Dunia Perempuan, 2012. Web. 10 Jan. 2012.

Firth, Rosemary. *Housekeeping among Malay Peasants.* New York: Humanities Press, 1966. Print.

Geertz, Hildred. *The Javanese Family: A Study of Kinship and Socialization.* New York: The Free Press of Glencoe, 1961. Print.

Heaton, Tim B., et al. "Why Is the Divorce Rate Declining in Indonesia?" *Journal of Marriage and Family.* 63.2 (2001): 480–490. Print.

Hull, Terence H. "Fertility Decline in the New Order Period: The Evolution of Population Policy 1965–1990." *Indonesia's New Order: The Dynamics of Socio-economic Transformation.* Ed. Hal Hill. New South Wales: Allen & Unwin, 1994: 123-145. Print.

Jaspan, Helen, and Lewis Hill.*The Child in the Family: A Study of*

Childbirth and Child-Rearing in Rural Central Java in the Late 1950s. Hull: University of Hull Press, 1987. Print.

Jayalaksana, Naomi "Berduasajacukup [Just Two of Us Is Enough]" *Femina* 41(October 2011): 22-28. Print.

Jones, Gavin W. *Marriage and Divorce in Islamic South East Asia.* Kuala Lumpur: Oxford University Press, 1994. Print.

Jones, Gavin W. "Modernization and Divorce: Contrasting Trends in Islamic Southeast Asia and the West." *Population and Development Review* 23.1 (1997):95–114. Print.

Jones, Gavin W. "Population and the Family in Southeast Asia." *Journal of Southeast Asian Studies*26.1 (1995): 184-95. Print.

Koentjaraningrat, R. M. *Javanese Culture.* Singapore: Oxford University Press, 1985. Print.

Mas'udi, Masdar Farid. *Islam dan hak-hak reproduksi Perempuan. Dialog Fiqih Pemberdayaan [Islam and Women's Reproductive Rights. The Dialogue on Empowering Islamic Law].* Bandung: Mizan 1997. Print.

Mdy, Acik. "Keberadaan Wanita yang Berprofesi Sebagai Ibu Rumah Tangga [The Existence of Women Whose Profession Is House Wife]." *Kompasiana,* 22 Dec. 2011. Web. 10 Jan. 2012.

Noor, Sofia Retnowati. "PeranPerempuandalamKeluargaIslami." Paper presented at the seminar on "Women's Roles in Family Building with Islamic Values."Wanita Islam [Muslim Women] and Forum PengajianIbu-ibu Al Kautsar Daerah Istimewa Yogyakarta [Women's Religious Forum Al-Kautsar in Yogyakarta].1 June 2002 Web. *8 Jan. 2012.*

Nurmila, Nina. "Indonesian Muslim Women's Dilemma of Dual Roles." MA thesis. Murdoch University, Western Australia, 1997. Print.

Nurmila, Nina. "When There Is No husband" *Inside Indonesia.* Inside Indonesia, Jan-Mar 2011.Web. 12 Apr. 2016.

Nurmila, Nina. *Women, Islam and Everyday Life: Renegotiating Polygamy in Indonesia.* 2nd edition. London: Routledge 2011. Print.

Qibtiyah, Alimatul. "Intervensi Malaikat dalam Hubungan Seksual." *Perempuan Tertindas? Kajian Hadis-Hadis "Misoginis."* ["The Angel's Intervention on Sexual Relationship." *Oppressed Women? The Study of "Misogynistic" Hadiths*]. Yogyakarta:

eLSAQ Press and the Center for Women's Studies 2003.

Republik Indonesia. "Undang-undang Republik Indonesia Nomor 1 Tahun 1974 tentang Perkawinan [Indonesian Marriage Law Number 1 Year 1974]: *Universitas Gadjah Mada*. Universitas Gadjah Mada, 2012. Web. 10 Jan. 2012.

Smith-Hefner, Nancy J. "The New Muslim Romance: Changing Patterns of Courtship and Marriage among Educated Javanese Youth." *Journal of Southeast Asian Studies* 36.3 (2005): 441-459. Print.

Suryakusuma, Julia I. *Sex, Power and Nation*. Jakarta: Metafor Publishing, 2004. Print.

The Study Quran: A New Translation and Commentary. Ed. and Trans. Seyyed Hossein Nasr. New York: HarperCollins, 2015. Print.

Tiwon, Sylvia. "Models and Maniacs: Articulating the Female in Indonesia." *Fantasizing the Feminine in Indonesia*. Ed. Laurie J. Sears. Durham: DukeUniversityPress, 1996.47-70. Print.

Wolf, Diane L. *Factory Daughters: Gender, Household Dynamics, and Rural Industrialization in Java*. Berkeley: University of California Press, 1992. Print.

11.
Confinement Practices of
Young Malay Muslim Mothers

FATIMAH AL-ATTAS

E XTENSIVE STUDIES HAVE BEEN CONDUCTED and compiled on the traditional confinemeant practices of Malay mothers in Malaysia in the twentieth century, both by Malaysian and Western researchers.[1] There has been significantly less research done to update the current situation, and like many parts of the world, Malaysia has been experiencing substantial change through globalization and urbanization. In this chapter, firstly, I review some literature on traditional Malay confinement practices and its relationship with Islam. I then present the findings from my research on the perceptions and practices of confinement among young Malay mothers. Finally, I discuss how my findings on contemporary urban mothers differ from the portrayal of mothers in previous research and address the relationship and distinctions between Islamic beliefs and traditional Malay postpartum practices.

LITERATURE REVIEW: HISTORICAL BACKGROUND

In Malaysia, the Federal Constitution Article 160 (2) defines a Malay as a Muslim who habitually speaks the Malay language and practices Malay customs. Islam plays an integral role in the formation of the contemporary national Malay identity with some inclusion of other cultures that conform with the original culture of the people in the region (Siddique 79). This includes influences from Indian, Chinese, Arab-Greek and Orang Asli (aboriginal Malay) languages and cultures.

Wazir Karim explains that *adat* and Islam are the two major forces that influence the everyday lives of Malay Muslims in Malaysia. *Adat*, as Karim describes it, is the "total constellation of concepts, rules and codes of behaviour which are conceived as legitimate or right, appropriate or necessary" (14). *Adat*, or Malay custom, is spread through everyday socialization; it navigates the everyday lives and practices of the people. Islam, on the other hand, was spread through a more institutionalized form of socialization, such as formal lessons at the mosque or schools (Wazir Karim 14). Over time, some Islamic practices have been integrated into the Malay *adat;* for example, saying *"Assalamualaikum"* (peace be upon you) upon meeting fellow Malays.

TRADITIONAL CONFINEMENT PRACTICE AMONG MALAYS

Traditional postpartum practices that are based on the humoral beliefs of hot and cold and involve the mother being confined in the home are common in many Asian cultures; the Japanese practice of *satogeri*, the Chinese and Taiwanese practice of "doing the month," and the practice of *berpantang* among the Malays (Kim-Godwin; Mori) are a few examples. Among Malays, the postnatal period is considered a vulnerable period, which demands the practice of confinement. This practise originates from ideas and social practices linked with medical beliefs based on a humoral system (Manderson, "Roasting;" Laderman, "Destructive"). Although the humoral system is not implemented completely, the balancing of hot and cold persists in popular Malay beliefs (Manderson, "Traditional"). Lenore Manderson explains that "[t]he classifi-cation of foodstuffs and medicines generally relates neither to the temperature of the item nor its spiciness or raw or cooked state, but to the reputed effect of the food on the body" ("Traditional" 510). Childbirth is associated with the loss of heat through the hot blood, leaving the mother in a cold, vulnerable, and dangerous state. The mother's body during the postnatal period is understood as dirty, cold, tired, and weak (Eshah et al.).The purpose of the forty day confinement period is to restore the mother's health, sexual ability, and pre-pregnancy shape as well as to reduce risk of sickness or infertility in the future based on the humoral understanding of hot and cold. The confinement period is a time for rest, treatment, and cleansing.

Traditionally, the confinement is supervised by a *bidan*'s (traditional midwife). Roziah Omar describes the *bidan* as follows: "The Malay bidan kampong (village midwife) is always a female who enjoys a high social status mainly because of her unique range of knowledge and skills relating to pre and post-partum practices" (110). In the literature surrounding Malaysian postpartum confinement practices, there are a number of different practices recorded. These include, but are not limited to, massages, *bertungku or bertuku* (hot compress), *mandi teresak* (herbal bath), *berdiang* (roasting), *berganggang* (vaginal washing and steaming) and *berbengkung* (wearing a corset).

In Lee Kick Kit, Grace Janet, and Ravindran Jegasothy's 1997 study, the majority of women in Malaysia still followed a special diet during the confinement period (89). However, in an older study by Laderman ("Destructive") in 1987, the majority of the participants did follow this strict diet for the whole period and gradually introduced otherwise restricted items, even within this period (363). As with many other aspects of confinement, practices surrounding food restrictions vary between regions and individuals. In Manderson's 1981 study, a small percentage of women did not practise this because they were either under medical supervision or deemed that the practice was a hassle and had no real effect ("Traditional" 513).

Food types include hot, cold, *bisa* (toxic), and *sederhana* (neutral). Hot and *sederhana* food is allowed. Conversely, cold and *bisa* food are best avoided. *Bisa*, which Carol Laderman translates as toxic, is not *essentially* a toxic food but is considered as such because it intensifies the disharmonies during this period (362). Manderson translates *bisa* as poison and describes it as having the ability to weaken the mother, inhibit her recovery, and to even cause convulsions, comas, and death ("Traditional" 513). As mentioned earlier, the descriptors given to the food types refer to the effect the food might have on the body rather than its physical state.

Haron and Hamiz report that all dieticians and gynaecologists in their study said that all food types can be eaten and are considered sources of energy (1307). However, it was noted that the dietician and gynaecologists believed that traditional practices were complementary to this, and they did not speak against traditional practices (1308). Studies in the 1970s and 1980s in the northern region of peninsular Malaysia reported that most mothers observed the confinement practices scrupulously both in rural and urban areas, even when the mothers had biomedical education and training (Laderman, "Destructive"; Manderson, "Roasting"; W. Karim). More recent studies by Eliana Naser and Aishah Eshah suggest that the number of mothers foregoing the traditional confinement practices has increased.

In the study by Naser, some mothers report that they see traditional practices as non-beneficial, so mothers have become selective in their adherence to the practice (869). It should be noted, however, that in the context of global communication technologies, there is easy access to other understandings of postpartum recovery (Naser et al. 869). The avoidance of confinement practice has been reported by Laderman ("Destructive"), who comment that "[f]ollowing these rules is a matter of individual volition; each person has autonomy of choice, and each must accept responsibility for the outcome. Some people interpret and manipulate the rules, continually testing the boundaries, while others, wary by nature or rendered cautious by past experience, obey them to the letter" (363). There are, and have been in the past, mothers that avoid the practise of confinement, but it would always be pointed out to them by their social circle of the consequences that it will bring.

METHODOLOGY

The data collected for this chapter are part of a sociological study drawing on phenomenological methods (Moustakas; Van Manen). A phenomenological research approach tries to provide a description of the nature or essence of an experience in its pre-reflexive state. Findings in this article were taken from twelve interviews with four Muslim couples, and two focus group discussions with five Muslim Malay mothers.

Participants in the dyadic interviews consisted of Malaysian Muslim couples, with first-time mothers between ages of twenty-five to twenty-eight who were about to return to work. Participants from the focus group discussions consisted of mothers between the ages of twenty-two and twenty-seven who had returned to work within the past year. All mothers had tertiary education.

DATA COLLECTION

The dyadic interviews were open ended and conducted three times with each couple; the interview lasted between fifty-five and nine-ty-five minutes each session. The time period between the three interviews varied between ten and fourteen weeks. Data collected from the dyadic interviews were used to guide questions for the focus group discussions. Focus group discussions lasted between ninety minutes to two hours each.

DATA ANALYSIS

Data for this article were taken from interview transcripts and textural descriptions of each interview. In keeping with phenome-nological method, the persisting elements were extracted and then classified as themes for the purpose of this chapter.

FINDINGS

The experience of confinement or lack thereof of the participants of this research revolved around two main themes: their perception of confinement and the practices of confinement.

Perception of Confinement

All of the participants in this research project knew of the practice of confinement. These mothers selectively practised and omitted aspects of the confinement period, and they attributed their practice to filial piety more than accepting or understand-ing the significance of each practice. Although the traditional confinement practices are still considered to be a part of the first weeks of motherhood, all the couples in the dyadic interview asserted that biomedical science has more authority than the traditional humoral explanations. When I asked Malik,[2] one of the fathers whom I interviewed, about the confinement period, he immediately responded with "[We will] follow the doctor. Whatever the doctor says, we would follow. We didn't really follow the prohibitions."

The participants in this study all gave birth at a medical centre, hospital, or family clinic. All participants except three spent the first few days at the maternal mothers' home after returning from the medical centres. "It is a common understanding to have confinement at your mum's," as one participant named Sarah said. The practice of spending the confinement period at the maternal home is part of the traditional practice. Two participants left their maternal mothers' home during the confinement period and both went to the mother-in-law's house.

The perception of confinement changed for one of the couples throughout the three dyadic interviews. During the first interview, Halim expressed his opinion as being cautious but receptive to the practices: "The advice has been there for a while. I think there has to be some truth in the tales (folklore) or whatever it is, says. They might have a point; why don't we try. If the particular practice is nonsense then we won't follow. Practices that might have to do with religion, we [have to] consider them." Farah, the mother, had a different opinion: "As for me, I'm more liberal. For example, in drinking cold drinks, I think that it's fine." At the final interview, the couple both agreed that they had more faith in biomedical explanations than the traditional practices after reading about the differences and contradictions between the traditional practices and biomedical science ones. The example they gave was the traditional practice of feeding the newborn with some water to ease digestion, which contradicted the biomedical advice to exclusively breastfeed infants before six months of age.

Pressure to follow the confinement methods were felt by all mothers. Maisarah narrated her experience: "Even though my husband is a [medical] doctor, he got scolded [by our mothers and aunties] because they say that that's just medical theory, these [practices] have been the practice for generations." One of the couples said that although there was real pressure to follow these practices, they did not want to because they felt it was against their Islamic beliefs. "There were constantly people asking us why we didn't follow it.... We always use the doctor as the scapegoat.... The *jamu* kit [herbal confinement kit] was a bit weird and Islamically we feel like it's wrong, like [there is] a *tangkal* [talisman or amulet]." A *tangkal*—commonly a black string placed either on the baby's wrist, ankle or abdomen—was typically used because of its perceived power to repel evil spirits and sickness and to provide protection for the baby according to Hindu and animistic beliefs. Two other couples mentioned that traditional confinement disagreed with their religious beliefs but did not specify which particular practice or restriction.

Knowledge and information about and obedience to the confinement practice were mostly transmitted through maternal mothers. Most participants when describing the confinement period began with a reference to the maternal mother. When asked about confinement, Lisa immediately said, "My mother doesn't really follow the Malay confinement methods." Other sources for information about the confinement practice included paternal mothers, confinement ladies, masseuses, or elder womenfolk around them. Confinement ladies and the masseuse were referred to through maternal mothers or aunties. Sources of information on traditional confinement practices other than these were not mentioned besides using phrases such as, "people say." This suggests that there exists a large body of commonly held thoughts or general wisdom on the practice, which attests to its longevity in Malay culture.

Practice

The practise of confinement involves restrictions and treatments. In general, only one of the participants spoke of doing the confinement diligently and following it through to the end. Most of the mothers selectively practised this tradition. For the purpose of this chapter, I have classified this restriction section into three aspects: diet, movement, and attire. Restriction in diet comprised most of the discussion around confinement for my participants. For these participants, following a healthy diet as prescribed by doctors and nurses was most important, as they were all breastfeeding. All the mothers spoke of not following the diet very strictly, except one. Damia described her mother's restrictions: "She even rationed the amount of water I took.... Food was strictly *singgang* [soupy dish], *ikan bakar* [grilled fish], *bakar* [grilled food], that's it. I was mad at my mum, because of the water; I had a fight with her about it. I said how can you expect me to produce enough milk when you ration my water intake? She was like, 'oh it's just how it is, and the people in the past didn't drink that much water.'"

Other first-time mothers spoke of their maternal mothers giving precedence to the prescribed diet given by hospital nurses and doctors. One of the participants followed a more "practical" and easy going diet. Misha, another participant, had a slightly strict experience, but some of the recommended humoral ingredients were removed because of side effects that she experienced. Most mothers commented that the food restriction could be challenging, but some expressed that they had actually enjoyed it and found that there was no trouble at all.

The consumption of hot and cold food was rarely mentioned overtly. Ginger and black pepper were very common ingredients during the confinement period, as they are understood as hot and to have the ability to help expel "wind." Lisa recalled: "When my mother cooked, she added ginger and black pepper. That's to expel wind."

Generally, women in confinement are also restricted in terms of motility and space. Most mothers in this study stayed at home for most of the period of confinement. Rahman's response when I asked what confinement meant for them said "She [Misha] did the usual, she didn't leave the house." The experience of being confined at home was challenging and stressful for most of the mothers. Some of the mothers took the liberty of finding ways to leave the house. Nurin, living away from family, recounted that she started going out after the second week despite the advice by family and having had a Caesarean section. As she said, "I couldn't stand staying at home."

Most of the other mothers, however, stayed at home under maternal supervision. As Lisa reported, "I didn't leave the house because my mother said I shouldn't go out. I left the house one week after Eid, which was to go to my in-laws house." Besides being confined to the home, mothers are advised to reduce the speed, amount, and patterns of movements that they make. Damia remembered in horror. "[My mother] said 'why are you sitting like this, you shouldn't sit like this'; I was like, oh my god, now even the way I sit is a problem." There were very specific restrictions and practices surrounding the attire or clothing for women in the postpartum period. The three main articles of clothing reported by the participants were *kain batik*, socks and *bengkung*. *Kain batik*, a type of cloth that has been sewn into a hollow shape, is wrapped around the lower body like a skirt. Most mothers either wore the *kain batik* or wore a skirt strictly during the confinement period. Socks were considered an important piece, wich helps preserve the mothers "heat." All the mothers observed the wearing of socks, although some did it only under observation to avoid negative comments. The *bengkung* can be considered both as a restriction and treatment. The *bengkung* is a traditional form of corset that covers the body from under the breast to the thighs. Most of the mothers observed the *bengkung*, as it was seen as personally beneficial despite its discomfort.

Treatments that were given to the participants of my study included massages, herbal baths, *tungku or tuku*, *pilis* and herbal medicines. Though not all treatments were practised by all the mothers whom I interviewed, most mothers, except one, received massages and herbal baths during this period. Massage was most common among the participants. Even though the dates on which these women received massages varied, it was commonly understood that mothers would receive massages within the first few days back from the hospital and on the last day of confinement.

Massages done during the confinement differ from the common massage treatments that are available at massage parlours in Malaysia. There are special techniques and equipment involved in the practice of postnatal massage for mothers as opposed to the massages typically given to either men or women for ache relief. These mothers contacted masseuses or confinement ladies that could do confinement massages. Massages are seen to have a myriad of benefits: besides helping the mother regain her body size by removing fats, the confinement massage helps reduce body aches after childbirth. Massages also involve the use of hot oils that help warm the body, increase blood circulation, and undo clots or blockages in the veins. Other benefits include assisting in the reduction of the uterus size.

Mothers also spoke of taking special baths for most of the confinement period. The baths are mostly made of a boiled mix of special leaves, and the mother used it while it was still warm. One of the mothers spoke of taking these baths once or twice a day for a month, another mother did the baths just for a week, the frequency and amount of baths taken vary between these mothers. Some of these mothers would apply oil and a paste on their abdomen and other body parts after the baths to help the regain pre-pregnancy shape. These paste and other requirements for the confinement period such as oils and traditional herbal mix are generally included in a confinement kit.

Confinement kits have now been made popular, coming in different commercial brands with a variety of contents. Some of the usual contents of a confinement kit include *bengkung*, *jamu* (herbal mix), special tea, massage oils, *pilis*, and some even a *tungku or tuku* set. Most of the mothers did not choose the confinement kits themselves; they referred to their mothers or had the set given to them. Not all of the contents of a confinement kits would be used either. Mothers selectively chose which items would be used.

DISCUSSION

Traditional confinement practices, as stated in recent studies by Naser and Eshah, are still widely practised. There are, however, significant differences between the experiences of participants in this study and the participants in previous studies on Malay confinement practices, which can be partly attributed to demographical differences. The participants of this research were younger mothers, who all had tertiary education, most lived in the central region of peninsular Malaysia, and many had experiences of living outside Malaysia for a period of time. The participants in previous studies (Eshah et al.; R. Karim et al., "Reproductive Health"; Laderman, "Destructive"; Manderson) in Malaysia were mothers from wide-age groups, ranging from primaparae mother (first time mothers) to multiparae mothers (mothers with multiple children) and most lived in traditional villages in the north and east coast region of peninsular Malaysia. Although I discuss the general concepts and acceptance of the confinement as a whole without scrutinizing the specific practices, it should be noted that the specific confinement practices might vary within regions and between families.

The main difference noted is that contemporary mothers in this study and in Aishah Ali's study from between 1997 and 1999 separate certain cultural beliefs from religious beliefs, unlike those described in Manderson's ("Roasting") and Laderman's ("Destructive") research. Confinement practices portrayed in Laderman's ("Destructive") article appeared foreign and almost unbelievable from a contemporary Malay standpoint. However, upon assessment of Laderman's book *Wives and Midwives*, I acknowledge that the general concepts are those commonly understood today, but some of the specific practices appear to be very remote and isolated to a particular village or family and do not represent the whole population. Laderman's use of the term "Islamic Malays" seems particularly contradictory and problematic. In her book, she describes the practices of the midwife as being condemned by the Islamic religious establishment for threatening Islamic integrity (*Wives and Midwives* 105). However, she continues to describe these practices as Islamic in her later article ("Destructive" 360). In fact, many of the explanations that were mislabelled as Islamic or having Islamic origin could be construed as more cultural in origin rather than religious. To illustrate, she writes, "Islamic Malays share the concept of destructive spiritual heat with the Orang Asli. They have, however, adapted this pre-humoral notion to correspond with the Greek-Arabic humoral model of the Universe and the Islamic myth of Man's creation" (360). Beliefs and practices of Malay magic might have been related and associated with Islam and Muslims in the past, but in contemporary times, my research participants acknowledged and pointed out that the practice of magic opposes Islamic beliefs and, hence, must have originated from culture and tradition. In fact, Wazir Karim argues that the practice of confinement is rooted in the cultural beliefs of animism and has no Islamic origins (153), and she further establishes the difference between Islam and *adat* within certain practices. *Adat* or customs were held very highly by the Malays, and parts of the practices were rooted in animistic beliefs. Although Muslims believe in the presence of unseen beings, animism and the practice of magic are forbidden and considered acts of disbelief.

Even though Islam was and is embraced in many of the divisions of the everyday Malay life, the animistic aspects of certain practices have persisted. W. Karim acknowledges that despite pressures from local religious authorities, certain animistic practices continue to be performed on the individual level but not in the public sphere (64). It is not uncommon that traditional animistic practitioners incorporate Islamic texts into their incantations to justify their practices. Moreover, some of the animistic beliefs and humoral practices are given "Islamic" explanations. Although these practices are not common in urban areas, some parents do place a talisman or amulet in the form of a bracelet, necklace, or stone with verses of the Qur'an to repel evil spirits perceived to be attracted to the mother and child. These talisman are placed either on the mother and child or under the pillow or sleeping area. There are some that believe that women during the postpartum period attract evil spirits or creatures because they are understood as spiritually weak and are excreting lochia, and, hence, they require extra protection. Although some Muslims in Malaysia might still practice some form of animistic belief, these practices are not commonly considered Islamic.

In recent times, however, with globalization, the Islamic resurgence (Omar 63), the Internet, and availability of educational resources, the younger generation have become invested in articulating differences between customary practices and Islamic practices. Islam acknowledges and accommodates to cultural or customary practices as long as they do not contradict Islamic beliefs. It was in relation to the contradictory practices that these mothers felt that they needed to distinguish and avoid certain customs—seeking protection through a talisman, for example. Such practices go against a basic tenet of Islamic faith, *tauhid*, which stresses the belief in the oneness of God. Asking for protection and depending on and worshipping other supernatural beings are considered forms of *shirk* or disbelief. Equally, establishing partners to God or placing faith in the power of other beings on the same level as God is also considered disbelief.

Islamic prescriptions concerning the postpartum condition mostly revolve around the lochia. Much like the ruling on menstruation, until the lochia has been fully flushed out, mothers are not supposed to have sexual intercourse, perform *salah* (prayers), or read the Qur'anic text, according to the *Shafi'i* school of thought. The end of this period, known as *nifas*, is marked by a cleansing practice of *ghusl* (major ablution), whereby the mother will cleanse her body by making a verbal intention (*niyyah*), performing ablution (*wudhu'*), and washing every part of her body. The specific order of *ghusl*, which part of the body to wash first, may vary slightly among the four Islamic schools of thought.

The *ghusl* is unlike the confinement baths practised by mothers in this study. The confinement baths are taken often more than once during the period. For some women, their *nifas* ends before the confinement period ends, and then they perform their *ghusl*, and begin their obligatory prayers again. However, there are no changes to their practice of confinement. For example, there are cases in which women still abstain from intimate relations with their husbands even after *ghusl* because the confinement period has not ended.

In terms of Islamic rulings, food prescriptions remain the same for mothers postpartum as with any other time. Muslims are encouraged to eat of what is halal and what is good. This is to say that Muslims, regardless of gender, are encouraged to consume what is beneficial and nutritious for the body. This can be translated into the type of food mothers might need more during this period. However, there is very little discussion about this matter regarding mothers in postpartum confinement.

The mothers involved in this study articulated their clear separation between religious belief, traditional postpartum practices, and contemporary biomedical practices. This is not to say that *adat* has been totally abandoned by the study population. *Adat* or customs constantly change and evolve (Omar 37), and although the traditional practices that involve animistic beliefs are being removed from the practices of these urban mothers, the Malay *Adat* is still alive. *Adat* can be clearly observed through the observance of filial piety, for example. Filial piety and keeping familial peace are still considered very important. When mothers in the present study needed to speak against their mother or mother-in-law, they found it very challenging. As Naser acknowledges, high value is placed on the importance of keeping peace and being respectful towards the family. This goes hand in hand with the Islamic value of respecting elders.

Much like Laderman's ("Destructive" 363) observation that mothers and their spouses know the advantages and risks of disregarding the confinement practice altogether, mothers in this study have also reported similar experiences. Although couples in this study knew of the spoken risks and repercussion of foregoing some of the practices, all have omitted some of the practices. The reason for this can be attributed mainly to the rise in popularity of biomedical sciences over traditional humoral medicine. All of the couples spoke of giving ultimate authority to biomedical sciences. None of the participants gave birth under a traditional midwife (*bidan*); they all went to hospitals and clinics to have their monthly check-ups and eventual delivery. This trend was already observed by Rita Raj Karim, when she studied young rural mothers in 2003; for them, hospitals and clinic were seen as a safer and more private alternative. For the participants in this study, delivering in hospitals and giving medical knowledge the ultimate authority were not things that they needed to justify or explain.

The rise of breastfeeding awareness alongside globalization has given even more authority to biomedical science than traditional humoral medicine through availability of reading resources. Information in books and on the Internet is among the main sources of reference for mothers in this study.

The term *bidan* was not used once by any of the participants in my study. The high social position once enjoyed by the *bidan*, as described by earlier writings, is almost non-existent in urban settings. This may be an outcome of policy changes brought about by the Ministry of Health to reduce mortality rates among mothers in rural areas (R. Karim and Ali). Traditional midwives or *bidan* are now required to be registered through the Ministry of Health and fulfil specific training before being able to practise. A smaller number of mothers spoke of a confinement lady. For most of the participants, it was a masseuse or their mothers who were the sources of guidance on the traditional practices.

In previous work written on confinement, the focus was given to the treatment of hot and cold, but for many of the mothers in my study, there were very few instances that elements of hot and cold were mentioned. The most spoken about aspect of confinement for most of these mothers was returning to maternal mother's home and the massage. Maternal mothers hold a significant role for first-time mothers; she is the point of reference for traditional postpartum knowledge; she helps prepare specific meals for the mother; she relieves the mothers from housework duties; and she helps out with taking care of the baby. Massage, unlike other confinement practices, was described. The mothers could physically feel the benefits of the massage, as it provided them muscle relief and increased their blood flow.

The confinement period plays a significant part in the attainment of the mother role because the first few weeks of motherhood are significant. Being under close supervision during the postpartum period, mothers either thrive under advice and guardianship of their maternal mothers or find themselves under pressure to become independently confident parents. There are instances when mothers find it especially difficult to be confident if and when their beliefs about mothering and childcare contradict their mothers' perspectives.

Some mothers accept what sociologist Talcott Parsons calls "the sick role" (259) and go through the first weeks in confinement smoothly. The sick role, according to Parsons, is a social phenomenon of sanctioned deviance whereby the sick person upholds certain rights and responsibilities. In this case, the mother is exempted from her social roles (relieved from household duties, intimate relations, activities outside the home, etc.), but she must try to get well by following the regulations of confinement.

But many of the mothers in this study no longer accept the sick role and do not wish to go through the experience of becoming a mother this way, even though they have given birth and might still be recovering from the birth and/or stitches. Instead, they would like to be able to go out, to perform certain tasks, and to participate in social life as soon as possible after giving birth.

CONCLUSION

The confinement period is very much a part of the mothering experience for most Malay Muslim mothers. Even though the specific practices have changed and some have been discarded, most mothers still observe the practice in the broader sense. In the present time, as the specific practices of confinement are weighed, mothers will choose practices based on Islamic principles or bio-medical explanations over humoral explanations. The traditional midwife (*bidan*), who once held a high social position, is no longer mentioned among young urban mothers. Nowadays, guidance on specific confinement practices is given by maternal mothers, paternal mothers, and confinement ladies or masseuses. The sample size for this research was limited, as is the nature of qualitative research. Mothers in the study belonged to a specific demographic group of young urban and tertiary educated mothers. Further research to provide a more detailed account of the practices among contemporary mothers in different regions of Malaysia would, thus, prove beneficial.

NOTES

[1] I would like to extend my sincere thanks to my research participants for spending their time and sharing their experiences and parts of their life with me for my research. I am also grateful to my academic supervisor, Associate Professor Rhonda Shaw, for her continuous support and helpful comments throughout this whole process. I would also like to thank Dr. Margaret Aziza Pappano for her comments on earlier drafts.

[2] All names in this chapter are pseudonyms. All interviews, transcriptions, and translations were done by the researcher. Most of the interviews were conducted in English, with a mix of Malay.

WORKS CITED

Eshah, Aishah et al. "Penjagaan Kesihatan Wanita Semasa Dalam Pantang: Amalan Dan Kepercayaan Women's Health Care during Postpartum: The Practice and Beliefs." *Malaysia Journal of Society and Space* 8.7 (2012): 20-31. Print.

Haron, Haryani, and M. Hamiz. "An Ontological Model for Indigenous Knowledge of Malay Confinement Dietary." *Journal of Software* 9.5 (2014): 1302-13. Print.

Karim, Rita Raj, and Siti Hasmah Mohamad Ali. "Maternal Health in Malaysia: Progress and Potential." *The Lancet* 381.9879 (2013): 1690-1691. Print.

Karim, Rita Raj et al. "Reproductive Rights and Reproductive Health: The Malaysain Experience." *Women in Malaysia: Breaking Boundaries*. Kuala Lumpur: Utusan Publications & Distributors, 2003. 169-185. Print.

Karim, Wazir Jahan. *Women and Culture: Between Malay Adat and Islam*. Boulder: Westview, 1992. Print.

Kim-Godwin, Yeoun Soo. "Postpartum Beliefs & Practices Among Non-Western Cultures." MCN: *The American Journal of Maternal Child Nursing* 28.2 (2003): 74-78. Print.

Kit, Lee Kick, Grace Janet, and Ravindran Jegasothy. "Incidence of Postnatal Depression in Malaysian Women." *The Journal of Obstetrics and Gynaecology Research* 23.1 (1997): 85-89. Print.

Laderman, Carol. "Destructive Heat and Healing Prayer: Malay Humoralism in Pregnancy, Childbirth, and Postpartum Period." *Social Science and Medicine* 25.4 (1987): 357–365. Print.

Laderman, Carol. *Wives and Midwives: Childbirth and Nutrition in Rural Malaysia*. Berkeley: University of California Press, 1983. Print.

Manderson, Lenore. "Roasting, Smoking and Dieting in Response to Birth: Malay Confinement in Cross-Cultural Perspective." *Social Science & Medicine* 15.4 (1981): 509-520. Print.

Manderson, Lenore. "Traditional Food Beliefs and Critical Life Events in Peninsular Malaysia." *Social Science Information* 20.6 (1981): 947-975. Web. 28 Aug. 2014.

Mori, Emi, K. Maehara, H. Iwata, et al. "Comparing Older and Younger Japanese Primiparae: Fatigue, Depression and Biomarkers of Stress." *International Journal of Nursing Practice* 21.1 (2015): 10-20. Print.

Moustakas, Clark. *Phenomenological Research Methods*. Los Angeles: Sage Publications, 1994. Print.

Naser, Eliana et al. "An Exploratory Study of Traditional Birthing Practices of Chinese, Malay and Indian Women in Singapore." *Midwifery* 28.6 (2012): e865–71. Web. 15 Aug. 2014.

Omar, Roziah. *The Malay Woman in the Body: Between Biology and Culture*. Kuala Lumpur: Penerbit Fajar Bakti, 1994. Print.

Parsons, Talcott. "The Sick Role and the Role of the Physician Reconsidered." *The Milbank Memorial Fund Quarterly: Health and Society* 53.3 (1975): 257-278. Print.

Siddique, Sharon. "Some Aspects of MalayMuslim Ethnicity in Peninsular Malaysia." *Contemporary Southeast Asia* 3.1 (1981): 76-87. Print.

Van Manen, M. *Researching Lived Experience: Human Science for an Action Sensitive Pedagogy.* 2nd ed. London: Althouse Press, 1997. Print.

12.
The Impact of Maternity Beliefs on Reproductive Health in Muslim Societies

NAZILA ISGANDAROVA

FROM ITS BEGINNING, Islam has encouraged its followers to marry in order to establish a loving relationship between spouses and procreate: "His proofs are that He created for you spouses from among yourselves, in order to have serenity and He placed in your hearts love and compassion towards each other. In this, there are sufficient proofs for people who reflect" (the Qur'an 30:21). This belief, to a great extent, has affected Muslims' attitude towards reproductive health education. Yet the importance of motherhood in patriarchal Muslim cultures facilitated misunderstandings about reproductive health issues among Muslims, largely because women became the "object of the womb"—the source of human relationships, reciprocity, and mutuality. In Islam, childbearing and childrearing are not only physical but also spiritual experiences; hence, the emphasis on childbearing and motherhood in the Qur'an and the *ahadith* (the narrations about the words, actions, or habits that later generations attributed to the Prophet Muhammad) literature has also contributed to the creation of a culture that gives importance to procreation. However, a reexamination of Islamic sources suggests that these sacred sources also encourage Muslims to acquire a proper basic knowledge of pregnancy and childbearing. For instance, according to Islam, pregnancy is developed in three trimester periods. The first forty days, or the first trimester of embryonic development, comprises the drop stage (*nutfa*), the leech-like clot or substance stage (*'alaqa*), and the tissue stage (*mudgha*). The other two periods of prenatal development mentioned in the Qur'an are the stages of *'adham* (bones) and the dressing of the bones with muscle. In addition, the Qur'an draws attention to the burden, *dhat al-haml*, of pregnancy and the special care legally due to pregnant women: "and every pregnant woman [*dhat al-haml*] will drop her burden" (the Qur'an 22:2); "And for those who have a burden [pregnant] their term is when they bring forth their burden ... If they have a burden [pregnant] then provide them with maintenance until they bring forth their burden" (the Qur'an 65:4-6).

Does the increase of reproductive health issues among Muslims indicate that a majority of Muslims are unaware of the significant aspects of reproductive health? Such aspects could include knowledge about fertilization; the facts and myths about menstruation; abstinence from unhealthy sexual behaviours; healthy sexuality; effective communication skills regarding consent; methods of transmission and symptoms of sexually transmitted infections; and prevention methods for sexually transmitted infections. The available literature suggests that Muslims have essentially three differing views about reproductive health education. The adherents of the first view argue that reproductive health education should be entirely secular; the second and opposing view is that, as with other aspects of education, sex education should be taught from an Islamic perspective. However, it is important to note that reproductive health education in Islam is also subject to heated discussion. Some hold more liberal position; others, however, hold a more conservative approach by arguing that the teachings of the Qur'an can be applied strictly to reproductive health education. The third view belongs to those who entirely reject reproductive health education, arguing that teaching it is against moral and cultural values and/or may engrain dangerous ideas in children's minds.

This chapter focuses on the religious and cultural perspectives on sexuality in order to discern the attitude of Muslims towards reproductive health education. I am especially interested in knowing to what extent Islam and culture inform this attitude. I use Qur'anic verses, *hadith* literature, and the works of traditional and contemporary Muslim scholars to briefly describe and analyze the overall Islamic theology of sexuality, marriage, pregnancy, and childbearing, and how this theology affects Muslims' attitude towards the understanding of reproductive health education. I also argue that reproductive health education constitutes a key strategy to increasing awareness and achieving an optimal state of reproductive health. With a proper religious education, the factors of shame and ignorance can be substantially reduced with regards to reproductive health education.

ISLAM AND SEXUALITY

The most important foundations for any argument about maternity and reproductive health in Islam are the Qur'an, *hadith* or the prophetic tradition, Islamic jurisprudence texts, and other Islamic sources (i.e., the Sufi tradition), which freely and without any restriction discuss human sexuality (one of the discussions in the Islamic classical sources was the consent in sexual relations). Under the influence of the patriarchal cultures, this discussion of sexuality was limited to men's sexuality (Ali). Such misogynistic practices resulted in (1) granting unlimited sexual rights to men; (2) reducing the mutual consent in sexual relations to men and excluding women's voices in this consent; and (3) demanding women to be sexually available for their men anytime.

Currently, Muslim scholars hold different views on the sexual norms of the Qur'an and the *Sunna* represented in the *hadith*. Moreover, Islam is not the only source of guidance to Muslims with regards to sexual norms and practices (Dialmy). Mass media (e.g., radio, television), education, and the social environment (a more liberal one) also affect the sexual behavior of Muslims (Agha). Nevertheless, Islam still has a tremendous influence on the attitudes of people. As Sohail Agha observes among Nigerian Muslim adolescents, Muslim communities exercise strict control, especially over the sexual behaviour of Muslim girls. Therefore, a complete secularization of sexual laws among Muslims in Nigeria is practically impossible. Dialmy proposes that the only solution to the problem would be reform within Islam through the reinterpretation of the Islamic sources. However, one reason for such oppressive attitudes towards women regarding their sexuality is the dominance of patriarchy, which has prevented women from new and creative rereadings of the Qur'an because only a male scholarly élite can claim "to speak authoritatively in God's name" (Barlas 41). Moreover, when it comes to discussions of reproductive health, the principle of modesty also became a patriarchal tool to control the discourse about women's sexuality. Nimat Hafez Barazangi presents the principle of modesty as an "individual autonomous consciousness and its balance with the social heteronymous action (socially imposed norms), while seeking equilibrium with Allah's guidance (*taqwa*)" (6). Barazangi argues that patriarchal interpretations of "*taqwa*" (God consciousness) as a "God-fearing" character have excluded Muslim women from active participation in the construction of Islamic knowledge and from being active in society; they, also, tended to idealize problems. These patriarchal readings of key Islamic sources present the Qur'anic examples for women, such as Maryam and the pharaoh's wife, "as ideal spiritual women or archetypes for being 'the silent pious, the pure, the virgin, and so on'" (Barazangi 40). Thus, patriarchal societies have effectively suppressed women's ideas from being developed and their voices from being heard in order to protect male dominance in the areas concerning the interpretation of women's sexuality and sexuality in general.

Islamic tradition considers sexuality a social phenomenon and regulates almost all aspects of it. It is usually men who control the sociological aspect of sexual relationships, and patriarchal societies use the Qur'an and the prophetic tradition to endorse male control over sexuality. Therefore, the Islamic tradition, in general, is viewed as a system that "favours men and certain ways of expressing one's sexuality. In other words, sexuality is constrained by patterns of masculine and heterosexual domination" (Dialmy 162). Nevertheless, the role of culture should not be disregarded as one of the important sources of influence over the understanding of sexuality. Since Muslims are not a homogenous group, ethnic, cultural, and linguistic factors also influence attitudes towards sexuality. Although the teachings of the Qur'an, *hadith* and *Shari'ah* provide a common framework to discuss themes of reproductive health, some Muslim communities prefer to follow their cultural values in some areas rather than the religious teachings (Sanjakdar).

ISLAM AND MARRIAGE

As one of the Abrahamic religions, Islam declares that human creation is one of the signs of the Creator: "And among His Signs is this, that He created for you mates from among yourselves, that you may dwell in tranquility with them, and He has put love and mercy between your (hearts): verily in that are Signs for those who reflect" (the Qur'an 30:21). The Qur'an further admonishes the believers by stating, "Marry those among you who are single, or the virtuous ones among yourselves, male or female: if they are in poverty, Allah will give them means out of His grace: for Allah encompasses all, and he knows all things" (24:32). The *hadith* literature also affirms the importance of marriage in the prophetic tradition. Prophet Muhammad himself educated his followers, both male and female, regarding every aspect of premarital and marital life. The Prophet was reported to have said, "Whoever marries has completed half of his *imaan* [faith], so fear Allah in the remaining half." He advised his followers, even those who lacked means to provide for family, to marry (Bukhari, vol. 7, book 62, number 80).

A majority of Muslim scholars argue that marriage is an act of *taqwa*—piety and God consciousness, a form of *ibadah*—worship of Allah and obedience to His Messenger and the only legitimate means of emotional and sexual fulfillment; it is a means of legitimate procreation and an approach to inter-family alliance and group solidarity (Noibi). Mutual contribution is expressed in an ideal marriage: the wife takes care of herself in order to be attractive to her husband, and the husband, too, should make himself attractive to his wife. However, male control over women before and after marriage is the troublesome reality that Muslims face today. By controlling women in every aspect of marriage life, including women's bodies and sexuality, men want to achieve a "social order" (Dialmy 167). Some scholars have even compared the Islamic marriage to the *milk* concept (the concept of ownership, dominion and control) in Islamic legal ruling. Kecia Ali points out that "[t]he basic understanding of marriage as a relationship of ownership or control is predicated on an analogy to slavery at a fundamental level, and the discussion of wives and concubines together strengthens the conceptual relationship" (xxv).

SEXUAL ENJOYMENT BETWEEN WIFE AND HUSBAND

Real life issues in marriage life, including the sexual enjoyment between wife and husband, challenge the ideal image of marriage in Islam. Aisha, the Prophet's beloved wife and scholar, considered sexual union as the practicing of an *ibadah* (worship) along with prayer, fasting, almsgiving, and performing the pilgrimage (Hoel and Shaikh). Discussions about sexual positions and sexual intercourse (termed as *dukhul, masis,* and *lamas* in *hadith* literature) recognize the wife's right to enjoy the sex.

However, religious teachings also link sexuality to the needs and desires of men (Hoel and Shaikh). For such teachings, even when Aisha considers sex as worship, convey the meaning that Muslim women need to be available to their husbands, since satisfaction of the husband also means pleasing God. With regards to sexual positions, for example, the early Muslim religious authority granted unrestricted sexual rights to men over their wives. They based their arguments on the Qur'an, which states, "Your wives are as a tilth unto you; so approach your tilth when or how you will; but do some good act for your souls beforehand; and fear Allah. And know that you are to meet Him (in the Hereafter), and give (these) good tidings to those who believe" (the Qur'an 2: 223). The early Muslim religious scholars argued that as a "sexual master," the husband should exert physical domination and should always be on the top of his wife. For them, such a sexual position was normal. The early advocates of this opinion tried to prove their argument by stating that this "normal" position enables the woman to conceive.

In addition to providing a framework for various sexual positions during sexual intercourse, Muslim scholars also discussed the wife's sexual pleasure within marriage. Dialmy argues that early Muslim scholars focused on the men's pleasure in sex and dismissed the wife's rights to enjoy sex (164). For them, the wife's only desire was to produce a large number of male children. Therefore, the "dominant narratives eclipse any potential view of woman as a sexual partner with an independent subjectivity requiring individual consideration. Her personal sexual needs and desires, or lack thereof, do not appear to factor into such discourses that frame sex as an act of worship" (Hoel and Shaikh 81). Nevertheless, Hoel and Shaikh explain the classical understanding of sexual enjoyment from a more complex and specific contextual and relational dynamic. For example, they argue that some Muslim women may "internalize religious perspectives that compromise their ability to make satisfying or even self-preserving sexual choices." However, in their qualitative study, they point out that there are other Muslim women who also "prioritize their right to a healthy and fulfilling sexual life as part of the dominant religious narrative" (77).

Furthermore, although traditional Islamic discourse views female sexuality in relation to male desire, it also presents more positive and affirming narratives of sexuality than the modern discourse of sexuality among Muslims (Hoel and Shaikh). A careful examination of the Qur'an and some aspects of the prophetic tradition clearly indicate that Islamic understanding of marriage hold potential for emancipation of women in marriage life. With regards to the pleasure in sex, for example, the following *hadith* illustrates the Prophet's dislike of the act of uncontrolled fasting. Sahih Bukhari states that:

'Abdullah ibn 'Amr ibn al-'As said, "The Messenger of Allah, may Allah bless him and grant him peace, said to me, 'Have I not been told that you pray at night and fast in the day?' I answered, 'Yes, Messenger of Allah.' He said, 'Do not do it. Fast and break the fast. Pray and sleep. Your body has rights over you. Your eyes have rights over you. Your wife has rights over you.'" (Bukhari, volume 7, book 62, number 127)

As reported by Bukhari, one of the authors of two canonical *hadith* literatures in Islam, the Prophet Muhammad disliked the fasting without break because such an act violated the rights of the body and of the wife. The Prophet also considered sexual intimacy within legal relationships as a charity and as an ethical virtue of generosity (Hoel and Shaikh).

In addition, reframing sexual enjoyment as a spiritual experience is also a dominant theme in the mystical tradition of Islam, as evidenced by Abu Hamid al-Ghazali (450-505 AH/1058-1111 AD). Another early spiritual writer Muhyiddin Ibn 'Arabi (1165-1240) is also associated with the merging of the spiritual and sexual:

sexual union is a state where an individual ego dissolves into another and as such, gives humanity a taste of complete union with God. Sexual intimacy thus serves at the most elementary level as an enticement for believers to proceed on the path of virtue, and at the level of spiritual seekers, it intensifies into a porthole of deep spiritual experience. (qtd. in Hoel and Shaikh 79)

The Qur'anic and the prophetic tradition's references to the importance of the mutual consent in marriage and pleasure in sex are proof that Islamic tradition endorses biological and psychological aspects of sexuality, such as eroticism, reproduction, affectivity, and gender. The prophet Muhammad, for example, recommended that spouses share pleasure between them. As narrated by Abu Zakaria Muhiy ad-Din Yahya Ibn Sharaf al-Nawawi (1233–1277), he used to say, "the marital coitus leading to pleasure is equivalent to alms.... When spouses make love, God looks at them, full of kindness" (Nawawi). He also said, "None of you must throw himself on his wife like an animal" (Dialmy 161). Muslim jurists, such as Omar Ben Abdelouaheb, stated that "it is necessary that the husband takes into account the rights (of his wife) during coitus. Sexual disagreement is the origin of discord between spouses ... the meeting of two waters at the same time is the finality of pleasure and the base of affection" (Dialmy 161). Many other jurists also considered the health benefits of sexual pleasure, but they limited it to marriage.

Thus, numerous Qur'anic verses and *hadith* show the importance of sexual pleasure, and a loving relationship. They also warn against harmful habits and behaviors. Based on these key sources of Islam, some Sunni schools of thoughts have even granted the wife a right to divorce her husband if he did not satisfy her needs. They also discussed the number of nights that a man is supposed to spend with his new wife.

ISLAM AND PREMARITAL AND EXTRAMARITAL SEX

Multiple sets of questions arise regarding the possibility of marrying without first seeing or establishing a loving relationship with a future partner. There is no doubt that patriarchal culture has diminished the role of girls and women in choosing their partners. However, the fundamental Islamic sources grant more rights to women and girls. For example, from Sahih Bukhari there is a *hadith* that narrates that the Prophet Muhammad was shown A'isha, wrapped in a piece of silken cloth: "You [A'isha] were shown to me in a dream. An angel brought you to me, wrapped in a piece of silken cloth, and said to me, 'This is your wife.' I removed the piece of cloth from your face, and there you were. I said to myself, 'If it is from Allah, then it will surely be'" (Bukhari, volume 7, book 62, number 57). Based on this *hadith* and many other narrations, Muslim jurists have allowed future partners to see each other in the presence of others, and they have also not prevented girls and women from participating in marriage proposals. As reported by Bukhari, the Prophet also said that "A matron should not be given in marriage except after consulting her; and a virgin should not be given in marriage except after her permission" (Bukhari, volume 7, book 62, number 67). Based on the Qur'an and the aforementioned prophetic tradition, a majority of Muslim jurists consider a marriage without the bride's consent invalid. Upon the complaint by a woman named as Khansa' bint Khidham al-Ansariyya, for example, the Prophet himself invalidated her marriage with a man because her father gave her in marriage without consulting her (Bukhari, volume 7, book 62, number 70).

Nevertheless, there are many areas in which men have control over women's sexuality. Islamic tradition allowed women to own slaves, but they were not allowed to have sexual intercourse with them, whereas Muslim men were allowed to enjoy sex with their slaves without marrying them (Ali). Furthermore, Islamic tradition also allows men to marry up to four wives by stating that it prevents men from committing adultery. Another important area of control is the emphasis on virgin brides. Many patriarchal societies have developed a virginity test as a tool to control women (Dialmy). Some Muslim communities have used early marriages as a tool (i.e., girls are married between the ages of twelve and fourteen) to control and prevent sexual misconduct (Agha). In patriarchal societies, an emphasis on marrying a virgin prevents the woman from being active in the sexual relationship and makes her dependent on her husband who is "her teacher in that domain" (Dialmy 164). Otherwise, women who dare to be active in sexual practices can be labeled a "whore."

There are many prophetic narrations that do not represent virginity as a best criterion for marriage. In one of the narrations, it is reported that the Prophet said, "A woman is married for four things, i.e., her wealth, her family status, her beauty and her religion. So you should marry the religious woman (otherwise) you will be losers" (Bukhari, volume 7, book 62, number 27). Yet in contemporary times, a virginal bride is still a significant measure of the successful marriage among Muslim men. Nevertheless, premarital and extramarital sex have become a frequent social phenomenon. Such a social and cultural change resonates well with the prophetic tradition, which clearly indicates that virginity is not an important criterion for a successful marriage: A'isha was the only virgin among the Prophet's wives (Sahih Bukhari, volume 7, book 62, number 14).

ABORTION

Any discussion about reproductive health must also tackle the subject of abortion, which, for Muslims, must strictly be based on the principles of the sanctity of human life and safeguarding its value. In difficult situations, abortion is allowed to prefer to the lesser of the two evils. Islam instructs its followers that it is God who gives life, provides sustenance, and takes it back (the Qur'an 30:4, 50:4, and 67:2). In this regard, the discussions around abortion in Islam are also about the debate on the dignity of human life. Muslims believe that life is a precious gift from God, but humans are responsible for how they use this gift. Humans are responsible for preserving their life and the life of others. However, the right for abortion is challenging to achieve if caregiver and patient do not share the same values. In this case, how can the professionals be helpful in this situation?

Islam clearly allows abortion when doctors declare with reasonable certainty that the continuation of pregnancy will endanger the woman's life or the existing children's health (Al-Qaradawi). In this case, the client has a right to choose between two evils, known in Islamic legal terminology as the principle of *al-ahamm wa 'l-muhimm* (the more important and the less important). It is narrated that the Prophet encouraged his followers to prefer the greater over the lesser when two forbidden things become an issue (Rizvi). In this case, the client chooses between aborting the unborn child or letting a living woman die. Islam, first of all, gives preference to the latter, and abortion is allowed to save the alive person. The Qur'an also commands that "A mother should not be made to suffer because of her child" (2:233).

Respect for autonomy, non-maleficence, and beneficence illustrates the Islamic principle of forbidding what is wrong and enjoining what is good. The Qur'an declares that taking the human life without a just cause is forbidden because God made the human life sacred (the Qur'an 6:151; 4:29, and 5:32). However, this instruction does not explicitly mention abortion. Indeed, the Qur'an does not make any explicit statements that abortion is a form of killing. Addressing infanticide but not the killing of fetuses, the Qur'an 17:31 states "Kill not your children for fear of poverty. We shall provide sustenance for them as well as for you. Verily the killing of them is a great sin." Another verse instructs Muslims: "Come, I will rehearse what Allah has prohibited you: Join not anything as equal with Him; be good to your parents; kill not your children on a plea of poverty for We provide sustenance for you and for them; do not approach to shameful deeds either public or private; take not life, which Allah has made sacred, except by way of justice and law. This He has commanded you that you may understand" (the Qur'an 6:151).

Some Islamic schools are more prescriptive than others on the issue of abortion. The Hanafi school—which is prevalent in Turkey, the Middle East and Central Asia—and the Shafi school—dominant in Southeast Asia, southern Arabia, parts of East Africa—allow abortions to be performed up to 120 days. The Maliki school, prevalent in Northern and Southern Africa, and the Hanbali school, predominant in Saudi Arabia and United Arabic Emirates, allow abortions until forty days. Some Shiite groups, such as the Ismailis, do not permit abortions to take place at all. Other Shiites, such as the Zaydites, allow abortions to be performed up to 120 days. The Grand Mufti of Jordan Shaykh 'Abd Allah Al-Qalqili issued a *fatwa* in 1964 in which he said that the methods for the prevention of childbearing was permitted. From this ruling, doctors decided that takings drug to prevent childbearing, or even to induce abortion, was permissible (Anwar, Sajid, Nosheen and Nawaz 23).

Nevertheless, there are different viewpoints and practices in Islamic countries, some of which express approval of abortion. In Azerbaijan, abortion is not an illegal activity. Tunisia's liberal abortion practice also allows for abortions to be performed up to the end of the third month without approval of the husband or of a male guardian. However, other countries have banned it in all cases. In Algeria, Egypt, Iran, Pakistan and Turkey (despite Turkey's secularism) abortion is fully prohibited (Al-Haq; Macintosh, Alison, and Jason; Mehryar, Ahmad-Nia, and Kazemipour). However, an exception for this law is made if the mother's life is endangered.

BELIEFS ABOUT REPRODUCTIVE HEALTH

After examining the attitudes towards reproductive health issues in the Islamic tradition, I believe that a number of factors play a role in reproductive health problems among Muslims. First of all, in patriarchal Muslim cultures, it is usually the women's responsibility to teach appropriate behaviours and the values of sexuality to their daughters. However, the society frequently restricts the scope of this "teaching" only to knowledge about menstruation or to administering warnings against extramarital affairs. Such an approach undermines the benefits of a broad discussion of reproductive health in the family and in society in general. Although there is not yet qualitative or quantitative research that measures reproductive health knowledge of the general population (i.e., what children and even adults know about fertilization; the facts and myths about menstruation; abstinence; effective communication skills regarding consent; methods of transmission and symptoms of sexually transmitted infections; and prevention of sexually transmitted infections), I have found that the reproductive health knowledge of Muslims is not at all adequate. This is also confirmed by studies on sexual health education among Muslim girls in Nigeria (Agha) and among Australian Muslims (Sanjakdar). There may be a general belief among Muslims that sexual education that teaches the children how to have safe sex is important.

Nevertheless, Muslims may also find certain language—such as dating, spending time together alone, and getting to know each other—goes against Islamic principles of decency, modesty, chastity, and sexual responsibility (Sanjakdar). Therefore, the factor of shame also limits reproductive health education. However, the Qur'an and the prophetic tradition are inspirational regarding reproductive health education. For example, in a response to one of the polytheists, who mocked Salman Farsi, who 'Ali lbn Abi Talib nicknamed 'Luqman the Wise' by saying that "Your prophet has taught you everything, even the manners of going to the toilet." Salman Farsi answered, "Yes, the Prophet forbade us from facing the Qibla when urinating or relieving oneself." He also said "The Prophet asked us not to use the right hand when cleaning ourselves and to use at least three stones for cleaning" (reported by Muslim, Abu Dawood, al-Tirmizi, al-Nasai and Ibn Majah). This narration alone shows that the Prophet Muhammad was open to address issues that the general society hesitated to talk about because of the culture of shame. Like the Prophet Muhammad, many Muslim scholars also acknowledge that the purpose of religion is to teach *akhlaq* (morals or character) or *adab* (comportment) in every aspect of life, including sex and sexuality. Therefore, without discussing reproductive health and sexuality, it is impossible to be vigilant about the personal and professional matters in society. In addition, many Muslim cultures have a "don't ask, don't tell" culture. It implies that a considerable number of customs and practices within the society that could be labelled as "illicit" are tolerated to a certain degree. The quantity and quality of this degree varies from culture to culture.

The examination of the fundamental sources of Islam points out that nothing prevents Muslims from acquiring a reproductive health education about sexuality, menstrual cycle, virginity, marriage, pregnancy, abortion, HIV/AIDS, etc. Instead, it is an important factor to achieve an optimal health. The Qur'an and the prophetic tradition encourage Muslims to consider reproductive health education as a key strategy for promoting safe and loving sexual behaviour. The existing literature on reproductive health and Islam also points out that reproductive health education plays an important role in promoting

> an ability to reproduce (have children) and regulate their fertility. A state in which women are able to go through pregnancy and child birth safely; outcome of pregnancy is successful in terms of maternal and infant survival and well being; and couples are able to have sexual relations free of the fear of contracting diseases. (Fathalla 1986)

I strongly believe that with the recent cultural and political changes in Muslim countries, the younger generations are more open to these discussions. Cultural and religious factors both should be taken into consideration regarding reproductive health education. First, women should be given sufficient space to benefit from reproductive health education. Second, taking into consideration the sensitivity of parents, reproductive health education should target secondary, college, and university students. Third, reproductive health education would be more efficient if men taught male students, and women taught female students. Both the medical professional and religious scholars in Muslim-majority countries and Muslim communities across Europe and North America must be involved in culturally sensitive reproductive health education.

CONCLUSION

The traditional Islamic discourse of pregnancy and childbearing must be a source of inspiration for Muslims to develop a positive attitude towards reproductive health education. Reproductive health education for Muslims is more effective if it is based on the Qur'an and other sources of Islam, and is both religiously and culturally appropriate. Compared to more secular approaches., it should pay attention to the fact that some elements of the Islamic tradition and patriarchal culture can be a source of misinformation. Reproductive health education for Muslims should also address the idea and practice that it is not only Muslim women responsible for childbearing and childrearing (the Qur'an 31:14; 12:4; 66:6; 2:233). This kind of reproductive health education will assign a new role and voice for Muslim women within Muslim societies, and, at the same time, will bring an Islamic dimension to reproductive health education.

WORKS CITED

Agha, Sohail. "Changes in the Timing of Sexual Initiation among Young Muslim and Christian Women in Nigeria." *Archives of Sexual Behavior* 38.6 (2009): 899-908. Web. 22 Sept. 2015.

Al-Haq, Sheik Ali Jad "An Interview with Grand Mufti of Egypt (1984)" *Populi* 2.2. Web. 10 Mar. 2006.

Al-Ghazali, Abu Hamid Muhammad ibn Muhammad. *The Proper Conduct of Marriage in Islam [Adab al-Nikah]*. Trans. Mukhtar Holland. Fort Lauderdale: Al-Baz Publishing, 1998. Print.

Al-Qaradawi, Yusuf. *The Lawful and Prohibited in Islam*. Oak Brook, Illinois: American Trust Publications, 1960. Print.

Ali, Kecia. *Sexual Ethics and Islam: Feminist Reflections on Qur'an, Hadith and Jurisprudence*. Oxford: Oneworld Publications, 2006. Print.

Anwar, Haq Nawaz, Nazir Ahmad Sajid, Farhana Nosheen, and Waseem Nawaz. "Perception of Religious Leaders about Family Planning in Rural Areas of Pakistan." *International Journal of Political Science, Law and International Relations* 3.2 (2013): 21-32. Web. 11 Mar. 2016.

Aziz, Rukhsana, Rahmatullah Shah, and Zafar Khan. "Attitude and Awareness of Bannu Community towards Reproductive Health Education." *Interdisciplinary Journal of Contemporary Research in Business,* 2.9 (2011): 280-285. Web. 19 Aug. 2015.

Barlas, Asma. *"Believing Women" in Islam: Unreading Patriarchal Interpretation of the Qur'an*. Austin: University of Texas Press, 2002. Print.

Barazangi, Nimat Hafez. *Woman's Identity and the Qur'an: A New Reading*. Gainesville: The University Press of Florida, 2006. Print.

Al-Bukhari, Muhammed Ibn Ismaiel. *Sahih. Bukhari*. Trans. M. Muhsin Khan. Vol. 7. Riyadh: Darussalam, 1997. Web. Print.

Dialmy, Abdessamad. "Sexuality and Islam." *The European Journal of Contraception and Reproductive Health Care* 15.3 (2010): 160–168. Web. 22 Sep. 2015.

Hoel, Nina and Sa'diyya Shaikh. "Sex as Ibadah: Religion, Gender, and Subjectivity among South African Muslim Women." *Journal of Feminist Studies in Religion* 29.1 (2013): 69-91. Print.

Fathalla, Mahmoud Fahmy. "Research Needs in Human Reproduction." *Draper Fund Report* 6 (1978): 1986-1987. Print.

Macintosh, Alison, and Jason L. Finkle. "The Cairo Conference on Population and Development: A New Paradigm." *Population and Development Review* 21.2 (1995): 223-60. Print.

Mehryar, Amir H., Shirin Ahmad-Nia, and Shahla Kazemipour. "Reproductive Health in Iran: Pragmatic Achievements, Unmet Needs, and Ethical Challenges in a Theocratic System." *Studies in Family Planning* 38.4 (2007): 352-361. Print.

Noibi, Dawood. "An Islamic Perspective." *Religion, Ethnicity and Sex Education: Exploring the Issues.* Ed. R. Thomson. London: National Children's Bureau, 1993. Print

Nawawi, Muhyi al-Din. *Al Arbai'n al Nawawia.* Tunis: Taftatzani Editions, 1877. Print.

Rizvi, Sayyid Muhammad. *Marriage and Morals in Islam.* Scarborough, ON: Islamic Education and Information Center, 1994. Print.

Sanjakdar, Fida. "'Teacher Talk': The Problems, Perspectives and Possibilities of Developing a Comprehensive Sexual Health Education Curriculum for Australian Muslim Students." *Sex Education* 9.3 (2009): 261-275. Web. 12 Sept. 2015.

The Study Quran: A New Translation and Commentary. Ed. and Trans. Seyyed Hossein Nasr. New York: HarperCollins, 2015. Print.

V.
MUSLIM MOTHERING AS ACADEMIC INQUIRY

13.
Theoretical Constructions of Muslim Motherhood

IRENE OH

O N THE SURFACE, the definition of a Muslim mother seems fairly straightforward. Presumably, a Muslim mother is a woman who identifies herself as Muslim and has given birth to a child or to children. Upon further examination, however, this definition of a Muslim mother makes a number of assumptions and leaves open other possible ways of understanding Muslim motherhood. Both the terms "Muslim" and "mother" are subject to controversy. Who "counts" as a Muslim, and how to define "mother" differ depending on context. As Evelyn Nakano Glenn observes, "a particular definition of mothering has so dominated popular media representations, academic discourse and political and legal doctrine that the existence of alternative beliefs and practices among racial, ethnic, and sexual minority communities as well as non-middle-class segments of society has gone unnoticed" (2-3). This essay seeks to explore the theoretical constructions behind notions of motherhood, specifically when motherhood is paired with Muslim identity, and to analyze the ethical implications of these approaches to Muslim motherhood.

Although there exists a small but substantive body of academic literature on mothering and motherhood, the most well-known theorists on mothers do not explicitly address mothering in the context of religion, much less in the context of Islam. Rather, seminal texts such as Nancy Chodorow's *The Reproduction of Mothering*, Adrienne Rich's *Of Woman Born*, and Sara Ruddick's *Maternal Thinking* take up the more general charge of defining motherhood from the perspective of mothers themselves. These texts, undoubtedly, revolutionized the study of mothers across multiple disciplines. Writing specifically about motherhood and Islam in a post-9/11 world, however, proves challenging in ways that could not have been anticipated and addressed prior to that critical event.

ARTICULATING THE CONTEXT

The events of 9/11 dramatically affected the way in which we, scholars of Islam, think about how our scholarship will be received. That day for many of us meant that suddenly the focus of our research, Islam, became more significant and relevant to a much larger audience. This also meant that we were writing about a religion with over a billion adherents who overnight shouldered the burdens of the acts of a tiny fraction of violent extremists. The "War on Terror" created a perplexing space between "us" and "them" for those of us who study and write about Islam. In addition, many specialists in the field of gender and Islam felt the added pressure of explaining in the "overwhelmingly male domain of terrorism" the role of Muslim women who were typically mentioned in studies on terrorism as simple victims of a patriarchal tradition (Lengel, Birzescu, and Minda 49). What was our responsibility, if any, to Muslims who would become the targets of hate crimes? What was our responsibility in representing a religious tradition that suddenly developed a reputation for unprecedented levels of violence? How do Muslim women, and Muslim mothers in particular, fare amid this complexity?

In frank discussions with colleagues who also work in the field of Islam, the overwhelming sense was that if we were writing or teaching anything remotely close to the topic of violence and Islam—especially about these topics as they relate to contemporary issues and events—that we had to emphasize the fact that only a very small number of Muslims supported violent extremism. The notion that our scholarship existed in a sanitized bubble, independent of the political demands of the day, was untenable for many of us. With the alarming rise of ISIS, we find ourselves once again in a position where we must stress in our scholarship that the violence, misogyny, and discrimination found in a small, distinct Muslim group must be distinguished from the religious practices and beliefs of the vast majority of the world's Muslims.

When we wrote in the aftermath of 9/11 about the topic of women and Islam, particularly in light of the media reports about the conditions of women under the Taliban in Afghanistan, we issued qualified statements about Muslim women's freedom, economic rights, and sense of autonomy. Not all Muslim women, we emphasized, live like the women under the Taliban. With a few exceptions, Muslim women are not forced by men to cover their hair with a hijab. When Muslim women do choose to cover their hair, we noted, the decision is often a choice and not necessarily the result of the demands of an oppressive and paternalistic culture. Indeed, Muslim women sometimes chose to wear the hijab as an assertion of their religious identity (Fayyaz and Kamal).

Writing as scholars in the early twenty-first century, however, should not prevent us from frankly addressing difficult matters within Islam or that affect Muslims in particular. Certainly, our responsibility as scholars means that we cannot turn a blind eye to realities that carry the risk of portraying some Muslims and some aspects of Muslim communities in a negative light. The fact of the matter is that there are Muslim women, girls, and mothers who are killed, deprived of basic rights, and suffer under Islamic states and in Muslim communities because they are female and living in patriarchal communities. Careful scholarship enables us to understand why and how members of these communities use Islam—rhetorically, politically, and legally—as a means of subjugating others. Careful scholarship also, on the other hand, enables us to understand why and how people understand Islam in ways that uphold the rights and dignity of all persons, regardless of their sex and gender. In other words, we can use the tools of our respective disciplines to demonstrate the complexity of Islamic traditions and Muslim communities.

WHY NOT FATHERS? OR PARENTS?

When I present my research to a broader audience of scholars, a question that often arises is why I focus on mothers, and not fathers or parents. Because scholarship on Islam and gender is necessarily normative—that is, by choosing to write about Islam and mothers, we are declaring that this intersection of topics is significant and worthy of investigation—are we somehow, perhaps even unintentionally, advocating for gendered parenting?

Although I cannot speak for others writing on the topic, my own normative perspective is that parents should share equally in the work of raising children. If anything, it seems that because the so-called primary parent in many societies is the mother, there needs to be greater incentive for fathers to participate in the care of children, especially infants and toddlers. However, because the bulk of parenting—including the day-to-day work, management, and responsibilities involved in raising children in most societies—typically falls on the shoulders of women, using the gendered term "mothering" coveys an accuracy that the gender-neutral term of "parenting" does not. Scholars in the field of gender studies repeatedly observe that parenting is, by and large, gendered labour (Porter). Moreover, because pregnancy and childbirth occur only through the female body, it also makes sense to call this part of parenting "mothering."

I acknowledge, of course, that exceptions to these gendered norms exist and are important to recognize. In many societies, men are becoming more involved in the care of children from birth, and many industrialized nations offer financial and/or workplace incentives for fathers to participate in the care of babies (Pattnaik and Sriram). There certainly are individual families wherein fathers are the primary caregivers for children. There are also single parents, both men and women; gay and lesbian parents; adoptive parents; and all varieties of familial arrangements that involve the raising of children. However, because around the world women overwhelmingly bear the brunt of parenting, and because the large majority of women do become pregnant and give birth, academic study of female-gendered parenting such as mothering is worthy of focused attention.

Scholars who write about mothers can be careful to note that simply because our work focuses on women as mothers, it does not invalidate or denigrate other forms of parenting. In fact, by better understanding why parenting is so often highly gendered—beyond pregnancy and birth—we may find reasons why this continues to be the case, even when it need not be. We can analyze the cultural, religious, political, and economic reasons for gendered parenting.

BIOLOGICAL AND CULTURAL CONSTRUCTIONS OF MOTHERHOOD

In writing about motherhood, we need to be clear about motherhood as biological or cultural or both. We might also consider how much self-identification as "mother" counts in our scholarship. There are, moreover, metaphorical connotations of motherhood, such as when writing about "Mother Earth" or about women who found particular movements, such as the Madres de Plaza de Mayo, which undoubtedly influence connotations of mothers as important in the public sphere mainly because of their care for future generations.

Scholars writing about motherhood should not assume that a woman who gives birth to a child will necessarily raise that child. She may give the child up for adoption or serve as a surrogate. If a woman ends up miscarrying, should we count her as a mother? In other words, under which circumstances can a woman be a mother without raising or have raised children? Much depends on the working definition of "mother" that we use in our scholarship.

Definitions of motherhood as a cultural term can be considerably broader than definitions of motherhood as a biological one. Who should we include under a cultural understanding of motherhood? We could, of course, include the biological mothers (with the caveats noted above) who also raise their children. However, many cultures consider women who become primary caregivers to children to be mothers, even when they are not biologically related. In other words, women who adopt children—whether it be legally recognized or simply recognized by the community—are also mothers. To be sure, when studying motherhood, legal status should matter because legal mothers are recognized by governments and are counted in census data, which is important when conducting quantitative research about motherhood. Moreover, laws often outline rights and protections as well as basic duties and obligations that mothers (and fathers) have with regard to their children. In scholarship that considers not just legal status but cultural status, however, both legal and cultural mothers should be considered.

When considering "motherly" or "maternal" as an adjective to describe girls and women, what are the assumptions that we make about mothers? In this case, the association is gendered and cultural—that girls and women have a tendency to act in caring ways, particularly towards children. But it can also reinforce the idea that such behaviour is hardwired in women and not in men. The notion, for example, that girls and women have "maternal instinct" may perpetuate the belief that girls and women should bear children and become their primary caregivers. It also may prevent boys and men from attempting to become primary caregivers to children. The impact of these cultural assumptions about maternal behaviours can be seen in policies that affect the family. Policies that allow working mothers to take time off without penalty are not necessarily extended to new fathers; if leaves are granted to fathers, they are shorter in duration.

The ways in which we define motherhood are varied but need to be specified in our scholarship. Because motherhood spans both biological and cultural spheres, definitions must be precise. It cannot be assumed that a mother is biological, cultural, or both. Also, when dealing with different sources in scholarship, it may be helpful to consider how the term mother is used. For those of us engaged in the study of Islam and motherhood, how the Qur'an defines mother is not always detailed, and it certainly can be interpreted in different ways. When we attempt to juxtapose texts from Islamic jurisprudence with contemporary medical or sociological studies, different results may emerge based on how we decide to apply these terms. Clear definitions, and consideration of the impact of such definitions, have ethical and policy implications.

HISTORY AND GEOGRAPHY

Because mothers exist in the context of histories, economies, politics, and within the intersection of race, ethnicity, and class, we must be aware of how these frames affect our understanding of motherhood. When studying Muslim mothers, we must ask ourselves: what does it mean to be a mother in twenty-first century North America versus seventh-century Arabia? How should we use narratives and texts from different eras and locales and apply them to the concerns of the present day in different locations? What does being a Muslim mean for mothers in widely ranging contexts?

Motherhood may very well differ dramatically over time and geographic region because of historic events, changes in technology, and shifts in cultural norms (Kawash). We know, for example, that the advancement of science and medicine means that today women are much more likely to survive childbirth and that children are much more likely to survive into adulthood. This fact of mere survival has tremendous repercussions regarding concepts that we often associate with motherhood, such as love, family, and kinship. Biological mothers are very likely more willing to attach emotionally to children who will survive past infancy.

Historic events, including wars, mass migrations, slavery, colonialism, industrialization, and social justice movements undoubtedly shape family structures. Some of the most insightful scholarship about the impact of major historical events on motherhood comes out of the work of womanist theologians and sociologists. Writings by scholars such as Katie Cannon and Patricia Hill Collins clarify how, given the history of slavery and racist institutions in the United States, the goals of the mainstream, majority-white, feminist movement of the 1960s and 1970s simply did not address the needs or desires of African American mothers. While the predominantly white, middle-class women of the second wave of feminism clamoured for the right to work and questioned expectations of domesticity and childcare, many African American women wanted nothing more than to be able to stay in their own homes and to care for their own children. Given the horrific legacy of children being separated from their parents by slave owners, and subsequent policies that perpetuated the fragmentation of African American families, motherhood held vastly different meanings and held starkly different associations for African Americans than for second-wave white feminists.

The question of context also frames how we address normative statements in the Qur'an, *hadith*, *sunna*, and other foundational scripture. We must be careful to articulate how we choose to understand these texts and towards what ends. Although it is commonly accepted that the Qur'an offers progressive views towards gender relations in the context of seventh century Arabia, the wholesale adoption of the Qur'anic texts into contemporary conversations about women's rights can prove challenging. As Aysha Hidayatullah concludes, "the contemporary expectations for gender equality at the heart of the feminist exegetical project perhaps cannot ultimately be reconciled with the Qur'anic text" (118). Accepting these texts as products of particular times means that our interpretation of these texts may differ from Muslims who choose not to understand these texts as bound by history. This may also mean that our willingness to interpret these texts more or less broadly affects normative conclusions. On issues ranging from breastfeeding to gay-lesbian parenting to artificial reproductive technologies, how we choose to locate foundational scripture may lead to very different conclusions.

LOCATING THE SELF: MOTHERS AND MUSLIMS

As human beings, we are unavoidably "participant-observers" when we study motherhood. Because we all have had personal, first-hand experiences with motherhood either as mothers ourselves or as the children of mothers, the question arises as to how much of our personal experiences and biases should be examined in our scholarship, if at all. Although completely objective scholarship is likely impossible, an honest and accurate assessment of our own views on mothers and mothering may be fruitful in articulating why and how we choose to write about mothering. Given this, scholars may also consider how much of this information to divulge to their readers, especially if these personal insights and reflections have some direct bearing on the object of study. As Pierre Bourdieu notes, "depending on what object she studies, the sociologist herself is more or less distant from the agents and stakes she observes, more or less directly involved in rivalries with them, and consequently, more or less tempted to enter the game of metadiscourse under the cloak of objectivity" (259).

All the scholars whom I know personally in the U.S., who write about religion and motherhood, are themselves mothers, including me. Granted that this is a small sample size, but the observation does suggest that giving birth to or adopting and raising children has a large amount of influence on our scholarship. We choose to write about motherhood because our experiences as mothers prove to be worthy of professional inquiry and reflection. Indeed, the impetus for me to research motherhood and religious ethics grew out of my personal experience of giving birth to and raising children as well as noticing a lack in scholarship about religious ethics and mothering. I rather quickly became aware of a number of ethical, social, and political concerns, especially around gendered notions of justice, that I had not been aware of before I became a mother. Perhaps because men (and fathers) were so long dominant in the academic study of religion, there were relatively few publications about the topic. This is, of course, not to discount the experiences of men as fathers; rather, it is a nod to the fact that in many communities, the work of parenting is often defaulted to women and mothers. Raising children, especially infants and young children, typically plays a much larger role in the lives of women than in men, including in academe.

In a parallel vein, when writing as a scholar about religion, the question arises as to whether or not one's personal affiliation with the tradition, in this case Islam, matters. The benefit of having some personal affiliation with a tradition may lead to unique insights that an outsider to the tradition may not be able to access easily. Also, as an insider within Islam, a Muslim scholar may have a much broader range of personal resources associated with the religion from which to draw. Given the political climate of the post-9/11 era, some Muslims may be hesitant to provide personal interviews with non-Muslims out of fear. However, the looming concern about Muslims writing about Islam remains that their scholarship may be apologetic or too biased to be taken seriously. Yet another perspective on this is that one's personal commitment to a faith tradition does not correlate to the quality of one's scholarship. That is, good scholarship comes from both Muslim and non-Muslim scholars and, conversely, questionable scholarship comes from both Muslims and non-Muslim scholars. The quality of research and writing cannot be predicted based on religious affiliation alone.

Certainly, experiences with parents and/or parenting and with a religious upbringing are powerful factors in determining worldviews. As a mother and as someone who was raised among multiple religious traditions, I acknowledge that these facts undoubtedly affect my choice of scholarship and how I approach the topics that I choose to study. For me, the experience of motherhood has had an equally profound impact on my scholarship, as have my experiences with religious traditions. Most importantly, the experience of raising children has led me as a scholar to think about issues that would not have gained my attention as a person without children.

CONCLUSIONS

A theoretical approach to the study of Islam and motherhood scrutinizes the assumptions surrounding common terms whose meanings we too easily take for granted. With this comes the realization that we must be careful to define our terms and to explain why we define these terms as we do. We must think reflectively about disclosing our own biases and agendas that may affect the scholarship. Even in seemingly objective social science research, articulating definitions, describing relevant contexts, and delineating boundaries help to uncover assumptions that may compromise the accuracy of scholarship.

In writing about Islam and motherhood, we bring together two topics that may be central to our personal and our political lives. It is somewhat ironic, then, that given how ubiquitous mothers and Muslims are in public discourse, this "blended" topic makes so many uneasy. Indeed, in searching for the terms "Muslim" and "mother" or "Islam" and "mother" online, the most popular results—aside from quotes about mothers in the Qur'an—are news articles about the role of mothers in North America and Western Europe in preventing their children from joining ISIS. Although this reveals the possible practical ramifications of scholarly research on Islam and motherhood, it also suggests that there is a need to think more broadly about why governments and the general public assume that mothers and mothering organizations may prevent teenagers from joining ISIS. Needless to say, questions about the role of fathers in all this as well as the roles of schools and friends are moved to the background, despite the likely reality that many teenagers associate more frequently with their friends and peers than with their mothers, and they do so via social media platforms that parents may not know how to access.

Although scholarly research about Islam and motherhood may lead to important insights about the current crises involving ISIS, it can also lead to insights about the raising of children, women and gender, and religious beliefs and practices more broadly. Such research will likely affirm the complexity of mothering in multiple contexts and bring to light the ways in which motherhood can cross cultural boundaries as shared, common experiences. Such research may also, however, reveal stark and perhaps incommensurable differences among mothers.

WORKS CITED

Bourdieu, Pierre, and Loïc Wacquant. *An Invitation to Reflexive Sociology.* Chicago: University of Chicago Press, 1992. Print.

Cannon, Katie. *Black Womanist Ethics.* Atlanta: Scholars Press, 1988. Print.

Chodorow, Nancy. *The Reproduction of Mothering: Psychoanalysis and the Sociology of Gender.* Berkeley: University of California Press, 1978. Print.

Collins, Patricia Hill. *Black Feminist Thought.* New York, Routledge, 2000. Print.

Fayyaz, Waseem, and Anila Kamal. "Practicing Hijab (Veil): A Source of Autonomy and Self-Esteem for Modern Muslim Women." *The Journal of Humanities and Social Sciences* 22.1 (2014): 19-34. Print.

Glenn, Evelyn Nakano. "Social Constructions of Mothering: A Thematic Overview." *Mothering: Ideology, Experience, and Agency.* Eds. Evelyn Nakano Glenn, Grace Chang, and Linda Rennie Forcey. New York: Routledge, 1994. 1-29. Print.

Aysha A. Hidayatullah. "Feminist Interpretation of the Qur'an in a Comparative Feminist Setting." *Journal of Feminist Studies in Religion* 30.2 (2014): 115-129. Print.

Kawash, Samira. "New Directions in Motherhood Studies." *Signs* 36.4 (2011): 969–1003. Print.

Pattnaik, Jyotsna, and Rajalakshmi Sriram. "Father/Male Involvement in the Care and Education of Children." *Childhood*

Education 86.6 (2010): 354-359. Print.

Lengel, Lara, Anca Birzescu, and Jennifer Minda, "Mothering in a Time of Terror." *Mothering in the Third Wave.* Ed. Amber E. Kinser. Toronto: Demeter Press, 2008. 48-69. Print.

Porter, Marie. "Focus on Mothering: Introduction." *Hecate* 36.1,2 (2010): 5-16. Print.

Rich, Adrienne. *Of Woman Born: Motherhood as Experience and Institution.* Tenth Anniversary Edition. New York: W.W. Norton, 1986. Print.

Ruddick, Sara. *Maternal Thinking: Toward a Politics of Peace.* Boston: Beacon Press, 1989. Print.

About the Contributors

Fatimah Al-Attas is a Malaysian doctoral candidate at Victoria University of Wellington, New Zealand, in the field of sociology. Her present PhD research is a phenomenological study of the experiences of first-time parenting and returning to employment among New Zealand and Malaysian families. Fatimah is currently one of the board members of Mothers Network Wellington, which works to provide more extensive support for mothers. Her other research interests include phenomenological research methodology, mothering, gender studies, migration and academe, emotion in research, and socio-linguistics.

Nouf Bazaz is pursuing her PhD in Counseling at George Washington University and holds a Masters in Trauma and Violence Transdisciplinary Studies from New York University. Ms. Bazaz frequently leads trainings on multicultural counseling, refugee resettlement, and vulnerable youth, and has served diverse populations, including refugees, asylum seekers, survivors of sexual trafficking, incarcerated males, ethnic minorities and immigrants, Indigenous women, and women in conflict zones.

Maria F. Curtis is an associate professor of anthropology and cross-cultural studies at the University of Houston, Clear Lake. She is interested in the topics of gender and family in Islam and American Muslims in the public sphere and the arts, festivals, music, media, and food. She has written on women's spirituality, performance, and globalization in Morocco as well as on Turkish and Turkish-American women's experiences in interfaith-based community projects, on Arab Americans in Houston, and on Muslim American identities. She has also written on issues of discrimination in the American Muslim context, and how they have responded in creative ways to countering Islamophobia in the post-9/11 era. Most recently, she has been working with Syrian and Iraqi refugees on a book that looks at how they tell stories about home through food and treasured family recipes.

Audrey Mouser Elegbede, PhD, earned her doctorate in cultural anthropology from Brown University and is senior lecturer of ethnic and racial studies at the University of Wisconsin-La Crosse. Since the 1990s, she has examined issues of gender, family, and mothering in Malaysia, with particular attention to middle-class Malay women. Her interests also include examination of white privilege, multiracial and multicultural identities, and Muslims in the US, and she is a speaker and advocate for children with autism and their families.

Rachel Fox is a postgraduate research student in the Department of English and Creative Writing at Lancaster University. Her PhD thesis examines and refigures West Asian female identities represented in post-millennial literature and photography. Her research interests include postcolonialism, neoimperialism, feminist literature, perceptions, and representations of Islam, and post-9/11 literature.

Nazila Isgandarova is spiritual and religious care co-ordinator at the Centre for Addiction and Mental Health, where she is specializes in spiritual care and counselling. She is a registered social worker (RSW) with the Ontario College of Social Workers and Social Service Workers (OCSWSSW) and a registered psychotherapist with the College of Registered Psychotherapists of Ontario. Dr. Isgandarova has served as an instructor for continuing education courses offered at Emmanuel College of Victoria University in the University of Toronto. She also has authored several articles that appeared in different academic books and journals. In recognition of her active and passionate focus on issues in Islamic spiritual care and multifaith counselling, she received the 2015 CASC (Canadian Association for Spiritual Care) Research Award. She is also a Forum for Theological Exploration award winner.

Aurélie Lacassagne holds a PhD from Science Po Bordeaux (France). She is an associate professor and teaches international relations at Laurentian University (Sudbury, Canada). Her research focuses on social theories, cultural studies, identity politics and motherhood. She has published numerous articles and co-edited a book entitled *Investigating Shrek: Power, Identity, and Ideology* (Palgrave, 2011).

Ulrike Lingen-Ali is a lecturer and researcher in the Cultural Studies Department and the Department of Education at the Carl von Ossietzky University of Oldenburg, Germany. She is currently conducting a research project on migrant one-parent families in Lower Saxony, Germany. She teaches in the areas of intercultural education and counselling, Migration Studies, Gender Studies and Educational Sciences. She received her PhD in education at Oldenburg University with a thesis on agency and biography in Palestinian and German feminist contexts. Lingen-Ali is a member of the working group Migration—Gender—Politics (MGP), the Centre of Interdisciplinary Research on Women and Gender (ZFG) and the Center for Migration, Education, and Cultural Studies at Oldenburg University (CMC). She has published on questions of single and lone parenting in migration contexts, doing difference and religious ascriptions. Her research interests include gender issues, family structures in migration contexts, postcolonial theory, and social constructions of difference and culture in Palestinian and Middle Eastern contexts.

Nina Nurmila is a senior lecturer at the State Islamic University (UIN) Bandung, Indonesia. She teaches gender in Islamic studies in the UIN Bandung postgraduate studies program. Her first degree was from UIN Bandung (1992). Her postgraduate degrees were from Australia: her MA was from Murdoch University (1997) and her PhD was from the University of Melbourne (2007). She was an Endeavour Postdoctoral Fellow at the University of Technology, Sydney (2008) and was a Fulbright Visiting Scholar at the University of Redlands, California, USA (2008-2009). She is the author of *Women, Islam and Everyday Life: Renegotiating Polygamy in Indonesia* (Routledge, 2009, 2011).

Irene Oh (PhD, University of Virginia) is Associate Professor of Religion and Director of the Peace Studies Program at The George Washington University in Washington, DC. She is the author of *The Rights of God: Islam, Human Rights, and Comparative Ethics* (Georgetown, 2007), numerous essays in peer-reviewed scholarly journals, and is currently working on a book about the ethics of motherhood. Irene currently teaches courses in peace studies, ethics, and world religions. She has been elected to the board of the Society of Christian Ethics, is a founding member of the Society for the Study of Muslim Ethics, and serves on the steering committee for the Comparative Religious Ethics Group of the American Academy of Religion.

Dana M. Olwan is assistant professor of women's and gender studies at Syracuse University and visiting assistant professor of sociology and anthropology at the Doha Institute for Graduate Studies. Dana's research is located at the nexus of feminist theorizations of gendered and sexual violence, solidarities across geopolitical and racial differences, and feminist pedagogies. In support of her work, she has received a Future Minority Studies postdoctoral fellowship, the Social Sciences and Humanities Research Council Art/Research Grant, and a Palestinian American Research Council grant. Her writings have appeared or are forthcoming in the *Journal of Settler Colonial Studies*, the *Canadian Journal of Sociology*, *Feral Feminisms*, *Atlantis: Critical Studies in Gender, Culture and Social Justice*, *American Quarterly*, and *Feminist Formations*. Shorter opinion pieces can be found on *Rabble, Richochet, The Feminist Wire*, and *Al Jazeera*. She is currently writing her first book manuscript, *Traveling Discourses: Gendered Violence and the Transnational Politics of the "Honor Crime."*

Margaret Aziza Pappano is associate professor of English literature at Queen's University, Kingston, Ontario, where she teaches courses on contemporary Muslim literature in English and gender issues as well as early literature. She is the co-author of *The Civic*

Cycles: Artisan Drama and Identity in Premodern England (Notre Dame University Press), and co-editor of *Premodern Artisan Culture* (Duke University Press) and the author of numerous articles in both scholarly and popular journals. She has held fellowships from the American Council of Learned Societies and the Erasmus Institute at the University of Notre Dame.

Mehra Shirazi is an assistant professor of women gender and sexuality studies at Oregon State University. Her research explores health inequalities through a lens of social justice with particular regard to class, race, gender, immigration, and environment, with an emphasis on immigrant and refugee Muslim women's health using a community-based participatory approach. Dr. Shirazi teaches courses on transnational feminism in film and media, violence against women, health inequities, and feminist research methods.

Nadine Sinno is assistant professor of Arabic and director of the Arabic Program in the Department of Foreign Languages and Literatures at Virginia Tech. Her research interests include modern Arabic literature and cultural studies, literary translation, contemporary Arab women's writings, and transnational feminisms. Her work has appeared in *The Journal of Arabic Literature*, *The Journal of Middle East Women's Studies*, *Interdisciplinary Studies in Literature and Environment*, *Arab Studies Quarterly* and *Middle Eastern Literatures*. Her current research focuses on the intersection of writing, war, and technology in contemporary war diaries by Arab women.